Australian Civilisation

AUSTRALIAN CIVILISATION

Edited by
Richard Nile

Melbourne
OXFORD UNIVERSITY PRESS
Oxford Auckland New York

OXFORD UNIVERSITY PRESS AUSTRALIA

Oxford New York Toronto
Delhi Bombay Calcutta Madras Karachi
Kuala Lumpur Singapore Hong Kong Tokyo
Nairobi Dar es Salaam Cape Town
Melbourne Auckland Madrid
and associated companies in
Berlin Ibadan

OXFORD is a trade mark of Oxford University Press

© Richard Nile, 1994
Authors retain copyright in respect
of their contributions to this volume.
First published 1994

This book is copyright. Apart from any fair
dealing for the purposes of private study,
research, criticism or review as permitted under
the Copyright Act, no part may be reproduced,
stored in a retrieval system, or transmitted, in
any form or by any means, electronic, mechanical,
photocopying, recording, or otherwise without
prior written permission. Enquiries to be made to
Oxford University Press.

Copying for educational purposes
Where copies of part or the whole of the book are
made under section 53B or section 53D of the Act,
the law requires that records of such copying be
kept. In such cases the copyright owner is
entitled to claim payment.

National Library of Australia
Cataloguing-in-Publication data:

Australian civilisation.

  Bibliography.
  Includes index.
  ISBN 0 19 553504 9.

  1. Australia - Civilization - Congresses. 2. Australia - Social
conditions - Congresses. 3. Australia - Social life and
customs - Congresses. I. Nile, Richard, 1958-
II. Australian Studies Conference (1992: Budapest,
Hungary).

306.0994

Edited by Cathryn Game
Typeset by Superskill Graphics Pte Ltd, Singapore
Printed through Bookpac Production Services, Singapore
Published by Oxford University Press,
253 Normanby Road, South Melbourne, Australia

Contents

ACKNOWLEDGEMENTS	vi
PREFACE	vii
INTRODUCTION Richard Nile	1
1. HISTORY Henry Reynolds	24
2. LEGEND John Barnes	41
3. MYTH Bruce Bennett	58
4. IDENTITY James Jupp	74
5. CITIZENS Laksiri Jayasuriya	93
6. HOMOSEXUALITY Dennis Altman	110
7. WOMEN Margaret Reynolds	125
8. POLITICIANS Sol Encel	141
9. INTELLECTUALS James Walter	162
10. CRINGERS Elaine Thompson	180
11. STRUTTERS Chris Wallace-Crabbe	199
12. CULTURE Andrew Milner	215
BIBLIOGRAPHY	236
CONTRIBUTORS	249
INDEX	252

ACKNOWLEDGEMENTS

Such an enterprise as this book could not have been completed without the efforts of many people, more really than I can properly acknowledge. My primary thanks go to the contributors, whose response throughout has been creative, collaborative and generous. The project was hatched in the UK, worked through in Hungary and completed in Australia. I acknowledge colleagues at the University of London, particularly Tom Millar and James Walter during their terms as head of the Sir Robert Menzies Centre for Australian Studies, and Peter Lyon from the Institute of Commonwealth Studies.

From the Lajos Kossuth University at Debrecen, I thank particularly Zoltan Abadi-Nagy and Agnes Toth; the Eotvos Lorand University at Budapest, Adam Nadasdy, Dorottya Hollo, Veronika Kniezsa, Gizella Kocztur; Curtin University of Technology where I was a research fellow in 1993, particularly Will Christensen and Peter Gadsden; and colleagues at the University of Queensland, where I finally landed in the last days of preparing the manuscript. I make special mention of Glenda Sluga, who is now at the University of Sydney.

For their editorial guidance and critical comments I thank Geoff Bolton, Stuart MacIntyre, Ffion Murphy and Tom Stannage. Thanks to Elizabeth Mitchell for the bibliography and Chris Nile for the story of the drovers.

Acknowledgement is due also to the participants at the 'Australian Civilisation' conference at the Eotvos Lorand University (there are too many to note individually), whose enthusiasm for the topic convinced many that this book ought to be done.

In memoriam, Marion Kerry Sullivan, 1964–93. Goodbye, sweet Marion.

Preface

In the early 1960s Peter Coleman edited a book by the title of *Australian Civilization*. He did so at the prompting of Andrew Fabinyi, an émigré from Budapest, who was at that time one of the most influential of Australia's publishers. A book with a bold title was in keeping with the period, and editor and publisher apparently liked the sound of *Australian Civilization*. Phrases based on book titles were becoming fashionable then, and a few bold ones would become part of the vernacular: 'the lucky country', 'the Australian ugliness', 'land of the long weekend', 'the tyranny of distance' and so on, all seem to belong to a peculiarly 1960s mindset. For whatever reasons *Australian Civilization* did not catch on to the same extent, but Coleman's volume did feature leading intellectual figures of the time whose names are now quite familiar to us: Robin Boyd, Vincent Buckley, Manning Clark, Sol Encel, Max Harris, Donald Horne, Robert Hughes, Ken Inglis, James McAuley, Douglas McCallum, A.A. Phillips, A.G.L. Shaw, Ronald Taft, Hugo Wolfsohn and, of course, Coleman himself.

On the cusp of the third millennium, a return to the theme of Australian civilisation might seem an ironic gesture back to the *belle epoch* of Australia's 1960s. It is clear that our present arguments are informed by the *fin de siècle* and *fin de millennium*, a period of extraordinary change and great communal soul-searching. By all accounts we are today in the midst of tremendous upheavals in our social, cultural and personal relationships, at a time when time-honoured intellectual, emotional and economic assumptions neither sustain nor comfort us. The complexion of the country seems to be transforming before our eyes. Things just aren't what they used to be. As individuals, within communities and as a nation, we are, whether we like it or not, actively engaged in a process of reinventing Australia, to borrow Hugh MacKay's

Preface

1993 phrase. Along the way we are remaking images of ourselves and those of others around us.

How could anyone have guessed any of this in 1962? I don't think the original contributors to *Australian Civilization* did. But this is not a criticism, simply an indication of the changes that have happened since those early heady days. Coleman, for instance, called his introductory chapter 'The new Australia'. It was something of a proud boast. And why not? Cold wars notwithstanding, 'The new Australia', like Australian civilisation itself, appeared to be a pretty good spot in 1962. Coleman's introduction was followed by the solid 'The old tradition' by A.G.L. Shaw. To be sure, you could look both forwards and backwards in 1962 and feel reasonably satisfied, perhaps not self-satisfied, but satisfied none the less that things were working out just fine.

The past really is a foreign country. Today Australians inhabit quite a different time and space. Nowadays we seem to take less for granted although we are perhaps no less brash as a collective. I sense also that we are as a nation less chauvinistic than we used to be once but I hope not less raw, which is a reason I like to use *we* when talking about Australians. In the longer run Australians might prove to be less expectant of the future as the bearer of cultural riches and of continued material prosperity, but we remain hopeful, if not always confident that the future will be the source of our bounty. We feel it is our reward for being Australian, our antipodean holy grail. Yet we know for certain also that many things are pretty crook. As the second millennium gives way to the third, uncertainty becomes one of the few real certainties we possess. And it's not just social dislocation, although dislocation might have triggered the response initially. Our problems go very much deeper into the soul. Spiritually we are revealed as a troubled people in search of philosophies of life itself. With a good deal of the hard yacka involved in laying the foundations for civilisation largely accomplished, we now turn inward to ask important questions of meaning.

The contributions to the present volume by Dennis Altman, John Barnes, Bruce Bennett, Sol Encel, Laksiri Jayasuriya, James Jupp, Andrew Milner, Henry Reynolds, Margaret Reynolds, Elaine Thompson, Chris Wallace-Crabbe and James Walter, and including my introduction, are written around these concerns and about those important changes that have affected Australian civilisation since Coleman's book appeared in the early 1960s. In the present

Preface

era, in this new book, Australia is both our glue and our solvent. Civilisation similarly draws us together and forces us apart. At times we appear to be expansive. At other times we are deliberately focused. Yet our intention to narrate the nation is clear. Individually we address the subject of Australian civilisation from what might be called monographic viewpoints, which is the reason we have opted for single-word chapter headings. Collectively we resist the notion of a master narrative, with the possible exception that we implicitly acknowledge Australia as a plural society.

Pluralism is a key. On the evidence of Coleman's *Australian Civilization* the striking impact of post-war immigration was readily contained within the 'Australian way of life', another phrase that owes its origins to the 1960s. Coleman's 'The new Australia', with its authoritative *the*, carries heavy associations of assimilation in its close semantic tagging of 'new Australians', as immigrants were called. Ronald Taft's 'The myth and migrants' is all about assimilation. At that time the colour bar was extended to indigenous Australians. Australian civilisation excluded Aborigines and Torres Strait Islanders in 1962 — five years before a nation-wide referendum created a space for their inclusion as Australian citizens. How different Australia was then. There is much to learn from but precious little to be nostalgic about in this past.

The term *land rights* in all likelihood in 1962 would have conjured up images of the squattocracy or of mining leases. *Multiculturalism*, if it were ever uttered, probably would have sounded like an exotic virus growing in a test tube, something from a science fiction comic book or one of those B-grade movies that gets a run on television very early in the morning very early in the week. *Post-modern* had been used by Bernard Smith in the 1940s but it did not catch on until the last decades of the century. In any case modernism had been shut out by Prime Minister Menzies who was still in charge of things in 1962, and anything post-modern was for most way out but not yet groovy. We confront the intriguing possibility in this volume that post-modernism pre-dates modernism, but not modernity, in Australia.

Today *native title*, *multiculturalism* and *post-modernism* are well-used terms and no longer exotic or confusing things. They are almost second nature to us. They appear to be the lived realities of our age — although we are still pretty vague about definitions, as we are about so many definitions and lived realities. A re-reading of the Coleman volume suggests that the cultural momentum in

Preface

1962, the force of Australian civilisation, was in the direction of an uncontested mono-identity. Australians probably felt safe inside this master narrative. On the edge of the millennium such a narrative has by force of circumstance dissipated — and there seems little chance of revival except among those conservatives who, concerned by the pace of change in contemporary society, cling to images of the 1950s and 1960s as Australia's golden age. The spectre of 2001 might have increased uncertainty for all of us, but I think we have also increased the potential for a positive Australian civilisation based on diversity and pluralism.

The present volume clearly demonstrates that the 1970s, perhaps more so than the 1960s, was a decade of considerable change in Australia. A generation on from the 1970s, the end of the century, the end of the millennium, and the quest to re-examine, to unpick and reinterpret many features of the Australian collective, our relations with one another and with the outside world, are the things that preoccupy us. Each new period probably ushers in a mood of re-examination. More generally, making identities is the hoary old gumnut of being Australian. The baby-boom generation, who are quite well represented in this volume, are in a position to relive the experience; only, where they were once the subversive generation, they are now the hegemonic generation. On the edge of the millennium, what do they say?

The insistence of our questions and our desire for some answers, if not closure, seem at times rather urgent. What is Australia? What brings Australians together? What makes us think we have enough in common to stay together? What are our states and states of mind? Who are the Australians? Fair enough questions, it might be said, for a first-world settler society in which the quest for identities is never far away, but increasingly Australians seem to be shifting out of those hard-won backyards, through living rooms and into the street where we presume, almost as a matter of course, as a birthright, the title *public intellectual*. Which is only to say that we all have a stake in, and take seriously the task of, narrating the nation. We can all be intellectuals in the sense that we make sense of and give shape to the worlds we inhabit, and Australians are among the most staunch peoples on earth. It is our right to be staunch, to be true believers if we wish, and there are no shortages of things to have opinions on in Australia. Equally it is our obligation as Australians to listen to and to consider carefully alternative views and ways of seeing the world, to weigh up the similarities and the differences patiently, to assess critically the weaknesses as well as the strengths of what we and 'others' say and, if need be, modify our opinions.

In the end, then, do we have an answer to the question: what is Australian civilisation? In the end I don't think there is one single answer, but there are many answers. Australian civilisation, as the contributors to this volume testify, is a wildly problematic, discursive and sometimes cranky thing. It can be a sensitive thing. It can still be chauvinistic. But I think our civilisation, like our culture, should remain in a provisional and contested state. In a more immediate sense we are still working through the questions. The twentieth century, that most barbarous of centuries, has educated us in the extreme limitations and human costs of definite civilisations espousing predetermined certainties.

Richard Nile
Australian Studies Centre
University of Queensland

INTRODUCTION

Richard Nile

A book on civilisation should very likely be full of wonderful lies, and a book on Australia would seem to require, almost as a matter of course, that lies be told. This much, at least, those two marvellously loaded words *Australia* and *civilisation* appear to share in common. 'It's all lies', wrote one of Australia's most civilised authors, David Malouf, in the closing scenes of his early autobiographical novel, *Johnno* (1975), 'And in the end perhaps it is . . . Maybe in the end, even the lies we tell define us. And better, some of them, than our most earnest attempts at truth.'[1] We live and die by the lies we tell and the lies we choose to believe. It seems to be in the nature of things that lies are the things that blind and bind us.

I choose to begin with my own lie, a story best told by my youngest brother. It concerns my maternal grandmother, Nanna as we knew her, Mum to everyone else in our community except for those few who had passed the test of equality to call her Ma. A bloke once called her Bill and she knocked his block off. Apart from Pop, nobody ever called her by her birth name. She was born on Anzac Day but before there was a war. For much of her adult life she worked as a drover and wood-cutter who supplied our local township in the wheat belt of Western Australia with its fuel for cooking and heating in winter. She wore dungaree overalls all her working days and, after she had given away the droving and the horses, when I was still a kid, she took to driving an old Dodge truck. In the end she died of axeman's heart. That was in 1974. I was aged sixteen.

As a kid, I took my turn at living with her — of hiding on the

Introduction

back of the Dodge, dodging school among the tool boxes, the tarps, the 44-gallon petrol drum and kangaroo dogs — whenever she went out to the ghost gums to axe down the dead trees. She delivered to her customers the chopped and sawn-up wood, which she had worked into manageable blocks on an engine-driven saw bench set up next to the old house. In return she collected dead beer bottles (as the empties were called), which, when her cache would fill a rail-truck, were despatched to the city in wooden crates on board the train. She had what was called a marine dealers' licence, which meant that she could collect and sell back to the Swan Brewery the empty brown 26-ounce bottles that seemed then to be such an abundant part of everyday life.

It was part of Nanna's repertoire to tell stories, and she was as good at spinning a yarn as she was at playing cards and gambling to supplement the family income, along with the bounty she received for the scalped ears and tales of verminous dingoes, foxes and rabbits she had trapped or shot with either of her .22 or .303 rifles. She was an excellent shot, nobody disputed, and once felled an old man emu, the biggest in the flock, fitting and threatening attack after the Dodge had broken down in the sandy plains. Perhaps her whistling at the dogs had set the emus off. They are normally more timid and nervous. This day you could hear the guttural clucking in the backs of their ugly throats.

At Nanna's command the passengers took cover under the truck. They swore they could hear in the ground — an old Indian trick — the slapping of cranky emu feet. She stood firm until the big bloke out front was close enough for her to blow his head off. A single shot. The dogs went mad. The big bloke dropped. The mob retreated. She worked quickly to retrieve the still-hot carcass and drain it of its oils. She took it home for a feed. It was a great banquet in the open air. Even the skinny dogs looked as if they would get their fill.

The five brothers in my immediate family, one cluster of many grandchildren among all kinds of kids who seemed quite naturally to gravitate towards her, huddled at night as she recounted her life's store. The story that I relate here, but only briefly, concerns the droving days before the sheep and cattle trucks took over.

There were three of them yarning around a campfire at the end of a run. Long days in the saddle, Nanna often said, give you a sore bum but time to think. The first drover, a man, told how he averaged several hundreds of miles along the Canning Stock Route,

Introduction

diverting across the Top End into Queensland. The second explained that he pushed even further north and south, across the Birdsville Track, before shooting back home across the Gunbarrel Highway. Nanna paused and, with that wicked twinkle in her eye, added how she droved throughout the west, across the Top End, down the east coast through Queensland, New South Wales and Victoria, and deep into Tasmania.

'What!' demanded her storytelling rivals, 'how the hell do you get across Bass Strait?'

'Ah,' said my Nanna, 'I don't go that way.'

For some this might seem an odd way to introduce a book that goes by the title *Australian Civilisation*. My Nanna is, after all, a minor historical actor obscured by the narrative of her times, which includes two world wars, a depression, a gold rush that almost killed her and a shark attack that claimed her young son in 1947, from which she never really recovered and which very nearly destroyed my own mother's life, but that is quite another story. Nanna participated in a lot during her life. She was, however minor, an agent of civilisation. Moreover, this story I want to claim as a metaphor and general tenet: that Australian civilisation 'does not go that way'.

Such an assertion is perhaps inevitable. Australian civilisation is almost unbearable as a contradiction. Viewed from the perspective of Europe, its traditional marker of civilised values, Australia is the Antipodes, meaning literally where things are the wrong way round. On the one hand Australia has been conceptualised romantically as a 'great south land', a place of noble human values, a place free from ancient conflicts, eldorado, Australia del Espiritu Santo. On the other, the satire of Jonathan Swift's much-wrecked sailor, Gulliver, who came upon the Yahoos among others during his imaginary travels into the Antipodes, signifies a tradition of ironic deflation against the conceit. And, as historian K.S. Inglis has reminded us:

> 'Australia' derives its name from a Spanish pun of 1606 by Quiros designed to flatter the Hapsburg emperor of Austria and Spain, Australia (del Espiritu Santo) being a play on the words for south and Austria.[2]

Yet Quiros, pun and all, never actually made it to Australia. In his great voyage in the name of theology, he believed he had discovered the great south land but had in fact turned back at the New

Introduction

Hebrides. So much for attempting to flatter the Hapsburgs with verisimilitude. Australia was from this moment of naming an imaginary place of boasting and drop-dead irony. We have been going forward and turning back in the Antipodes ever since.

There are two 'incompatible pictures' of Australia, argued J.D. Pringle in the early 1960s: 'one of a barbarous, uncivilised, land of cultural yahoos. The other of a land of young but flourishing art and literature'.[3] This antipodean paradox has been articulated by many Australians, among them the grand and most serious Patrick White and the iconoclastic Barry Humphries, creator of Edna and the 'Ocker' who, like Swift, rarely let the moment pass without a knock-down. In the tradition of many grand authors, White commented that, from time to time as a young man, he had wanted to be an actor but was too shy to live out the fantasy. A more natural extrovert, Humphries' initial theatrical flurry in the early 1960s was to understudy Fagin in London's West End adaption of Dickens' *Oliver Twist*, an antipodean twist if ever there was one. The root of absurdity and therefore humour, Humphries would later observe, is the juxtaposition of unlike things such as a can of diced vegetables, an airsickness bag, a plastic spoon and a domestic flight with turbulence between Australian cities. In a similar rearrangement of opposites it might be supposed that no other culture, apart from New Zealand, which geographically approximates the Antipodes even more than Australia, would produce the oxymoronic Yahoo Serious, writer, film-maker and star of *Young Einstein*, which was an Australian box-office success in the late 1980s, and the less successful *Reckless Kelly* released in the early 1990s. On account of its antipodeality, *Australian civilisation* seems to have a similar oxymoronic ring to it. It is at very least a term to approach with a mind to double illusion.

If *Antipodes* is tricky as a designation, *civilisation* is virtually guaranteed to cause problems, and where there is smoke there is fire. Did Freud really say that civilisation began when man first urinated on fire and thus brought it under his control? This appears to be the Blainey view in *The Triumph of the Nomads* (1975). Blainey's Tasmanians had access to fire — they even carried fire sticks — but they did not possess the means to master it. Civilisation was within their grasp quite literally, but the Tasmanians had been pissing into the roaring forties for tens of thousands of years.[4] In 1993, in what became known as his Wagga Wagga address, the National Party leader, Tim Fischer made a similar claim, that

INTRODUCTION

because they had no carts nor buildings of substance, the Aborigines lacked civilisation.

But what is civilisation? In his best-selling book and television series, *Civilisation*, British historian Kenneth Clark posed just that question only to answer, 'I don't know — yet', holding out hope with that 'yet' of an unproblematic but complex disclosure. '*Civilisation*,' Clark admitted, 'it was this word alone that persuaded me to undertake the work. I had no idea what it meant, but I thought it preferable to barbarism.'[5] Clark's Australian namesake, Manning Clark, beginning a few years earlier, came to a similar conclusion by opening his own can of vegetables. Civilisation and barbarism, Manning Clark maintained, are antonyms, and the history of the western world, including former colonies like Australia, has been a continuous tussle between the two.

Yet, it would appear, civilisation and barbarism are not simple oppositions; rather they are complementary 'others' linked on a continuum, coexisting within the same space and moment, like good and evil, light and dark. Barbarism is the very shadow of civilisation, the reverse side of the coin, without which civilisation could not exist or be defined.

Civilisation is a powerful and time-honoured concept, but the term itself is more recent. It came into common English usage at the height of the enlightenment, around the time of European exploration in the Pacific.[6] One of civilisation's two primary synonyms is *courtesy*,[7] the substantives of which include: *urbanity, polish, politeness, gentility, comity, civility, amenity, suavity, discretion, diplomacy, gallantry* and so on. In the Antipodes the qualities of courtesy slump without grace alongside some of the more muscular and erect self-images of the settler society, the substantives of which include *practical, rough and ready* and phrases such as 'quick to decry any appearance of affectation in others'.[8] There is little time for courtesy if you've got a country to build. Precious little time for manners. There is work to be done. The second synonym, *mankind*, might appeal more. Its substantives include: *people, race, society, community, commonality, nation, state, realm, commonwealth, republic, nationality* and so on. These practical demarcations — solid nation-building stuff — are more in keeping, it would seem, with the no-nonsense values of Australians.

In his history, *Australia*, which became a prototype of a good deal of historical writing that followed, W.K. Hancock argued in 1930:

INTRODUCTION

the British have imposed themselves upon [Australia] with their barbed wire and railways and commercial journalism and modern liberal ideas. Their advance resembles the forward scattering of a horde, and sometimes, like the onrush of a horde, it has been devastating.⁹

In other contexts *horde* and *civilisation* might appear oddly, perhaps ironically, juxtaposed. Hordes usually signify the barbarians. Great walls have been built to keep them at bay and in their place. Not so, it would appear, in the new world but, if civilisation was ready-made in the old world, it seems equally clear that it did not arrive in Australia complete and uncontested.

The actual term *civilisation* is only occasionally used by Australians. There is, for instance, no entry in the *Australian National Dictionary* (1988), although there are entries for the verb *civilise*, referring to the assimilation of the Aborigines, and the participial adjective *civilised*, meaning 'domesticated' or 'tame'.¹⁰ The omission, I'd wager, is not simply a condition of antipodeality but a commentary consistent with the historical processes by which the uncivilised is said to be brought into civilisation. Australian civilisation is never quite an achieved state — it is always developing but not quite yet developed — but a primary process towards achievable and practical goals. It embraced the enlightenment but could not in the least celebrate an achieved condition of refinement.

Hancock put down a template. Manning Clark made it his ambition to manufacture histories out of Australia and the Australians. Clark argued that 'civilising' concerns the process by which 'people are brought together out of barbarism'. The proper direction of human history, he maintained, is in progression out of darkness towards higher civilised values. But what of a people who migrate to far-off lands? How is such an orderly progression affected? Clark's life's work was to understand how well civilisation transplanted in the Australian environment and, in common with Hancock, he explicitly identified civilisation as a European condition — although he acknowledged also Hindu, Chinese and Islamic civilisations — not a condition of the Antipodes. The coming Australians had to apply themselves with dexterity and tremendous endurance, the great subtheme of Clark's six tomes, in order to make civilisation viable. Volume 1 of *A History of Australia* opens: 'Civilisation did not begin in Australia until the last quarter of the eighteenth century.'¹¹ In epic form, over five succeeding volumes and the ensuing decades of his life, Clark resolved to know something of the shape of civilisation in the Antipodes. Gazing across seas and wondering about the nature of the hordes to the north, west and east, he ruminated in pessimistic moments: 'have we become bored survivors, sitting comfortless on Bondi Beach, citizens in the Kingdom of nothingness who booze and surf while waiting for the barbarians?'[12]

If *civilisation* is a double entendre in the Antipodes, then indolence brings its own demise. As a scholar of the enlightenment, Manning Clark conceptualised Australia as a barbarous continent inhabited originally by barbarous peoples. The Australian barbarians, the Aborigines, he maintained, 'created cultures but not civilisations!'[13] They had refused the greatest gift of all:

> the gift of the greatest civilisation in the history of mankind; the civilisation which had produced the plays of Shakespeare, Bach's *Mass in B Minor*, the piano concertos of Mozart, the Authorised version of the Bible, Milton's *Paradise Lost* and the *Book of Common Prayer* — to mention but a few . . .[14]

But 'What was puzzling', puzzled Clark, was 'why the Aborigines spurned the gift of European civilisation'. Aboriginality had made 'no progress', he said, out of barbarism despite a long residence in this continent, and in the post-contact period Aborigines had turned their backs on the great opportunities to acquire civilisation.[15] Hancock, during meditative walks through the Monaro, perhaps guessed why civilisation had been rejected but was not brave enough to say so aloud. During his weekly 'open air seminars' with protégé Humphrey McQueen, Clark came to appreciate in the last years of his life, when the great volumes were all but done, that Aboriginal non-compliance was actually resistance to dispossession and more generally that, in the new world, '"Civilisation", like "freedom" and "democracy", is a word that kills', as Ronald Wright put it so succinctly in *Stolen Continents* (1992), a history of indigenous peoples in the Americas from the time of Columbus. If civilisation 'means anything at all', Wright maintained, 'it means only this. Civilised peoples have practiced the Roman Circus, the Aztec sacrifice, the Spanish Inquisition, the burning of witches, the gassing of Jews. Uncivilised ones have acted no worse'.[16] A bit harsh, we might feel, but effective in making a powerful point. We might add to the civilised ledger the ethnic cleansing of the Australian Aborigines, the Western Front, Changi, Hiroshima, 'rolling thunder' and so on.

INTRODUCTION

Barbarism, that is to say, is contained within civilisation. It came to Australia on board the tall ships along with the Bible, Shakespeare, Bach, Mozart and Milton. The dichotomy of the enlightenment, civilisation/barbarism, applies to contact history but on the side of the invaders. An alternative dialectic, civilisation/savagery, was required to provide the semantic and philosophical manoeuvrability to renegotiate civilisation in its new space. Specifically, it provided the slippage needed in the vexed question of defining worlds beyong the limits of civilisation — the Antipodes — where, by extrapolation if civilisation did not exist, barbarism also did not exist. Savagery fulfilled the outer condition.

Savagery, unlike barbarism but very like primitivism, which is its correlative condition, is a romantic disposition popularised during the European upheavals of the late eighteenth century, which grew out of, but as a point-counterpoint to, the enlightenment. While its source of meaning is thoroughly European, savagery turns away from notions of improvement through progress — from barbarism to civilisation — towards entertaining the possibilities of virtue in the uncivilised state. It is this disposition that we find at the heart of contemporary environmental politics in Australia, which makes good and bad use of terms like *wilderness* and *pristine areas*. More widely, the sometimes deeply conservative, sometimes subversively radical, repositioning of presumed opposites became not so much a source of humour but a possible new dialectical explanation of civilisation itself, savagery as 'Other'. Yet civilisation comes to the savages, not the other way round. It remains privileged and superior. Hancock might well have been right after all. *Hordes* might well, indeed, be the right word to describe settlers in a settler society.

Civilisation claims superior technology on its side, but it also learns lessons from the primitive and the savage. In the official bicentennial series, *The Australians* (1988), McQuilton and Camm spoke confidently about the richness of Australia's 'prehistoric art', and they used the term *gallery* to describe significant sites. 'Although many galleries remain unrecorded', they pointed out, 'this heritage forms one of the world's largest art collections and probably some of the pictures rank among its oldest.'[17] In such conceptualisations of Aboriginality we witness an important shift away from scientific archaeology, that precision instrument of the enlightenment and of modernity, to cultural aesthetics. With certainty palaeontologists in 1993 announced they had recovered the

INTRODUCTION

world's oldest art gallery in a rock shelter in the Northern Territory. The paintings were dated back at least 53,000 years. And so we acquire not only new time-clocks but also cultural barometers by which we measure human creativity in Australia.

Such antiquity renders tautological Tim Fischer's complaint that, yes, it is true, Aborigines had no carts — they had no need of carts — yet slowly other wheels and wheels within wheels are turning. Brave graffiti accompanying the bicentennial celebrations in 1988 announced that 'White Australia has a black history'. The graffiti hit the mark and, with important political and legal implications, the stories of colonisation and decolonisation in Australia are changing, providing flexibility, legitimacy and agency for the re-conceptualisation of Aborigines as one of the oldest continuous cultures on earth. Pioneering sagas of the white settlers, on the other hand, are being reconsidered to take account of the dispossession that occurred as a result of 'unlocking the lands' for 'productive usage'. Such historical and philosophical reappraisals are close to the heart of legal challenges to and bench decisions against *terra nullius*.

A decade before the High Court Mabo decision overturned *terra nullius* as Australian law and as an article of faith, Colin Tatz (1982) argued 'Aboriginality as Civilisation' but cautioned that 'far too often white society equates Aboriginal culture only with facets of their ornamental culture, such as bark paintings'.[18] In the ensuing decade Aboriginal dot paintings became a million-dollar industry at a time when native title was set to become one of the most intensely and publicly contested issues among Australians. When it has suited, non-indigenous Australians have made indigenous Australians *our Aborigines* — when they have been successful in the arts and sport in particular, when their names have been the likes of Lionel Rose, Evonne Goolagong, David Gulpilil, Tracey Moffatt, to mention a few. We have been rather more suspicious of 'Aboriginal intellectuals' — they have meant trouble for us, those 'smart-arse black-fellas' and 'troublesome gins' — and we habitually disregard those in poverty. The overrepresentation of Aborigines brought to book by the criminal justice system is a clear indication that something is terribly wrong.

There are courts and Courts. The succession of Charles by Richard in Western Australian politics looks like the ambitions of a dynasty. Richard Court became Premier of Western Australia in the early 1990s on the back of popular resentment at Labor's financial mismanagement in the 1980s. On election night Court's adopted Aboriginal daughter appeared on the dais with the premier-elect, his wife and natural son. Richard Court clearly loves his daughter but, as a politician, he has proved a resolute antagonist in any debates on native title in Western Australia. In 1993 the Court Government legislated against what were called 'Mabo-style claims' and set up a fighting fund of $2 million to be used against such claims. The essentialist heart swells easily inside non-indigenous rib-cages, but clearly, as Tatz has signalled, the claims of Aboriginal civilisation go very much deeper than the fluting of our pride.

If civilisation has been both a destroyer and creator, if we have been both settlers and disrupters, it stands to reason that there might be arguments for reconstituting the term *savage* as a signifier of the Antipodes. I don't mean this fully in the sense suggested by Levi-Strauss, for instance, in *The Savage Mind* (1962), who none the less observed:

> nothing in our civilisation more closely resembles the periodic pilgrimages made by the initiated Australians, escorted by their sages, than our conducted tours of Goethe's or Victor Hugo's house, the furniture of which inspires emotions as strong as they are arbitrary.[19]

Nor do I mean this fully in the darker side of our dreamings as narrated, for instance, in the tragic irony of James Savage who discovered his Aboriginality all too late. As a child James Savage was removed from his natural mother, adopted by white parents and raised in the USA. He knew nothing of his background, but was on the streets by the age of twelve; he grew up fast, as the expression goes, and now awaits execution for murder. Who are the guilty parties in this case? The savage saved by civilisation only to experience the fullness of barbarism. The metaphors are pregnant, yet for me there is a related, if more modest, less obviously tragic, sense in which savagery might be reclaimed as an Australian condition. I grew up as a wadjella in Nyoongar country and, as children, we all spoke creole in the playground — naturally it was banned in the classroom. Our Nyoongar creole drew heavily on common English but among the many verbal subversives was the phrase: 'Ngah cruel savage, unna', meaning quite the opposite: 'You're a real civilised human being'.

Aboriginal dreamings across the continent hold that death means 'going into the country', attaching yourself spiritually to place, which is quite a different rationalisation from that oft-noted Euro-

INTRODUCTION

pean dread of sleeping perchance to dream. Aboriginal dreamings are clearly journeys from which travellers can and do return. But it requires a leap in faith, a shift in perception or, as Judith Wright would say, a new axis, to begin to wander beneath southern skies. D.H. Lawrence crossed the equator in the 1920s but Australian ghost gums reflected in the full moon terrified him. He retreated to the security of the drawing room and made the observation that Australia needs to be populated by centuries of ghosts before Australians can properly call themselves a civilisation. He was, of course, talking about non-indigenous Australians. In a like manner, when Voss disappears into the interior in Patrick White's masterful novel, Laura says: 'He did not die . . . He is there still, it is said, in the country, and always will be. His legend will be written down, eventually, by those who have been troubled by it.'[20] Voss enters a space that resists our best attempts at appropriation. The space is elusive and metaphysical, which is one reason why the early realists had difficulty with White as a writer; but if the imagination remains troubled, it might well be because we still have journeys to travel.

Over tens of thousands of years possibly hundreds of millions of Aborigines have lived and died in Australia. Their stories will not be written down but their ghosts fill the continent. They, rather than the more recent immigrants, in the words of Mudrooroo, are *Master(s) of the Ghost Dreaming* (1991). Tragically and prophetically, the Aborigines who first came into contact with Europeans identified the invaders not as conquerors but as returning spirits of the ancestral dead. We learn to write different stories, I think, from this beginning. It is a more honest place to start, a common base to our Australian-ness and our humanity. It provides a sounder philosophical logic to our often confused and sometimes contradictory mythologies. The spaces we occupy in Australia were Aboriginal first.

Non-indigenous Australians habitually find themselves between a rock and an ocean when they try to match their stories with place and history. They can yack and yack about work, tell jokes and tall tales and spook one another about strange occurrences, but they publicly baulk at suggestions of a metaphysical attachment to place. There are many restless spirits in this vast land, among them the ETs, the bolters, the fugitives, the refugees, who exist in a kind of spiritual exile, of unbelonging, and for whom Australia has been not only the last great region of the world to

Introduction

come under the influence of the Europeans — the 'last challenge of European civilisation'[21] — but also the least endowed of the continents. Least and last, Australia enters the imagination as a place of forced necessity and last resort where displaced souls have had to travel first and work hard to remake their lives.

Among the great migratory peoples of the nineteenth century, the Irish hoped and prayed for their *émigré* sons and daughters fleeing starvation and the blight. Their first choices of exile were invariably England, Scotland and North America, but the Irish ritually performed wakes for those destined for Australia — because the Antipodes were too far away for any return to be practical. Going to the other side of the world, going to Australia, was akin to dying — and if you had already died at home there was no need to do it a second time round in an alien environment. Death became an accepted condition for exiles from Erin. The Antipodes implied limbo — the most diabolical of all spiritual conditions. For the Irish, then, Australia was the land of the living dead. Industrial and agrarian revolutions might have put an end to similar enactments of funeral rites for those other Britons facing exile who instead substituted legendary stoicism for superstition. The end result, however, was remarkably similar. They were still aliens in an alien environment. Work was their salvation and, as long as you could work hard, you did not have to think too hard. The wisdom of Solomon said as much.

Deep anxieties of unbelonging run pretty close to the bone of being Australian. They are ritually re-enacted in Anzac remembering each 25 April. They are present in the care taken by the Commonwealth Graves Commission with its tens of thousands of marked but not always identified graves over Europe, markers of the Australian dead in European wars. Unbelonging fills out the backpacks of those thousands of young Australian tourists who each year make the pilgrimage to the killing fields of Gallipoli. It is the narrative running through stories of the lost child in the bush, the nineteenth-century concern to repatriate the remains of Burke and Wills, the continued obsession with the 'lost figure' of Ludwig Leichhardt, the model for *Voss*, and the obsession with Lindy Chamberlain as a witch figure.

Not all Australians have been fugitives out of necessity, but many have been fugitives none the less. Poet Les Murray made the observation that the British working class got away to Australia — that they escaped far worse conditions in the old world to lay

Introduction

claims eventually to a vernacular republic in the new world. A few more besides made their way south to live out complicated lives in Australia — of being both runaways and outcasts, of possessing not only pasts but also histories that have been consciously suppressed. These Australians carry the mark of Cain in their DNA. They are simultaneously guilty and free of responsibility and, unable to 'cultivate the land' properly, to bring it under civilisation, they have made national heroes instead out of itinerants, wanderers and travelling soldiers. Squads of four-wheel-drive vehicles with aggressive radial tyres parked in the suburban driveways bear witness to the continuous nature of this particular fantasy. 'So we leave them dumbfounded at their optimism, astounded that belief in material progress and mateship could be their only comforters against earth, man and beast,' wrote Clark.[22]

Robert Drewe has observed that Australia is a place where, if the dingoes don't get you, the sharks will. My mother's brother was never seen again after his sudden disappearance in the surf in 1947. Nobody actually saw a shark, and when a small skeletal hand was later found inside a monster, a year or so after her son had disappeared, my Nanna refused to believe it was the hand of the child she had once held. 'It can't be,' she wept as she looked down on the scrawny bones. She never gave up this belief, and the image of those few bones has haunted my family ever since in a similar way, I suspect, but without the attendant publicity, as the baby's jumpsuit that has dogged the poor Chamberlains. Dare I make such a comparison? I think so. In both cases there are only fragments of the presumed beastly annihilation and the ghastly lingering images of the terrifying last moments. Public consciousness, on the other hand, requires forensic proof, and I sometimes wonder whether this might be partly the reason why Australians are such bloody good soldiers in other nations' wars but the most reluctant organ donors in the western world. We desire to be committed whole to earth, water or fire.

Fred Hollows, a pioneer surgeon whose life's work was as a practical man and a man of vision, a man who could make others see, was sung in death into the quiet earth that has made so many so nervous. He was buried at the back of Bourke. At Broken Hill — in Australia the land is so old hills can be broken, rocks can decay — twelve statues were erected to honour his memory. Ozymandias in the outback, they were said to recreate a '30,000-year-old stone-carving tradition of the Aborigines from beyond the

Introduction

Darling River'.[23] Hollows died into the country in a way that artist Sidney Nolan could not. Nolan's family pleaded for Australians to understand why the corpse ought not be repatriated from the UK where the artist had lived for the last half of his life. Perhaps Nolan was haunted, as his Kelly series of paintings might suggest. These contrasting spirits, what might be called our Hollows–Nolan complex, are part of our spiritual dilemma — our Australian being — the very things that bring us together and keep us apart.

Part of the reason for our nervousness and often prodigious energies in work and war is, I suspect, as David Malouf has eloquently put it in *Remembering Babylon* (1993), because Australians have been cut off not only from their pasts but also from their dead, a theme that also rises and falls in Patrick O'Farrell's history, *Vanishing Kingdoms* (1992). As a nation of immigrants, Australians have often preferred to call 'Home' somewhere else, making classic television out of Telecom advertisements in the 1970s and 1980s. And for many, until relatively recently, 'Home' connoted the United Kingdom. So long, it would seem, as there was an empire through which they could enjoin themselves to Greater Britain or, in Churchill's phrase, Australians could defer thoughts of civilisation towards the 'history of the English-speaking peoples', there was surely some comfort in being an exile. But it is now a school history lesson that Churchill sacrificed Australia in two world wars — at Gallipoli in 1915 and Singapore in 1942 — and the empire is all gone even in name. We turn inward.

Exiles turn but can rarely return — not properly — and, while the Australian imagination turns in on itself readily enough, Australians have maintained some steadfast traditions of the great cultural achievements of older worlds against which their own enterprises seem to pale. 'Australia was too young' to be able to call itself a civilisation, wrote a despondent Louis Esson on the eve of World War II,

> it had no culture — there were no castles or abbeys, no folk-songs — there was no Bloomsbury or Montemartre or Latin Quarter of Paris, with exciting bohemian life — no-one interested in arts or literature — it was crude, materialistic, Philistine.

Australia lacked 'style and taste', it was a 'far-off land . . . rather vague and empty'.[24] Bloomsbury would soon be surrounded by fire and rubble, while Montemartre and the Latin Quarter, with

INTRODUCTION

less evident destruction, submitted more readily to the authority of Nazi jackboots. Esson only just survived the war and died rather pathetically in 1946. He did not record how he might have felt about the second devastation of Europe this century — he was saved the barbarous truths concerning the holocaust — but already he was inclining Pisa-like towards the positive values of Australia.

Between 1939 and 1945 Europe, the cradle of civilisation, demonstrated for the second time in the twentieth century how even the most civil societies can also be the most barbarous. In the wake Australia began its drift away from core Anglo-Celtic values, itself a problematic designation, which none the less remains at the centre of multiculturalism,[25] when for the first time people from European countries other than Britain began to arrive in substantial numbers. Like those before them, these immigrants were displaced in Australia, only they had the added disadvantage of having to negotiate displacement against the claims of the already dug-in 'independent Australian Britons', another antipodean oxymoron.[26] The first wave — the 'DPs' (displaced persons), the 'reffos' and the 'Balts', as they were called with almost expectant antipodean tickiness signifying the absconder — came because they had nowhere else to go. They belonged nowhere. Nobody would take them. Of the eight and half million refugees in Europe at the end of the war there were at least two million whom, according to Sir Robert Jackson, the first head of the United Nations Relief and Rehabilitation Administration, 'no country in the world would accept'. 'Finally, in desperation', Jackson admitted, 'I went to Australia.' There he allegedly found a receptive ear in Prime Minister Chifley, who was concerned that Australia had to 'populate or perish'. A good railway man and engine-driver before he became a politician, 'Chif' cleared the log-jam — although, as Sir Robert's comments make clear, even in these horrendous circumstances, Australia was a last resort.[27]

Clearly the Antipodes can of its own accord be a '"horrid and diabolical" condition'[28] but, if Australia is a place of contrarieties, not of order, it is also a place to be wary of what appear to be the inversions. If things are not what they seem to be, there can be no certainty that they are what they appear to be not — civilisation in topsy-turvy land. One of Australia's more recognisable cultural icons of my childhood, Rolf Harris, kick-started his entertainment career with three boots by impersonating a deformed man in a trenchcoat. Harris included in his repertoire a song concerning a hapless jackeroo and his obliging mate who agreed with almost pathological simplicity to 'Tan me hide when I'm dead, Fred' — 'So we tanned his hide when he died, Clyde. And that's it hanging on the shed'. This really is shocking post-mortuary mutilation, but I am tempted to think I should now know why 'Jake the peg' and 'Tie me kangaroo down, sport' were popular when I was a kid and why a transnational petroleum company and later a paint company used Harris as evidence of their Australian-ness. These black humorous characterisations, like those of Paul Hogan in the 1970s and 1980s, in particular the laconic hero Mick Dundee, take the edge off Henry Lawson's more hardened observation that 'Death is about the only cheerful thing in the bush'.[29] They are similar in each case, and the bush is what Australia has had plenty of. The bush has been civilisation's project in the Antipodes. Civilisation needs gardeners.[30]

Legend has it that actress Ava Gardner, while on a film set in the garden state of Victoria for the shooting of Stanley Kramer's *On the Beach* (1959), when asked the inevitable — 'What do you think of Australia, Miss Gardner?' — responded coolly that it was a good place to make a film about the end of the world. Anyone with even limited local knowledge could have told her that Melbourne has no decent beaches. Off Bondi but apparently not awaiting the barbarians, the Sydney-based film company Kennedy Miller took the siren at her word in the 1980s with the shooting of Mad Max. In doing so they assured both the film career of Mel Gibson and enough money for not one but two sequels. How many times does the world have to end? It comes very close very often in the imagination and again in *Stark* (1993), an ABC–BBC coproduction costing the ABC more money to make than had ever previously been spent on a single production, written by and starring British comedian Ben Elton. Ms Gardner might have been right after all. In these narratives Australia retains its exotically defined but commonly accepted outer condition, the duality that brings Elton periodically back to Australia but which sent Ava Gardner in the opposite direction, scurrying home to the comfort of dream factories located in metropolitan centres. It is the duality that makes tourism a multimillion dollar industry in Australia — 'it's a good place to visit' — and an imagined location for a multifunction polis, a post-modern, futuristic city.

The term *civilisation* derives from the Latin *civis*, meaning the citizens of cities. Cities, then, have traditionally been the sites of civilisation. In the old world civilisation is signified by ancient ruins and solid modern buildings. In Australia the foundation stones were manufactured by convicts. Thus Australian civilisation belongs to a worthy tradition of civilisations built on the labour of slaves. So, if the jails are burning, take note. Australia boasts in convict-free Adelaide the first garden city in the world, signifying both civilisation and culture, while Sydney and Melbourne, which tries to pretend it had no convicts at all and by extension therefore possesses more culture, are metropolitan centres of considerable importance. In the late twentieth century Brisbane issued a formidable challenge to displace Melbourne as Australia's second city. Staunch banana-benders refer to anything south of their border as Mexico.

On the far west coast, an equally parochial bunch defied the scriptures and built their city on sand. They built Perth to be the 'most isolated city in the world'. In *The Merry-Go-Round in the Sea* (1965) Randolph Stow turns these metaphors round and round within the limited vision of his young protagonist Rob Coram who, on his first visit from the rural hinterland to the city, is impressed by the appearance of antiquity. Perth!

> They were fascinated by the customs of this new country.
> It was a mystery to them what they were doing there, how it was possible to be transported from the known world to a place so utterly foreign. Simply, their mother had said that they would go for a holiday, because they had never had that sort of holiday within their memory. And the holiday had been, first, a brown panelled nineteenth century sleeping compartment in the shuddering train, in which they had spent sixteen hours, and then this extraordinary, huge ancient metropolis, which must be, Rob thought, as old as London, to judge from the romantic grime on the buildings near the railway station....
> 'It's really only about twenty years older than Geraldton,' his mother said. But that meant nothing emotively. Perth was ancient, an ancient civilisation. Soot darkened buildings proved it, and the existence of a Museum, and the fact that it was a seat of government.[31]

There are many ironies played out in Rob's misplaced awe — in this scene the city itself, which began modestly with the felling of a tree in 1829, the houses of parliament and civilised institutions, including particularly the museum. Perth is made a civilisation on account of its presumed antiquity. Its tenuous hold is eventually realised not because it is a very young city, nor because of the sand; rather the atomic bombing of Hiroshima: 'They reckon it is big enough to wipe out anywhere . . . Just one of 'em'll wipe out a city.'

The end of Australia, then, as much as its unconventional beginnings, inscribes the Australian imagination much of the time. There were the Japanese in the 1940s, a few scares during the early cold war, in the 1960s there were those Vietnamese dominoes, and in the 1990s in apocalypse revisited — the clash of civilisations thesis — Australia was made a frontline state in yet another reworking of that ever-recurrent, easily evoked, phobia called the old yellow peril. According to this thesis, the world is divided into nine civilisations: 'European and North American; Confucian; Japanese; Islamic; Hindu; Slavic–Orthodox; Latin American and African'. The particular danger for the most 'isolated fragment of western civilisation in the world', Australia, is that 'powerful reaction is setting in among the elites of other civilisations in the form of de-westernising, return to roots movements'. Australia's location makes it especially vulnerable because the main challenge to the West is said to come from a 'de-facto anti-western co-operation between the Confucian and Islamic civilisations of Asia'.[32] The result is that Australia is living on the 'edge of the most dangerous "fault-line" in the world — and is the softest target on that line'.

The 'fault line' described by the clash of civilisations thesis pretty accurately corresponds with what is called the Wallace line, which separates Australasia from Asia. On the one side there are predatory mammals, such as the tiger, and tropical birdlife, including woodpeckers and thrushes, which have ventured no further. Today, *tigers* refer to the NICs or newly industrialising nations of Asia. On the other side there are cockatoos and honeysuckers but no comparable predatory mammals. Indonesian expansionism has crossed the line and moved into Melanesian West Irian. Timor has also been colonised. But in the last 60,000 years the only successful civilisation to cross this way into Australia were the Aborigines. The Europeans came from a different direction.

From a historical perspective Manning Clark has pointed out that ancient 'Hindu, Chinese, and Muslim civilisations' did not get to Australia, partly because of the internal histories of these civilisations.[33] We might very well be in a similar situation now, but it

INTRODUCTION

is important to bear in mind that what can be mapped as the Asia–Pacific region is demographically one of the most plural of all the world's areas. The sheer plurality, not to mention lack of will on the part of Asian countries to form some mega-Asian Confucian–Islamic bloc, would seem to militate against any East-versus-West clash of civilisations within cooee of Australia. The clash of civilisations scenario is really a symptom of anxiety on the part of western intellectuals looking for new definitions in the post–cold war era. It is also lazy scholarship. None of the world's land masses moved during the cold war. None have shifted since.

The Asians are not coming, although Australia's most Asianised city, the wonderfully named Darwin, signifying both the ascent and the descent of man, has been our most battered city. It was bombed by the Japanese in 1942. A generation later it disappeared from the face of the earth, blown away by a big wind on Christmas Day 1974, and had to be completely rebuilt. Santa never made it into Darwin but Gough Whitlam, a man who understood well the decline and fall of ancient European civilisations, Promethean man in the Antipodes, the man who woke Australians from their Menzian slumber, was prime minister at the time. Whitlam had come to government, just two years before the destruction, determined to 'buy back the farm'. In the end he was outflanked by the 'squatter mounted on his thoroughbred'. There are powerful vested interests in this old democracy.

In the middle of 1974 Whitlam was forced back to the polls by hostile senators, so soon after his election. He secured a second term for his government but with a reduced majority. The second election also marked the end of twelve months of rain and massive flooding throughout eastern Australia. But when the floods subsided the fires began, first in the outback and then in New South Wales jails, which had been torched by rioting inmates. 'Is Bathurst burning?' asked the *National Times*. 'You bet . . . ', came the reply. The Promethean legend was being played in reverse. Ignoring the signs, Whitlam embarked on a six-week world tour, covering around 150,000 air kilometres and setting a cracking walking pace through the ruins of the old world. Journalist Robert Haupt reported: 'When he visits ruins, he does not do things by halves. He is voracious, walking at a rapid pace, climbing up and down, invariably taking longer than expected and always wanting to visit the furthermost site.' Early on Christmas morning the cyclone came to Darwin. More than sixty people were killed, hundreds were injured. All souls had to be evacuated, requiring the biggest 'manpower' effort since mobilisation for war in the 1940s.

With his own ruins now to tend to and a new city to build in its place, Whitlam defied calls to return home but instead intensified his concentration on Europe. And he became testy when quizzed about his absence. Could his government have been held responsible for a natural disaster? he shot back at reporters. When asked by an intrigued Dutch observer, a man who clearly would have put his finger in the dyke, whether this 'odyssey' was like being a 'farmer on holiday when the barn is burnt down', Whitlam snapped, 'Who the hell are you?'[34] Whitlam was greeted on his scheduled return with headlines such as 'Home to a crisis he doesn't know about' and 'Does he know where he is heading?', the cover story from the *Bulletin*, in which Peter Samuel maintained: 'Whitlam will hardly be back from the archaeological sites and palaces of Europe in all their quiet splendour before he has to throw himself into intense politicking.'[35] You can't be prime minister and stay out of the country when a whole city in your own civilisation disappears from the face of the earth. You can't be away from home, as William Morris Hughes and Robert Gordon Menzies discovered before Whitlam, when your civilisation is calling. You have to put your heart as well as your soul into the place.

All Australian prime ministers seem to be attracted by international travel, although they don't all visit ruins. In the footsteps of many other Australian travellers, Malcolm Fraser, Bob Hawke and Paul Keating each made it a prime ministerial duty of remembrance to visit the European killing fields of the 1914–18 war. Fraser would later lose his pants in the US, but only after he had given up his seat in parliament. Bob Hawke became a roving reporter specialising in Australian prime ministers travelling overseas after losing the top job to Keating in 1991. In 1993 Prime Minister Keating took to the Queen his message that Australia wished to be a republic and was greeted in London with tabloid headlines that he was a 'barbarian'. 'The Lizard of Oz' and 'Bleating Keating' were also popular. The reason for these outbursts was a long-running battle over Australia's recent historical past and Britain's part in it. He also appeared as a prime minister very much in favour of Australia concentrating on its region rather than endlessly gazing across oceans to the old worlds of Europe. Such a shift in perceptions required of Australians and of the world quite different rules for Australian civilisation.

INTRODUCTION

Nationalism, then, is our Australian point of reference but not in the rigid nineteenth-century sense of the term nor indeed in the sense of the blind furies and the barbarous certainties of our earlier colonial mentalities and those of a number of present-day old-world societies. If the collective chooses to define itself as Australian then it also moves with little conscious effort between adjective and noun to signify and give meaning to our many and varied conditions and identities, usually based on region, ethnicity, religion or class but also on just about any other grouping or identification we choose to make for ourselves. The collective consciousness, that is, has travelled well beyond the depiction offered by Alan Seymour in his classic play, *The One Day of the Year*, where Alf proclaims himself simply as a 'bloody Australian'. Present-day Australian nationalism offers great versatility and flexibility. It is one of the real achievements of *our* civilisation.

Australia continues to see itself as a place of the future still in the making, of a civilisation that is always arriving but which has not yet quite arrived. We are a community of perpetual provisionality. Added to the versatility of our nationalism, our provisional condition is a charm against delusions of grandeur and of national chauvinism. We have come together out of fragments, out of bits and pieces from here and there, out of crosses and double-crosses, out of colonialism and modernity. The fourth estate of our civilisation, then, is to remain critical of our histories. Scepticism is an Australian trait, but we have not always approached the past honestly; partly, I suspect, because we have lacked the time and often the patience to think deeply about our spiritual or emotional being, the metaphysics of being Australian. The time has now come, I'd reckon, to take a break from the sun, to shake off some of the flies and to take a swig from the waterbag, to spell under the ghost gums and to listen for a moment to the breathing of this quiet land. Melanomas and all, we are Australians. We need to think ourselves into the place. We have made our lives here. In the end that is something pretty considerable. It is time to reconcile our spirit and our stories to place, the beginning point, I would say, of our peculiarly Australian civilisation.

NOTES

1 David Malouf, *Johnno*, University of Queensland Press, St Lucia, 1975, p. 170.
2 K.S. Inglis, 'Anzac revisited: Australia, New Zealand and the Anzac

INTRODUCTION

tradition', in Alan Seymour and Richard Nile (eds), *Anzac: Meaning, Memory and Myth*, Sir Robert Menzies Centre for Australian Studies, University of London, 1991, p. 13.
3 J.D. Pringle, *The Australian Accent*, Chatto & Windus, London, 1961, p. 134.
4 Geoffrey Blainey, *Triumph of the Nomads: A History of Ancient Australia*, Macmillan, Melbourne, 1975.
5 Kenneth Clark, *Civilisation*, BBC Books and John Murray, London, 1992, pp. 1, xvii.
6 See Bernard Smith, *European Vision and the South Pacific*, Yale University Press, New Haven, Conn., 1985.
7 Raymond Williams, *Keywords: A Vocabulary of Culture and Society*, Collins, Glasgow, 1981; D.C. Browning (ed.), *The Everyman Edition of Roget's Thesaurus*, Sphere, London, 1989.
8 Russel Ward, *The Australian Legend*, Oxford University Press, Melbourne, 1958, pp. 1–2.
9 W.K. Hancock, *Australia*, Benn, London, 1930, p. 29.
10 See W.S. Ramson (ed.), *The Australian National Dictionary*, Oxford University Press, Melbourne, 1988, which has entries for *civilise* and *civilised* but not for *civilisation*.
11 C.H.M. Clark, *A History of Australia*, Melbourne University Press, Melbourne, paperback edition, 1979, vol. 1, p. 3.
12 C.M.H. Clark, 'A discovery of Australia' in *Manning Clark: Occasional Writings and Speeches*, Fontana, Melbourne, 1980, p. 39.
13 Clark, op. cit., p. 48.
14 Ibid, pp. 48, 47.
15 Ibid.
16 Ronald Wright, *Stolen Continents: The 'New World' seen through Indian Eyes since 1492*, Viking, Toronto, 1992, p. 100.
17 J.C.R. Camm & John McQuilton, *Australians: A Historical Atlas*, Fairfax Syme & Weldon, Sydney, 1988, p. 38.
18 Colin Tatz, 'Aboriginality as civilisation' in Gillian Whitlock and David Carter (eds), *Images of Australia*, University of Queensland Press, St Lucia, 1992, pp. 87–8.
19 Claude Levi-Strauss, *The Savage Mind*, Weidenfeld & Nicolson, London, 1962, p. 244.
20 Patrick White, *Voss*, Penguin, Ringwood, 1974, p. 448.
21 Op. cit., p. 164.
22 Peter Coleman, *Australian Civilization*, F.W. Cheshire, Melbourne (paperback edition), 1963, pp. 3, 7.
23 Patrick Lawnham, 'Sculptors carve outback tribute to Hollow', *Weekend Australian*, 22–23 May 1993.
24 See David Walker, *Dream and Disillusion*, Australian National University Press, Canberra, 1976, pp. 11–30.

25 See Charles Husband, 'Multiculturalism as official policy in Australia', in Richard Nile (ed.), *Immigration and the Politics of Ethnicity and Race in Australia and Britain*, Sir Robert Menzies Centre for Australian Studies, University of London, and Bureau of Immigration Research, Melbourne, 1991, pp. 118–27.
26 W.K. Hancock used this phrase to describe the Australians in his 1930 history *Australia*; he also spoke about Australians as being transplanted Britons.
27 Robert Jackson in evidence to the Independent Commission on International Humanitarian Issues, Geneva, 1983, cited in Gough Whitlam, *The Whitlam Years: 1972–1975*, Viking, Ringwood, 1985, p. 489.
28 David Lowenthal, 'Antipodean and other museums', *Working Papers in Australian Studies*, No. 66, 1991, p. 1.
29 Brian Penton, *Think or be Damned*, Angus & Robertson, Sydney, 1941, p. 55.
30 On the development of 'civilisation' through 'culture' and 'cultivation' see Williams, op. cit.
31 Randolph Stow, *The Merry-Go-Round in the Sea*, MacDonald, London, 1965, pp. 142–3, 145.
32 Owen Harries, 'Clash of civilisations', *Weekend Australian*, 3–4 April 1993.
33 C.H.M. Clark, *A History of Australia*, vol. 1, p. 3.
34 *National Times*, 13–18 January 1975.
35 *Bulletin*, 25 January 1975.

1
HISTORY

Henry Reynolds

Peter Coleman's 1962 symposium *Australian Civilization* celebrated the emergence of the 'new Australia' and the retreat of the old bush legend as well as the 'way of life it expressed and encouraged'. Central to this change were developments in Australian historical writing that represented a 'counter-revolution in Australian historiography'. Seen in retrospect the changes signalled were less significant than those that took place subsequently in the 1970s and 1980s. The differences between the 'old' and the 'new' traditions are less obvious, and we can now see that they share much more than was apparent in the early 1960s.

One of the features of Coleman's book that strikes today's reader is the lack of any consideration of Aboriginal culture or history. There are just three brief mentions of Aborigines. They are noticed in passing and used only to illustrate aspects of other themes — particularly police attitudes and the role of the press. While there is a chapter on immigrants and numerous references to racism, there is not so much as an index entry for Aborigines. The outsider reading *Australian Civilization* would have to assume that in the early 1960s indigenous Australians played no role whatever in local society, culture or politics.

Neglect of the Aborigines was clearly apparent in the work of the two historians who were thought to best illustrate the old tradition and the new: Russel Ward and Manning Clark. In his classic 1958 work, *The Australian Legend*, Ward celebrated the outback traditions but virtually ignored the owners of the land, who resisted the 'nomad tribe' of pastoral workers, or the black guides, trackers and stockmen, who assisted them in every district from the earliest years of settlement. Manning Clark's first volume of his *History of Australia* (1962) deals with the coming of European civilisation but pays scant regard to the society and culture that was destroyed in the process. In later years both Clark and Ward sought to remedy what increasingly came to be seen as a surprising and unacceptable oversight in their work.

The total neglect of the Aborigines was a characteristic of Australian historical scholarship in the first sixty years of the twentieth century. This had not been the case with colonial historians. The most serious scholars — men like John West, George Rusden and James Bonwick — dealt at length with the continuing tragedy of dispossession and destruction. But that concern diminished during the following generations.[1] Histories of Australia written before the 1970s typically began their tale with the arrival of the European explorers or with events in eighteenth-century Britain — the overcrowding of the gaols, the decision to dispatch the First Fleet, the appointment of Governor Phillip and suchlike. Fleeting mention was made of the blacks around the pinpoints of European settlement while a few individuals were given walk-on parts in the drama of early Sydney. Inland clans met and sometimes harassed intrepid explorers and hardy pioneers; black spears symbolised the hostility of an alien environment there to be mastered. Many writers discussed and deplored the fate of the Tasmanian Aborigines, but after the mid-nineteenth century interest faltered and there was little further mention of the blacks at all. Racial conflict was portrayed as a feature of the earliest period of Australian history with little relevance to the present.

In a lecture that surveyed historical scholarship over the thirty-year period from 1929 to 1959 Professor J.A. La Nauze of the Australian National University pinpointed lack of interest in the Aborigines as one of the distinguishing features of national historiography that marked it off even from the scholarship of other colonies of settlement. He explained that:

> even among countries of modern European settlement we are peculiar in having no real experience of formidable opposition by the native inhabitants. Unlike the Maori, the American Indian or the South African Bantu, the Australian aboriginal is noticed in our history only in a melancholy anthropological footnote.[2]

The contrast is immediately apparent if we compare general histories of Australia and New Zealand written in the 1950s and specifically Sinclair's *History of New Zealand* (1959) and Greenwood's *Australia: A Social and Political History* (1956). Sinclair begins with an account of Maori New Zealand. Half the book is taken up with colonial history in a section entitled 'Maoris and settlers'. Maoris take up thirty-three separate entries in the index. When we turn to Greenwood we enter another world. The book is entirely Eurocentric. There is nothing about Aboriginal culture, economy or traditions. They are mentioned twice — but only in passing — and do not appear in the index at all.

Why were the Aborigines written out of the historical record early this century? Many influences were probably at work. Some of the major ones can be noted here. Until the 1940s the overwhelming opinion — both popular and scientific — was that the blacks were 'dying out', condemned by the iron laws of evolution to eventual extinction. With only a minor black role in the present and none in the future, the Aboriginal past could be discounted. Early twentieth-century history was self-consciously nationalistic and written to foster patriotism in the present and pride in the past. Racial violence was an embarrassment best forgotten, especially as the heroes of the pioneer legend — squatters, prospectors, explorers and overlanders — had helped to bloody the billabongs. To create doubts about the means of European occupation was to question the morality of settlement, even the right to the continent. Such questions had no place in works that celebrated steady material progress, the creation of free institutions and the evolution of a happy, hedonistic lifestyle.

Attitudes towards the Aborigines have changed dramatically. Dissatisfaction with conventional historiography grew during the 1960s and stimulated new scholarship in the 1970s and 1980s. A prominent early critic of the historical profession was the celebrated anthropologist Professor W.E.H. Stanner. In his 1968 Boyer Lectures for the ABC Stanner sharply criticised the nation's historians for neglecting the Aborigines. In a lecture entitled 'The great Australian silence' he argued that 'inattention on such a scale could not possibly be explained by absent mindedness'. Rather it was a

> structural matter, a view from a window which has been carefully placed to exclude a whole quadrant of the landscape. What may well have begun as a simple forgetting of other possible views turned under habit and over time into something like a cult of forgetfulness practised on a national scale.[3]

But change was already under way when Stanner spoke. Stimulus for change came from many sources. Australia has been influenced by the worldwide reassessment of European imperialism that followed in the wake of decolonisation and Third World assertiveness. Indigenous peoples embedded in European settler societies — American Indians, Maoris, Bantus, Aborigines — have linked arms, assessments and aspirations.

Aboriginal political activism has challenged assumptions about the past as surely as it has questioned contemporary attitudes and current policies. The establishment of the Tent Embassy on the lawns of Parliament House in Canberra in 1972 and the unfurling of the Aboriginal flag were events resonant with historical as well as political significance. The pivotal issue of land rights is above all about history. Its roots go back to the first days at Sydney Cove when the colonists, adopting the view that Australia was *terra nullius* — a land without legitimate owners — annexed a continent of which they knew less than one hundredth part. The Aborigines and their supporters are not only struggling for land but for a radical reinterpretation of the past as well. The results of the new historical scholarship also reach far beyond the study and the conference room, feeding both political and cultural springs of the Aboriginal renaissance.

Australian prehistory has been transformed in the last generation. What archaeology existed before the 1960s was old-world archaeology. The first university appointment in Australian prehistory was not made until 1961, at which time the Aborigines were thought to have been in the continent for 10,000 years. Since then our view of ancient Australia has been totally reshaped. Prehistory has become a field of intense activity, of intellectual excitement, of popular interest. These developments were summarised in an article published in the journal *World Archaeology* in 1981:

> In 1961 the oldest date was some 9,000 years, by 1968 four sites older than 20,000 years were known and by the early 1970s at least two sites older than 30,000 years were accepted. For the last five years, 50,000 years has been generally agreed on as a likely limit, though a few believe that considerably greater antiquity will be revealed.[4]

When set against a history of such depth the European era in Australia shrinks in significance, representing a mere half of one per cent of the time of human occupation — only eight generations out of 1600.

It is not the great antiquity of Aboriginal society alone that has impressed contemporary scholars but also the evidence of creative adaptation to a vast and varied continent over periods of dramatic environmental change. D.J. Mulvaney's book, *The Prehistory of Australia* (1969), was probably the first work to draw this to the attention of a wider audience. Australia, he wrote in the introduction:

> stretches from about 43 degrees south latitude to within 11 degrees of the equator, while a third of the continent lies within the Tropics; in recent times an equal area has received an average rainfall of less than ten inches; it is further from Perth to Melbourne than the distance separating London and Moscow. The dispersal of the Aborigines throughout this vast land, their responses and adjustments to the challenges of its harsh environment, and their economical utilisation of its niggardly resources, are stimulating testimony to the achievements of the human spirit.

In the opening sentence of the book Mulvaney directly challenged traditional historiography with its emphasis on the achievements of the European explorer and pioneer. 'The discoverers, explorers and colonists of the three million square miles which are Australia', he wrote, 'were its Aborigines.'[5]

In a more recent survey of Australian archaeology, Josephine Flood has made use of the 'amazing acceleration in archaeological studies' to establish that 'Aboriginal culture has changed and evolved over more than 40,000 years'. Moreover, she observes, 'Aboriginal society has the longest continuous cultural history in the world, its roots being back in the ice age . . . when the Australian continent was both larger and greener than today':

> Australian Aborigines have been called by world renowned anthropologist Claude Levi-Strauss 'intellectual aristocrats' among early peoples. Outstanding features of traditional Aboriginal society are highly sophisticated religion, art and social organisations, an egalitarian system of justice and decision-making, complex far-flung trading networks, and an ability to adapt and survive in some of the world's harshest environments.[6]

The dramatic discovery of a vast prehistory was important enough in itself. Its significance was increased because it coincided with an international reassessment of the nature of hunter–gatherer societies summed up in the phrase the 'original affluent society' coined by the celebrated American anthropologist Marshall Sahlins. In

Australia this radical re-evaluation was popularised by historian Geoffrey Blainey in a book celebrating the *Triumph of the Nomads* (1975). Blainey argued that the Aborigines enjoyed a far higher standard of living than previously thought, their nomadism not withstanding. He explained:

> If we specify the main ingredients of a good standard of living as food, health, shelter and warmth, the average aboriginal was probably as well off as the average European in 1800. [They] could not match the comfort and security of the upper-classes of Europe, of the wealthiest tenth of the population, but they were probably much better off than the poorest tenth. In the eastern half of Europe the comparison favours the aboriginals, they probably lived in more comfort than nine-tenths of the population of Eastern Europe.[7]

After a generation of research spanning many disciplines the Aborigines now appear not the aimless wanderers of traditional accounts but as people who systematically exploited their environment by means of a profound knowledge of its resources. In open grasslands the local clans harvested vast fields of self-sown yams and indigenous cereals. On sea coasts and permanent rivers sophisticated fish traps were constructed; in the Western District of Victoria archaeologists have discovered a massive system of canals and drains that allowed exploitation of eels passing from fresh water lagoons to the sea. We have also come to appreciate the importance of the controlled and systematic use of fire over many generations in shaping the environment. The lightly timbered eucalypt woodlands that first attracted the sheep farmers were not an untouched wilderness but a human artefact shaped by centuries of deliberate 'fire-stick farming'.

The implications for traditional historiography are clear. European settlers did not tame a pristine continent but turned a usurped land to new uses. While exploring its surface and testing its potential they followed Aboriginal paths, drank at their wells, slept in their gunyahs and were highly dependent on the sophisticated bushcraft of black guides. Writing of the south-west corner of the continent, the prehistorian Sylvia Hallam emphasised that local blacks had 'opened up' the landscape in which the settlers were able to 'move around, to pasture their flocks, to find good soils ... and water sources'. The Europeans, she argued, 'inherited the possibilities of settlement and land use from the people they dispossessed'.[8]

Australian scholars have broken the Great Australian Silence and have transformed our knowledge of the Aboriginal past — multiplying the length of human settlement by four or five, challenging accepted notions of population density, reassessing our view of the quality of life of hunters and gatherers and the creative achievements of Aboriginal society. But what of the relations between the Aborigines and the European interlopers?

While archaeologists have employed a wide range of new techniques to unlock the ancient past, historians, uncovering new source material and asking fresh questions of old, are examining the Aboriginal response to European invasion and settlement and exploring the other side of the frontier. At the same time there is a tremendous upsurge of interest in the past among Aboriginal communities seeking to preserve their history both for its own sake and to buttress claims to traditional land. All over Australia communities are researching and recording their history; individuals are writing notable stories, novels and autobiographies. An increasing number of historians are drawing on Aboriginal oral history to help understand the past and enliven their story.

Much research awaits to be done but it is now possible to piece together a generalised picture of the impact of European settlement. There are numerous stories of the awe and alarm felt by coastal people at the arrival of the first sailing ships. Swan River Aborigines told confidantes among the early settlers:

> with great vividness their impressions when they saw the first ship approach the land. They imagined it some huge winged monster of the deep, and there was a universal consternation. One man fled inland for fourteen miles without stopping and spread the terrifying news amongst his friends.[9]

Europeans have left many accounts of first meetings with Aborigines in which the actors on both sides display that uneasy amalgam of anxiety and curiosity, the sudden unpredictable shifts from amity to aggression and back again, the mutual discovery of commonality and novelty. 'We were so novel to one another', wrote the French scientist Peron of his meeting with the Tasmanians in 1802. As in other parts of Australia, the island Aborigines were fascinated by the Europeans' white skins, their clothes and shoes and strange possessions. The gender of the fully-clothed, clean-shaven Frenchmen was a matter of earnest debate and insistent exploration. As Peron explained:

the natives wanted to examine the calves of our legs and our chests, and so far as these were concerned we allowed them to do everything they wished, oft repeated cries expressing the surprise which the whiteness of our skin seemed to arouse in them. But soon they wished to carry their researches further. Perhaps they had doubts whether we were the same sort of beings as themselves, perhaps they suspected we were of a different sex. However it may be, they showed an extreme desire to examine our genital organs, but as this examination was equally displeasing to us all, they insisted only in the case of Citizen Michel, one of our sailors, who by his slight build and lack of beard seemed he must be more likely to set their minds at rest. But Citizen Michel, who I begged to submit to their entreaties, suddenly exhibited such striking proof of his virility that they all uttered loud cries of surprise mingled with loud roars of laughter which were repeated again and again.[10]

But the experience of coastal clans was not typical. For most Aborigines the Europeans did not arrive unannounced. News of them travelled inland well in advance of the wave of settlement while straying domestic animals and assorted European commodities long preceded the bullock drays into the interior. We know that iron, glass and cloth, axes and tobacco were received by Aborigines far in the interior as long as thirty years before the appearance of the first permanent settlers, having passed along the traditional trade routes that criss-crossed the continent. Iron and glass were quickly and successfully incorporated into traditional tool kits. Skilfully crafted glass spear heads were fitted to traditional shafts; sharpened scraps of iron were hafted with wooden handles. European animals escaped from settlements all around the continent and strayed into the interior. There are many stories of the Aborigines' amazement and fear when they came face to face with the exotic animals. A North Queensland story tells of a meeting with a stray horse sometime during the middle of last century:

> Somebody lost a horse — first time they ever saw a horse . . . and they got their spears and boomerangs and nulla-nullas and they chased this horse and they speared the horse and they put so many spears in the horse that the old horse fell down. And they walked up and had a look at him and they lift his head up and said, 'What sort of creature is this?' They never seen an animal so big. They said, 'I wonder where this animal has come from, it's so big.'[11]

Information about the white people also travelled quickly back from the fringes of European settlement. News of the danger and mysterious power of guns passed on to tribes all over the continent before they came into physical contact with Europeans. Explorers found that blacks were highly apprehensive of guns even before they had been fired. The artist and writer Dick Roughsey recalled that on Mornington Island in the Gulf of Carpentaria his father was told of guns before he had seen white men. Mainland blacks had related 'how white people could kill a man with thunder that sent down invisible spears to tear a hole in his body and spill his blood in the sand'.[12]

The origin and nature of the white men provoked an intense debate in Aboriginal society. Initially it was commonly thought that Europeans were spirits returned from the dead, although eventually it was concluded that they were 'nothing but men'. All over the continent in areas of early settlement the Aborigines applied to Europeans traditional terms meaning 'ghost', 'spirit', 'departed' or 'the dead'. In many cases whites were thought to be not merely reincarnated blacks but actually returned relatives, a fact that often saved the lives of convict escapees and wrecked sailors, as well as shielding fragile infant settlements from black hostility. Settlers so designated were given the names of recently deceased relatives and the vacant place in the kinship network. George Grey, explorer and later colonial governor, related his experiences in Western Australia when claimed as the son of an old Aboriginal woman:

> A sort of procession came up, headed by two women, down whose cheeks tears were streaming. The eldest of these came up to me, and looking for a moment at me said ... 'Yes, yes, in truth it is him', and then throwing her arms around me, cried bitterly, her head resting on my breast ... she then cried a little more, and at length relieving me, assured that I was the ghost of her son, who had some time before been killed by a spear wound in his breast ... My new mother expressed almost as much delight at my return to my family, as my real mother would have done, had I been unexpectedly restored to her.[13]

It was commonly suggested in histories written before 1970 that Australian settlement was uniquely peaceful due in part to the inability of the Aborigines to mount any resistance to the Europeans. They were, W.K. Hancock wrote in 1930, 'pathetically helpless' when confronted by the newcomers.[14] The anthropologist Raymond Firth argued that the Aborigine reacted 'in a simpler manner' than the Maori when 'his way of life is rudely thrown out of gear by the impact of an alien civilisation . . . he mutely dies'.[15] In 1958 Russel Ward celebrated the life of the outback worker who 'seldom had to go armed' because the Aborigines were unable or unwilling to confront the interloper.[16]

Recent studies from all parts of Australia have emphasised the ubiquity of frontier conflict. The traditional picture of peaceful pioneering by unarmed frontiersmen has been shattered. Frontier settlements bristled with guns, and almost every district settled during the nineteenth century had a history of conflict between local clans and encroaching settlers. A small town pioneer explained in 1869 that his community 'had its foundations cemented on blood'.[17] Another looked back ruefully on a decade of frontier conflict during which 'our cowardly fears led us to believe that our safety lay in reckless appeals to powder and lead'.[18] Black resistance in its many forms was an inescapable feature of life on the fringes of European settlement from the first months at Sydney Cove until the early decades of the twentieth century. Edward Curr, pioneer, squatter and amateur ethnographer, provided an overview of Australian frontier warfare. Writing in 1883, he explained:

> In the first place the meeting of the Aboriginal tribes of Australia and the white pioneer results as a rule in war, which last from six months to ten years, according to the nature of the country, the amount of settlement which takes place in the neighbourhood, and the proclivities of the individuals concerned. When several squatters settle in proximity, and the country they settle is easy of access and without fastnesses to which the Blacks can retreat, the period of warfare is usually short and the bloodshed not excessive. On the other hand, in districts which are not easily traversed on horseback, in which the Whites are few in numbers and food is procurable by the Blacks in fastnesses, the term is usually prolonged and the slaughter more considerable.[19]

In the early stages of contact conflict often resulted from mutual fear, anxiety and misunderstanding. Once settlement had been established deaths occurred in the course of conflict about property. Innumerable small skirmishes involving European possessions, which on the surface appear to be little more than unseemly brawls, were manifestations of a fundamental conflict between the Aboriginal concept of reciprocity and sharing and the European one of private property. Many whites were put to death in revenge for specific injuries or for serious transgression of traditional law frequently relating to sexual relations between Aboriginal girls and womanless white frontiersmen. Such action was aimed at particular individuals or groups of offenders with the intention of inducing them to behave in morally acceptable ways. Initially, then, the blacks attempted to deal with the Europeans as though they were Aborigines. Their actions were judicial rather than martial. But as violence escalated and European competition for land and water intensified, many Aboriginal groups moved decisively from feud to warfare, engaging in concerted guerrilla attacks on the settlers and their crops and flocks, huts and herds.

Considering the advantages possessed by the Europeans, Aboriginal resistance was surprisingly prolonged and effective, exacting a high price from many pioneer communities in tension and insecurity as much as in property loss, injury or death. Aboriginal attacks on property had devastating effects on the fortunes of individual settlers and at times appeared to threaten the economic viability of such pioneer industries as squatting, farming, mining and pearling. There were occasions — as in Tasmania in the late 1820s, New South Wales in the late 1830s and early 1840s and Queensland in the early 1860s — when Aboriginal resistance emerged as one of the major problems of colonial society. An editorial in Queensland's leading newspaper in 1879 assessed the impact of Aboriginal resistance in the colony:

> During the last four or five years the human life and property destroyed by the Aboriginals in the North totals up to a serious amount . . . Settlement on the land, and the development of the mineral and other resources of the country, have been in a great degree prohibited by the hostility of the blacks, which still continues with undiminished spirit.[20]

Yet Europeans were only rarely willing to recognise the intelligence and courage that informed the resistance. When they did their comments were particularly interesting. In 1830 a writer in the Hobart paper, the *Colonial Times*, referred to a 'cunning and superiority of tactics which would not disgrace some of the greatest military characters'.[21] Another island settler remarked that the blacks had 'oftentimes evinced superior tact and clearness of head'.[22] The official Tasmanian Aborigines Committee thought the blacks a 'subtle and daring enemy', a 'sagacious and wily race of people'.[23] A report of 1831 observed that the island blacks 'now conduct their attacks with a surprising organisation and with unexampled cunning, such indeed is their local information and quickness of perception, that all endeavours on the part of the whites to cope with them are unavailing'.[24]

In 1834 Governor Stirling informed his superiors in England that West Australian settlers had found the blacks 'very formidable enemies, and if they could avail themselves of the advantages of combination it would be useless to attempt a settlement in this quarter with our present numbers'.[25] A pioneer colonist concurred, remarking in 1833 that if, in addition to their knowledge of the country, the local Aborigines had 'firearms and a little discipline', they would 'put an end to the settlement in less than a month'.[26]

But perhaps the most generous tribute was paid by Edward Eyre who wrote:

> It has been said, and is generally believed, that the natives are not courageous. There could not be a greater mistake ... nor do I hold it to be any proof that they are cowards, because they dread or give way before Europeans and their firearms. So unequal a match is no criterion of bravery, and yet even thus, among natives, who were labouring under the feelings, naturally produced by seeing a race they were unacquainted with, and weapons that dealt death as if by magic, I have seen many instances of open manly intrepidity of manner and bearing, and a proud unquailing glance of eye, which instinctively stamped upon my mind the conviction that the individuals before me were very brave men.[27]

The cost of frontier conflict was high. It seems probable that about 2000 Europeans and more than 20,000 Aborigines died violently in the course of Australian settlement, and many others carried scars of shot and spear with them into a more peaceful era. Such a degree of violence might surprise outsiders less than it has Australians raised on historical works that stressed peacefulness of national development. Australian was the 'quiet continent', which has been colonised, not conquered; settled not invaded. The numbers killed greatly overshadowed those involved in all other forms of internal conflict and can only be compared with the death rate in Australia's overseas wars. Many white Australians are acutely embarrassed by findings of the new history of the frontier. They would prefer that past bloodshed be forgotten. But in black communities memories are fresh and wounds have not healed. Oral history has already tapped some of these sagas of bitter skirmish and sudden death. A chilling example is a story of the 1870s and 1880s related a few years ago by an old man who had probably heard it as a boy from eye-witnesses to the events. It tells of an attack by the Queensland Native Police on a group of Aborigines who had taken bullocks from nearby settlers and were caught while cooking them. Such 'dispersals' happened many times in colonial Queensland. Despite the lapse of time, despite the broken English, the story has a powerful impact:

> All the Native Police come up All got the rifle, all got handcuffs. Shoot im altogether, Shoot im altogether Chuck im in the fire. All the revolvers going on. Talk about smell. Nobody gonna be alive. Chuck im in the fire, half alive Sing out. Native police shoot im all. Widow come back cryin. She lose im husband. All finished, they shot em live. All cryin come home To this valley here.[28]

But conflict and resistance were not the only notable features of the Other Side of the Frontier. There was much else besides. Enough work has been done since the 1970s for us to see that the Aboriginal response to invasion was far more positive, creative and complex than generations of white Australians have been taught to believe. Indeed the story that is now emerging has many parallels with the chosen themes of nationalist historiography.

The courage of European explorers pushing out into the interior was matched by that of the Aborigines who met them on the way and by those who travelled in towards the settlements to observe and evaluate the interlopers. Voyages of discovery were never the preserve of white frontiersmen. The explorers' fear of savages was echoed in Aboriginal alarm about evil spirits and malignant alien magic. The improvisation and adaptation of Europeans settling the land was paralleled by tribesmen who grappled with a new world of experience on the fringes of white settlement. The stoical endurance of pioneer women was matched by that of their black sisters who bore children and battled to keep them alive in conditions of stark adversity. All over the continent Aborigines bled as profusely and died as bravely as white soldiers in Australia's twentieth-century wars.

How Australians will relate frontier conflict to cherished military traditions, to the Anzac legend itself, has yet to be determined. Will white Australians come to accept fallen tribesmen as national heroes who died defending their way of life against powerful invaders? Will their actions ultimately seem more relevant than those Australians who died overseas pursuing the tactical ends and strategic objectives of a distant motherland? That such questions now confront us is the clearest indication that the Great Australian Silence has been shattered, the cult of forgetfulness abandoned. Slowly, unevenly, often with difficulty, white Australians are incorporating the black experience into their image of the national past.

This process was apparent during the bicentennial year of 1988. The official celebrations ignored the unpleasant facts of two hundred years of conflict and dispossession, an oversight brilliantly dramatised by the frequently seen graffiti, 'White Australia has a black history'. The arrival of the tall ships in Sydney on the morning of 26 January was answered in the afternoon by a mass march and rally of Aborigines and their supporters. During the year Australians of European descent were forced to reconsider the Aboriginal past. Novelist Thomas Keneally celebrated the ancient past. 'So, among everything else', he wrote, 'let's drink to pre-Australia, its mysteries, its glories, and even its demands. Until we've both imagined and dealt with it, we'll never be fully at home.'[29]

Fellow writer David Malouf observed that what Australia needed was 'a sense of continuity, a line passing from the remotest past into the remotest time to come if one is to get a grip on the future'.[30] A legal historian pursued the issue even further. M.P. Ellinghaus argued that Aboriginal elements should be integrated into the legal tradition. Until then Australian civilisation could not 'come to maturity without the complete integration of its indigenous component'. Our history of ideas included 'that of more than forty millennia of Aboriginal presence'. Indeed we must 'recover and re-instate the Aboriginal past before we can be at ease on this continent'.[31]

In an article in *Island* magazine the architect B. McNeill reflected on his response to the discovery of Australia's ancient past and in particular the spectacular archaeological finds made at Lake Mungo in south-west New South Wales:

> I know that in my own case it took many years to shake off the power of the childhood images of landscape, cottage and country house that characterised the Arcadian thrust of English children's literature and comics. For me, second generation Australian, the real turning point came when I learned of the significance of Lake Mungo from John Mulvaney. There on the shore of a lake in Western New South Wales a red ochre sprinkled burial of some 30,000 years ago showed that spiritual concerns of humankind had

a very long history in Australia. With the realisation that despite the absence of a built tradition more than 200 years old, I lived in a continent with a cultural tradition longer than any other place on earth, I suddenly felt at home.[32]

The new historiography has had an impact on both law and politics. In June 1992 the High Court of Australia handed down its judgement in the Mabo case, which recognised the native title of the Meriam people of the Murray Islands in Torres Strait. In doing so the court carried through a legal revolution. The changes that had taken place in Australian life over the previous generation had broken through into the hitherto insulated world of jurisprudence. The law had been brought into alignment with the new historiography. The doctrine of *terra nullius*, affirmed in the Gove Land Rights case of 1972, was decisively rejected. In its place the court adopted the concept of native title, which had been part of North American and New Zealand law since the nineteenth century. The Murray Islanders had title to their land as a consequence of prior occupation, not as a result of a grant from the Crown. Neither the claim of sovereignty in 1879 nor anything else the Queensland Government had done in the intervening years had extinguished the native title. The islanders were 'entitled as against the whole world to the possession, occupation, use and enjoyment of the lands of the Murray Islands'.[33]

The court did not confine the scope of the judgement to the Torres Strait. Instead it set out basic principles that were to apply throughout the country. Where Aboriginal groups could claim a traditional association with vacant Crown land or land held under various forms of lease or licence native title is likely to have survived and can be claimed at common law. The full implications of the Mabo judgement are still unfolding.

The dramatic changes in the historiography of Aboriginal–European relations have deeply influenced politics since the 1970s. Aboriginal campaigns for land rights and more recently for sovereignty have been grounded on the facts of dispossession and destruction as outlined in the new historical scholarship, which has found outlets in countless books, articles, films, television and radio programs and even songs, plays and paintings.

Political leaders have also responded to the changed perceptions of the past. In 1983 the federal Minister for Aboriginal Affairs, Clyde Holding, delivered a speech entitled 'Aboriginal past: Australia's future'. 'We have to admit and accept the past', he argued, noting that 'we have, only recently, begun to admit to ourselves that the widely accepted version of our beginnings', of the Europeans bringing 'the benefits of civilisation to benighted heathens, is rather less than the whole truth'. He believed that the approaching bicentenary provided Australians with the opportunity 'not merely to contemplate our achievements as a nation, but also to come to terms with our history'.[34]

Nine years later the Prime Minister, Paul Keating, was much more forthcoming. In an address launching Australian participation in the International Year for the World's Indigenous People he said that any reconciliation would have to start with an 'act of recognition' that it was the Europeans who 'did the dispossessing', who 'took the traditional lands and smashed the traditional way of life'. His message was that there was 'nothing to fear or to lose in the recognition of historical truth'. Referring to the Aboriginal contribution to national life he listed: 'Economic contributions, particularly in the pastoral and agricultural industry. They are there in the frontier and exploration history of Australia. They are there in the wars. In sport to an extraordinary degree. In literature and art and music. In all these things they have shaped our knowledge of the continent and of ourselves. They have shaped our identity. They are there in the Australian legend'.[35]

Since the 1970s many people — scholars in numerous disciplines, writers, artists and activists — have transformed our knowledge and understanding of Aboriginal Australia in the past and in the present. It has been one of the major achievements of Australian intellectual and cultural life since World War II. White Australians in increasing numbers have come to accept a less flattering image of the past but a much more realistic one. In coming face to face with black Australians they have at last come face to face with themselves, with their claims to civilisation.

Notes

1 See Stuart MacIntyre, 'History, the university and the nation', Trevor Reece Memorial Lecture, Sir Robert Menzies Centre for Australian Studies, University of London, 1992.
2 J.A. La Nauze, 'The study of Australian history, 1929–1959', *Historical Studies*, vol. 9, no. 33, 1959, p. 11.
3 W.E.H. Stanner, *After the Dreaming*, ABC, Sydney, 1969, p. 25.
4 J. Murray and J.P. White, 'Cambridge or the bush? Archaeology in Australia and New Guinea', *World Archaeology*, vol. 13, no. 2, 1981, p. 257.

5 D.J. Mulvaney, *The Pre-history of Australia*, Thames & Hudson, London, 1969, p. 12.
6 J. Flood, *Archaeology of the Dreamtime*, Collins, Sydney, 1983, p. 16.
7 G. Blainey, *Triumph of the Nomads*, Sun Books, Melbourne, 1975, p. 225.
8 Sylvia Hallam, *Fire and Hearth*, Australian Institute of Aboriginal and Torres Strait Islander Studies, Canberra, 1975, p. 65.
9 George Fletcher Moore, *A Descriptive Bibliography of the Language in Common Usage Among the Aborigines of Western Australia*, W.S. Orr, London, 1842, p. 108.
10 N.J.B. Plomley (ed.), *The Baudin Expedition and the Tasmanian Aborigines, 1802*, Blubber Head Press, Hobart, 1983, p. 84.
11 Henry Reynolds, *The Other Side of the Frontier*, Penguin, Ringwood, 1982, p. 10.
12 D. Roughsey, *Moon and Rainbow*, Rigby, Sydney, 1971, p. 13.
13 G. Grey, *Journal of Two Expeditions of Discovery*, T. & W. Boone, London, 1841, vol. 1, pp. 301–2.
14 W.K. Hancock, *Australia*, Jacaranda, Brisbane, 1960, p. 20.
15 R. Firth, 'Anthropology in Australia', *Oceania*, vol. 3, no. 1, 1932, p. 9.
16 Russel Ward, *Australia*, 2nd ed., Prentice-Hall, Englewood Cliffs, NJ, 1967, pp. 26–7.
17 *Port Denison Times*, 1 May 1869.
18 Ibid., 21 May 1870.
19 E. Curr, *The Australian Race, Its Origins, Languages, Customs* (4 vols), Victorian Government Printer, Melbourne, 1886–87, vol. 1, p. 100.
20 *Queenslander*, 15 February 1879.
21 *Colonial Times*, 16 July 1830.
22 Ibid., 1 June 1834.
23 Papers of the Aborigines Committee, Tas. State Archives, CSO/1/319.
24 Aboriginal Tribes in British Possessions, British Parliamentary Papers, 1834, p. 158.
25 Dispatches to Colonial Office, 14 September 1834, 6 December 1838, Battye Library, Perth.
26 *Perth Gazette*, 30 March 1833.
27 E.J. Eyre, *Journals of Expeditions of Discovery*, T. & W. Boone, London 1845, vol. 2, pp. 216–17.
28 Reynolds, *The Other Side of the Frontier*, p. 127.
29 *Age*, 1 January 1988.
30 *Age*, 23 January 1988.
31 M.P. Ellinghaus et al. (eds), *The Emergence of Australian Law*, Butterworths, Sydney 1989, pp. 66, 68.
32 B. McNeill, 'Sources for Australian design', *Island*, no. 40, p. 51.
33 *Australian Law Review*, no. 102, 1992, p. 2.
34 Clyde Holding, speech to House of Representatives, 8 December 1983.
35 Speech by P.J. Keating, Redfern, 10 December 1992.

2
LEGEND

John Barnes

Aborigines have never appeared as more than marginal figures in the 'Australian legend'. By this term I mean the collection of stories about the coming-into-being of 'the Australian', embracing both what Russel Ward (1958) delineates as the 'national mystique' in his famous book, *The Australian Legend,* and what John Hirst (1978) calls the 'pioneer legend'.[1] The essence of the Australian legend is the struggle of man (read 'European man') with the land. According to the legend, the conquest is of land and not of people. It is, at the one and same time, a story of success in making the land fruitful and a story of sacrifice and suffering, which, paradoxically, is also a kind of success.

The importance of the legend is that the Australian (read 'white man') has earned the right to possess the land. The white settlement of the continent is part of the triumphant spread of civilisation around the globe. There is only a 'blank' before the coming of the whites.

In this version of nation-building the heroism and suffering of the whites is to be celebrated and the Aborigines are 'primitive', regarded as incapable of reaching the level of white 'civilisation'. In 1902 a member of the Commonwealth Parliament could say, in all seriousness, that 'there is no scientific evidence that the Aboriginal is a human being at all'.[2] Social Darwinism offered a ready-made explanation of the decline in numbers and the visible degradation of the Aboriginal population; a process of evolution, about which no member of the superior race need feel any guilt, was under way. Nature was taking its course, and while the compassionate might seek to ameliorate their condition, 'to smooth the pillow of the dying race', the 'passing of the Aborigines' could be seen as inevitable and natural.

Meanwhile, a sense of national identity was emerging; Australia was being 'invented', as Richard White puts it. The 'Coming Australian' was a theme of many commentators, especially towards the end of the nineteenth century, as Federation neared.[3] The notion of an evolving national type runs through the literature of the 1890s, which later generations took as fixing a mould of Australianness. The so-called 'legend of the nineties' has been revised and reinterpreted a great deal in recent years, but I doubt that literary historians have recognised how thoroughly racist were the writers of the time. Humphrey McQueen has asserted that 'Racism is the most important single component of Australian nationalism';[4] but the implications of this claim have not been explored in creative writing. To a literary critic and cultural historian like A.A. Phillips, who could be seen as an apologist for the Australian legend, the racial exclusiveness on the part of major exponents of the 'democratic theme', like Lawson, Paterson and Furphy, seemed to be a failure of sympathy rather than an expression of inherent racism; and that is still the most common reading.[5] Their racism was overt in their hostile portrayal of Asians, notably Chinese, who seemed to pose a threat to the new Australian society; and it was no less strong, although less conscious, in their attitudes towards Aborigines.

In his most famous short story Lawson praises a black woman who came to the aid of the drover's wife, but the language betrays his sense of racial hierarchy:

> The last two children were born in the bush — one while her husband was bringing a drunken doctor, by force, to attend to her. She was alone on this occasion, and very weak. She had been ill with a fever. She prayed to God to send her assistance. God sent Black Mary — the 'whitest' gin in all the land. Or, at least, God sent 'King Jimmy' first, and he sent Black Mary. He put his black face round the door-post, took in the situation at a glance, and said cheerfully: 'All right, Missis — I bring my old woman, she down alonga creek.'[6]

There could be no higher praise than to describe the Aboriginal woman as 'white', that is, as if she were a fully human being. In Lawson's vision the Aborigines were associated with the very harshness and desolation of the 'bush': they could survive in what he once described as the 'Out Back Hell', which could only be a place of suffering for whites. In his poem, 'The men who made Australia', written on the occasion of the royal visit to Australia in 1901, he pulls out all stops to honour the 'bushmen', the nation-builders. (I'm assuming that the sexism of the writing is so obvious as to need no comment.) The fifth stanza reads:

> Dragged behind the crawling sheep-flock on the hot and dusty plain,
> They must make a cheque to feed the wife and kids —
> Riding night-watch round the cattle in the pelting, freezing rain,
> While world-weariness is pressing down the lids.
> And away on far out-stations, seldom touched by Heaven's breath,
> In a loneliness that smothers love and hate —
> Where they never take white women — there they live the living death
> With a half-caste or a black-gin for a mate.[7]

Taking a black or half-caste woman as a sexual partner is represented as the ultimate hardship — endured by the white man who is 'making Australia'.

The subject of black–white sexual relations was not one that the nationalist writers cared to dwell on. Lawson was more comfortable with the theme of mateship — the bond between men, which he idealised — than with the mating alluded to in the quotation. And mateship became a central theme in the Australian legend, reinforced by the war legend of the Anzacs.

The war historian C.E.W. Bean defined the 'typical Australian' as 'seldom religious in the sense in which the word is generally used', but believing in a creed of mateship. The belief that a 'man should at all times and at any cost stand by his mate' was, according to Bean, the 'one law which the good Australian must never break'. It was an essential part of the national character, which Bean saw as a creation of Anglo-Saxon racial characteristics modified and enhanced by the physical environment. In Australians the 'characteristic resourcefulness of the British was perforce developed further'. Bean seems to be creating a new hierarchy when he writes: 'It was a fact often observed, that in a ship-wreck or bush-fire one man of British stock could compass the work of several Germans; and this capacity the Australian possessed in an extreme degree.' The Aborigines are not mentioned; they do not figure in Bean's thinking about the condition of Australia in 1914. Remarking on the newness of the Commonwealth, Bean notes that state loyalties tended to be stronger than the national: 'Only in one point was the Australian people palpably united — in a determination to keep its continent a white man's land.'[8]

It is as if the original inhabitants had never existed. They are excluded from the notion of an Australian identity. Bean's account was published in 1921. Twenty-one years later, when Australia was under threat of attack from Japan, Vance Palmer was writing far less confidently about Australian characteristics. Palmer was a key figure in the promotion of 'Australian-ness' in local writing and commanded great respect as a *littérateur*. His views are representative of Australian nationalism at the time:

> The next few months may decide not only whether we are to survive as a nation, but whether we deserve to survive. As yet none of our achievements prove it, at any rate in the sight of the outer world. We have no monuments to speak of, no dreams in stone, no Guernica, no sacred places. We could vanish and leave singularly few signs that, for some generations, there had lived a people who had made a homeland of this Australian earth. A homeland? To how many people was it primarily that? How many penetrated the soil with their love and imagination? We have had no peasant population to cling passionately to their few acres, throw down tenacious roots, and weave a natural poetry into their lives by invoking the little gods of creek and mountain.

Palmer goes on to argue that there is an 'Australia of the spirit', the 'Australia of all who truly belong here', and that it is expressed in the writing of the nationalists such as Lawson. He believed that this Australia has something to offer the world in the form of 'ideas for the creation of that egalitarian democracy that will have to be the basis of all civilised societies in the future'.[9]

Palmer's essay is sincere and deeply felt in its idealism, far from mere patriotic sentiment, which makes it all the more revealing. I should be surprised if anyone reading the essay fifty years ago would have been disturbed by its blindness to the Aborigines, the people who, for tens of thousands of years (as Henry Reynolds points out in chapter 1, 'History'), had 'made a homeland of this Australian earth', who had 'sacred places', who 'truly belong here'. Palmer's phrasing exposes a deep-seated anxiety that runs through much white Australian writing, an anxiety about the relationship of white Australians to the land.

Ten years earlier Nettie Palmer had been concerned with what she thought of as the colonial outlook:

> Three or four generations have not been enough to allow us to get thoroughly rooted in the soil. Waves of uncertainty sweep over us. Is this continent really our home, or are we just migrants from another civilisation?[10]

It is an awkward question. The Australian legend, in its various forms, offered the 'right' answer, the answer that the white inhabitants wanted to hear. It told them that they had earned the right to the land, they belonged — or rather, it belonged to them. Hodge and Mishra (1990) have talked of the 'dark side of the Australian dream', the 'dark secret of the Australian consciousness', by which they mean the repression of the knowledge of the dispossession of the original inhabitants; and they have many interesting things to say about the ways in which the inherent contradictions of the white Australian position are manifested.[11] Fifty years after Palmer's essay, the Australian legend is being deconstructed, Australian history is being rewritten and in the process Australia is being reinvented, with the Aborigines now in the centre of the picture. Aborigines are now telling their side of the story and whites are listening.

'One day, perhaps, an Aborigine will write a book in his own language, or in English. On that day we will learn much about our ignorance and conceit.'[12] These are the words of Professor A.P. Elkin, then Professor of Anthropology at the University of Sydney, in an introductory note to a book published in 1949. They were prompted by the nature of the book's narrative — an autobiography of an Aboriginal woman, written not by the woman herself but by a white station-owner. In the preface to his book, *Tell the White Man: The Life Story of an Aboriginal Lubra*, the author, H.E. Thonemann, vouched for the authenticity of the raw material and explained how he had produced a readable English version of what he had been told in an Aboriginal language:

> This is the story of Buludja, an Aboriginal woman of the Mungari tribe, whose territory is situated at the Elsey on the Roper River in the Northern Territory of Australia. It should have been her autobiography but, had she recorded it in her own language, or even in 'pidgin English', few white people would have understood it. Unfortunately, in translation much of the poetic quality of the aboriginal tongue is lost. And, although I have tried to keep the style as simple

as possible in order to give some idea of the way in which the story was told to me, I have been forced at times, when a complicated or technical description demanded it, to use words and phrases that Buludja would not recognise, nor understand if she did. For these, and other small liberties, my apologies are due to her, for this is the story of her life which I am telling only because she has not the means to do so herself.

There are a number of issues raised here about the production of a text — and specifically, the production of what purports to be a narrative by a black woman — but I am not so much concerned with that topic in this chapter. My focus is, rather, the impact on white readers of the increasing number of texts that, in various ways, are telling the whites about Aboriginal experiences.

Tell the White Man was one of the early attempts to represent an Aboriginal version of Australian experience. Thonemann was genuinely anxious to help the Aborigines on his station and to point out the degradation resulting from white influence. At several points in the narrative Buludja moralises about black–white relations and gives the whites some advice. These are, of course, the white man's words in which the black attitudes are interpreted. For example:

> The white man is clever at his own work, but we can do much better than he does in bushcraft, easy living and happiness. He builds up many possessions which cause him a lot of trouble, and then spends his life getting out of trouble. We spend a life of ease and contentment, and avoid any unnecessary work and trouble.
>
> I should like to see your white men let loose in our country dressed and equipped as we are, then they would not think us so simple. But we do not mind what they think of us as long as they leave us to go our own way.[13]

Although Thonemann has his narrator caution whites against the notion that Aborigines are simple, *his* construction of Buludja's narrative does not challenge that view; and in his preface the author actually tells his readers that this 'is a simple story because the aborigines are a simple people — but in their simplicity lies their strength. Sophistication was their undoing'. This stereotype is somewhat undercut by the fact that Thonemann had difficulty in understanding the tribal organisation and customs which, as Professor Elkin notes, are very complex.

Part of the interest of *Tell the White Man* stems from the fact that it purports to give the Aboriginal side of a story that had been told from a white perspective. Two of the most commercially successful books ever written in Australia were Mrs Aeneas Gunn's *The Little Black Princess* (1905) and *We of the Never-Never* (1908), both about the year she spent on Elsey Station in 1902 as wife of the manager. The 'Little Missus' is a childless young wife, unfamiliar with the life of the outback, who writes about her experiences with a gentle amusement, making a joke of the difficulties and crudities, and carefully omitting from her narrative anything that would blemish the image of pioneering bushmen. She writes in the spirit of the Britisher Abroad — in true imperial fashion a bullock is roasted to celebrate Edward VII's coronation — and she observes the Aborigines with a sympathetic but distant eye as simple, lovable children of nature. Her role as the Missus means that she has to learn how to manage the Aboriginal labour force. She tells the reader in *The Little Black Princess* how she indulges the black women who do the washing: 'You see, I was what white people would call a "bad mistress"; but the blacks called me "goodfellow Missus", and would do anything I wanted without a murmur.'[14]

The image of white benevolence and black acquiescence is created with a charm that one feels even today when one knows the great gap between the image and the reality. *The Little Black Princess* was a book for children and so it is not surprising that there is no hint of one of the things that troubled Mrs Gunn most: sexual relations between white men and black women. In the book she even hides the fact that the little girl has a white father, a fact that she did not make public until half a century later, although it was the real reason why she took charge of the child.[15] The story of Bett-Bett, the 'Princess', a title not wholly free of mockery, is constructed as a narrative of white benevolence; there is no mention of her black mother or her white father, and the white Missus assumes a feudal right to decide the future of the child.

Mrs Gunn viewed the Aborigines from a position of power, as a member of a higher race viewing a lower. The possibility that the Aborigines might one day own the station and be capable of running it would never have occurred to her. In *The Little Black Princess* she remarks how 'wonderful' the Aborigines are, after discovering their sign language; she says that she 'never laughed at their strange beliefs', which she found 'wonderfully interesting' as she realised that 'under every silly little bit of nonsense, was a great deal of good sense'.[16] In the atmosphere of the time — in 1907 the *Bulletin* changed its slogan from 'Australia for the

Australians' to 'Australia for the White Man' — Mrs Gunn was sympathetic, if not enlightened, in her portrayal of Aborigines.

With the portrayal of whites it was a simple matter of idealisation. Like *Geoffry Hamlyn*, Henry Kingsley's nineteenth-century novel of pastoral life, *We of the Never-Never* offered a flattering view of the process of civilisation and was accepted as 'an Australian classic'. It celebrates the bushmen as chivalrous, selfless, nation-building pioneers. The Aborigines are always around, but their role in the running of the station is passed over; it seems that there is 'the inevitable black "boy"'[17] on hand all the time to work under white direction, as a servant rather than an employee. In Kingsley's novel the Aborigines are one of the hazards faced by the settlers, one of the natural obstacles, as it were, along with flood, fire and drought. In Mrs Gunn's narrative the Aborigines are considered a potential rather than a real threat, and there is a remarkable absence of friction between black and white. She concludes with a reference to the death of her husband, mourned by the white men on the station:

> And as those great hearts mourned, ever and anon a long-drawn out sobbing cry went up from the camp as the tribe mourned for their beloved dead — their dead and ours — our Maluka, 'the best Boss that ever a man struck'.

It is a fascinating image of the two races sharing a common emotion. The tribe is a kind of chorus in relation to the main actors, the great-hearted whites.(The Aboriginal word *maluka*, meaning 'old man', indicated the respect of the tribe.)[18] It is an image of colonialism at work; out of context, it could be read as typifying the situation in a number of British possessions, in which indigenous peoples have been subjugated. It is a reminder that, as Hodge and Mishra have emphasised, Australia 'adopted the classic attitudes of imperialism in its treatment of the Aboriginal people of Australia'.[19]

Many factors have contributed to the creation of a white readership eager for Aboriginal narratives. The work of anthropologists has enlarged and deepened knowledge of the Aboriginal past; in recent years historians — pre-eminently Henry Reynolds — have revealed much that was forgotten or deliberately repressed about the history of black–white encounters over two centuries of white settlement; and the Aborigines themselves have become a political force, with a very capable leadership articulating the case for land rights and insisting that the white community recognises the social deprivation they have suffered. In a world where racism is under attack, white Australians have felt increasingly uncomfortable about the situation of the black minority. At the same time, Aborigines have been writing plays, stories and poems; Aboriginal artists have become fashionable; and in the media and in education Aborigines have become very visible in a variety of roles. Against this background the stories of how Aborigines see their own lives have found acceptance.

Of the Aboriginal writing that has so far been published, Sally Morgan's *My Place* has had perhaps the greatest impact on the white community, achieving the sort of sales that few white Australian authors could ever hope to equal. Her book is an account of her early life in a lower-middle-class suburb of Perth in Western Australia, the main focus being her search for the truth about her Aboriginal origins. As a schoolchild she has to face questions about her family. She tells her mother: 'The kids at school want to know what country we come from. They reckon we're not Aussies. Are we Aussies, Mum?'[20] The possibility that they are *black* Aussies apparently doesn't occur to the other children. Her mother tells her to say that the family are Indian, an answer that she accepts, until the truth is eventually forced on her. She then finds that her sister Jill has already faced the truth that she has been repressing. The sisters react in different ways to the social stigma of being Aboriginal — Jill anxious to hide the fact, Sally curious and wanting to know more. Neither girl has any first-hand knowledge of Aboriginal culture. In their ignorance they both express stock white attitudes of the 1960s:

> 'You know, Jill,' I said after a while, 'if we are Boongs, and I don't know if we are or not, but if we are, there's nothing we can do about it, so we might as well just accept it.'
> 'Accept it? Can you tell me one good thing about being an Abo?'
> 'Well, I don't know much about them,' I answered. 'They like animals, don't they? We like animals.'
> 'A lot of people like animals, Sally. Haven't you heard of the RSPCA?'
> 'Of course I have! But don't Abos feel close to the earth and all that stuff?'
> 'God, I don't know. All I know is none of my friends like them.'[21]

Her mother and her maternal grandmother — who is recognisably Aboriginal in appearance — try to deflect Sally's questions. But

Sally is determined to dig into the past, and the narrative traces her success in locating the family 'place', which includes the literal place where her grandmother was born.

Although *My Place* is stylistically dull, it is shaped with very great skill to affirm Aboriginality. In the words of the narrator herself, after a visit to her grandmother's country where, for the first time, she meets her extended Aboriginal family, the search for information becomes an experience of self-transformation:

> We were reluctant to return and pick up the threads of our old lives. We were different people, now. What had begun as a tentative search for knowledge had grown into a spiritual and emotional pilgrimage. We had an Aboriginal consciousness now, and we were proud of it.[22]

The 'digging into the past', which Sally's mother and grandmother resist at first, becomes for the whole family a liberating and enriching experience. The narrative climaxes with the grandmother telling her story shortly before her death. *My Place* includes three tape-recorded oral narratives told to Sally, by her great-uncle Arthur, her mother Gladys and her grandmother Daisy; a strategy that increases the whole work's claim to authenticity. 'Could be it's time to tell. Time to tell what it's been like in this country,'[23] says Daisy, who nevertheless keeps to herself some of the things that Sally wants to know, including the identity of her grandfather. It seems clear from the text that incest has occurred and that Howden Drake-Brockman, the white station-owner, was the father not only of Arthur and Daisy but also of Daisy's child, Gladys. The once-taboo subject of sexual relations between white men and black women is at the very centre of the family history that Sally reconstructs.

The story of Daisy Corunna — the surname is that of the station — is contemporaneous with that of Mrs Gunn's 'Little Black Princess', and in each instance the future of the 'half-caste girl' is determined by whites, who pride themselves on their benevolence in taking the child away from the Aboriginal mother and training her to be a domestic. Bett-Bett's story ends happily enough with her absorbed into white society, translated into a respectably married lady with a white husband. Daisy's story, however, is one of servitude to a powerful family.

Alice Drake-Brockman, Howden's second wife, is interviewed by Sally Morgan about her memories of Daisy. In her nineties,

Alice typifies white attitudes. Alice either didn't know or didn't admit that her husband was the father of Daisy and of Daisy's child; and she had rose-coloured memories of the years when Daisy worked for the Drake-Brockman family as a domestic and children's nurse: 'She grew up loving us and we were her family, there were no servants. It was just a family life.'[24] It is basically the same attitude that Mrs Gunn has towards her Aboriginal servants, seeing their lives as fulfilled in service to whites.

Daisy grew up knowing Drake-Brockman as her father. And of her daughter Gladys she says: 'Everyone knows who the father was, but they all pretended they didn't know. Aah, they knew, they knew. You didn't talk 'bout things, then. You hid the truth.'[25] Of her feeling about the Drake-Brockman family, she says: 'I was owned by the Drake-Brockmans.'[26]

In her portrayal of her grandmother, Sally Morgan presents her as lovable, slightly eccentric 'Nan', but as the narrative unfolds she is seen both as the victim of a patriarchal white system and as a precious link with the past, possessing a racial gift, a capacity for spiritual awareness, which Sally believes that she has inherited. What originally seemed to be a social stigma is revealed as a blessing.

There are problems with this notion of genetic Aboriginality and with Sally Morgan's portrayal of Aborigines generally. As Eric Michaels has pointed out, in *My Place* Sally Morgan

> constructs criteria for evidence and truth which are self-referential: 'Aborigines do not lie, do not selectively interpret their memories, and so their stories are true . . . beyond even the context of their presentation (i.e., neither the narrative genre nor the translation from oral to written modes influences the story).'[27]

Most readers, I think, do not stop to reflect on such considerations, although they could hardly fail to note how completely the narrator dismisses the paternal inheritance of herself and her mother. The tragedy of her white father, wrecked by his war experience, is passed over rather quickly. She deliberately chooses the Aboriginal inheritance and finds in herself what she takes to be Aboriginal characteristics. In a total reversal of the colonial attitude she finds good *only* in her Aboriginal inheritance.

By comparison with a life like that of Ruby Langford,[28] Sally Morgan's life as she constructs it does tend to simplify the whole issue of what it means to be an Aborigine — and indeed what it meant at the turn of the century when Daisy was growing up on the Drake-Brockmans' station. There is much about the relationship of Daisy to the Drake-Brockmans that the narrative leaves unexamined, partly, it is true, because Daisy will not go beyond a certain point. The narrator interprets her silences as signifying 'great dark depths'[29] too terrible to talk about, but other readings are possible. The oral narratives of both Daisy and Arthur do suggest that some aspects of the past are not fully comprehended in Sally's narrative.

However, the authority of the narrative is hardly affected in the eyes of most readers, even when such reservations are expressed. *My Place* has the authority of autobiography, a genre which has become exceedingly popular at the very time when fiction has been asserting its fictiveness. More than history or anthropology, black autobiography is able to 'tell the white man' about the experiences of being Aboriginal, because its appears to offer the immediate experience of the individual human being. With writers like Sally Morgan, Jack Davis and Mudrooroo, who were educated in white society and had, in various ways, to educate themselves into Aboriginality, there aren't the textual problems that there are with narrators like Elsie Roughsey or even Ruby Langford, who need to have the assistance of white editors — although not as much as did Buludja back in the 1940s.[30] Yet it is as well to emphasise that any text is a cultural production and that readings are not fixed. Which is to say that *My Place* might be read differently in the future from the way in which it is being read now.

It belongs to a period in which old myths of inherent white superiority are being destroyed and racial value systems up-ended. In *My Place* Sally Morgan has searched for her Aboriginal roots at the same time as denying roots elsewhere; her father's family were Irish, and the Drake-Brockmans were English. Her grandmother in her oral narrative confesses that she had wanted to be white, she had been made to feel ashamed of being black, and at the end of her life what she looked for was respect: 'I like to think the black man will get treated the same as the white man one day. Be good, wouldn't it? By gee, it'd be good.'[31] Throughout her life she had been powerless, sexually violated by white men, deprived of all choice in living her life, and even in old age she was still fearful of the authority in the hands of the whites who had taken her children away from her — the fear that lay behind the fiction that the family were Indian. The very act of writing *My Place* is a form of empowerment for black women, and what it reveals of the exploitation of black women is a damaging comment on the actuality behind the Australian legend.

More than that, *My Place* identifies Aboriginality with spiritual depth. Sally and her mother both describe having religious experiences in conventional Christian terms, but at the end of the narrative Sally claims to possess the psychic power of her grandmother, symbolised by the mysterious bird-call. When an interviewer questioned her about the relationship between the 'spirituality of your heritage' and 'your Christian beliefs', Sally Morgan replied:

> I think one can enhance the other. I have many relations who wouldn't have the same beliefs as me, and would probably disagree with my religious beliefs, but they still have that Aboriginal spirituality, which I just think comes as part of that culture and as part of that inheritance. Having that in you tends to make you sensitive to other forms of spirituality, whether it comes in Christian terms or any other.[32]

The term that she uses here is now widely accepted — *Aboriginal spirituality* — and has become a distinguishing feature of the new image of Aboriginality that is emerging. And here again we have an interesting reversal of white attitudes and a further subverting of the Australian legend.

To the nineteenth-century Europeans it seemed that the Aborigines lacked a religious sense, were generally incapable of what was understood by these Christians as religion, or at best could rise to a simple childlike faith. The concept of 'the Dreaming' or 'the Dreamtime', which anthropologists formulated around the turn of the century, has come to signify Aboriginal spirituality in popular discourse, but originally it, in effect, identified the Aborigines as lacking the capacity for rational and abstract thought displayed by European civilisation.

The transformation of the Dreaming or Dreamtime from a negative to a positive concept has occurred gradually. Perhaps the most decisive moment in the evolution of the concept was the anthropologist W.E.H. Stanner's essay, 'The Dreaming', which was published in 1956. Arguing that it is 'much more complex philosophically than we have so far realised', Stanner makes the interesting comment: 'I greatly hope that artists and men of letters who (it seems increasingly) find inspiration in Aboriginal Australia will use all their gifts of empathy, but avoid banal projection and subjectivism, if they seek to honour the notion.'[33]

He was registering the effect of the literary movement that called itself Jindyworobak and (on the basis of a superficial acquaintance with Aboriginal culture) was attempting to create an Australian literature that would express the spirit of place. He can hardly have foreseen the power of the notion that he hoped artists would honour. Much of that power comes from his own eloquent demonstration that the Aborigine is a 'metaphysician in being able to transcend himself' and a 'philosopher in being able to use his power of abstract reason'. In expounding the integrity of the Aboriginal vision, Stanner stresses the disability of the Europeans in trying to come to terms with it:

> The truth of it seems to be that man, society and nature, and past, present and future, are at one together within a unitary system of such a kind that its ontology cannot illumine minds too much under the influence of humanism, rationalism and science. One cannot easily, in the mobility of modern life and thought, grasp the vast intuitions of stability and permanence, and of life and man, at the heart of Aboriginal ontology.[34]

In the course of the essay Stanner quotes an Aborigine who said:

> White man got no dreaming.
> Him go 'nother way.
> White man, him go different.
> Him got road belong himself.[35]

When he collected his essays twenty-five years later, Stanner gave the volume the title, *White Man got No Dreaming*. More recently Ronald McKie, a journalist and novelist, entitled his autobiography, *We have No Dreaming* (1988). The very pragmatism, the lack of religious passion, that the exponents of the Australian legend were inclined to see as a mark of strength is now a mark of weakness, an indication of a vital lack in the Australian psyche.

The legal recognition of Aboriginal 'sacred sites' has emphasised that, whatever meaning or value land might have for white Australians, it has a religious value for Aborigines. Far from being a blank, the landscape that Europeans entered in 1788 was full of meanings not accessible to the whites. The changing attitude to the environment, the battle now to preserve not destroy the wilderness, has altered the perspective on the Aborigines as inhabitants. They are not seen now as having failed to tend the land, of lacking civilisation, but as having lived in harmony with it. As more and more of the Aboriginal past is recovered — the restoration of Aboriginal names, for example — the white relationship to the land is subtly challenged at an emotional and psychological level.

The desire to feel at one with the land is age-old. In Aboriginal communities, despite the cultural deprivation and dislocation of two hundred years of white dominance, the sense of 'our place', of belonging, is unproblematic. In her autobiography Ruby Langford says: 'I thought of the difference between white people saying "I own this land" and blacks saying "We belong to this land".'[36] Land rights are a crucial issue for Aborigines in a way that many whites simply don't yet understand and must be part of a treaty or whatever form of reconciliation or accommodation is eventually worked out.

For whites the whole issue of 'home', 'place' and 'belonging' has become problematic; not yet at the public or political level, but at the level of feeling, of individual, private awareness. An interesting example of this disturbance to white identity is to be found in Cassandra Pybus' *Community of Thieves*. Pybus is anxious that her fellow Australians should understand and acknowledge the dispossession of the Aborigines. At the same time she feels a deep attachment to the part of Tasmania where her family have lived for five generations. She is, in a phrase of Judith Wright's, 'born of the conqueror' and wants to confront this reality honestly; and she is a Tasmanian who feels that the place where her ancestors settled is 'my place'. On her morning walks past the house of her great-grandfather, 'I can feel my ancestral bonds to this place. It is my place: the landscape of my dreaming'.[37] Taken at its face value, the phrase — 'landscape of my dreaming' — might seem to mean that it is the place where she dreams or the place of which she dreams; but it clearly means more than that. The walk she takes is a 'profound and constant source of spiritual renewal'. In the context of her book, she is appropriating the term used by whites and Aborigines alike to signify a complex Aboriginal conception and implicitly claiming a connection with place that matches the Aboriginal.

Cassandra Pybus sums up the white dilemma when she writes: 'We need to know how it is we white Australians call this country home.'[38] The myth of white heroism and endurance in settling an empty land and creating an egalitarian society is fading, and a new myth is starting to take shape around the central fact of white dispossession of the Aborigines. The bicentennial celebration hastened the process by dramatising the history of white migration. White Australians don't have that sense of belonging to the land that is taken for granted in Aboriginal civilisation. Right now they are learning to think of themselves as non-Aboriginal Australians, the first painful but necessary step in 'reinventing Australian civilisation'.

Notes

1. Russel Ward, *The Australian Legend*, Oxford University Press, Melbourne, 1958; John Hirst, 'The pioneer legend', *Historical Studies*, vol. 18, no. 71, 1978, pp. 316–37.
2. King O'Malley, American-born Labor politician; quoted in W.E.H. Stanner, *White Man got No Dreaming: Essays 1938–1973*, ANU Press, Canberra, 1979, p. 322.
3. See Richard White, *Inventing Australia: Images and Identity 1688–1980*, Allen & Unwin, Sydney, 1981, ch. 5.
4. Humphrey McQueen, *A New Britannia*, Penguin, Ringwood, 1970, p. 42.
5. A.A. Phillips, *The Australian Tradition*, Cheshire, Melbourne, 1958, p. 45.
6. Henry Lawson, 'The drover's wife' (1892).
7. Henry Lawson, 'The men who made Australia' (1901). See *Collected Verse* (ed. Colin Roderick), Angus & Robertson, Sydney, 1968, vol. 2, p. 8.
8. C.E.W. Bean, *The Story of Anzac* (Vol.1, *Official History of Australia in the War of 1914–18*), Angus & Robertson, Sydney, 1933, pp. 3–7.
9. Vance Palmer, 'Battle', *Meanjin Papers*, March 1942, cited in Ian Turner (ed.), *The Australian Dream*, Sun Books, Melbourne, 1968, pp. 304–6.
10. Nettie Palmer, 'Colonial wares', *Talking It Over*, Angus & Robertson, Sydney, 1932, p. 25.
11. Bob Hodge and Vijay Mishra, *Dark Side of the Dream: Australian Literature and the Post-colonial Mind*, Allen & Unwin, Sydney, 1990.
12. As well as contributing an introductory note, Elkin assisted the author with anthropological detail. See H.E. Thonemann, *Tell the White Man: The Life of an Aboriginal Lubra*, Collins, Sydney, 1949, p. 9.
13. Ibid, pp. 90–1.
14. Jeannie Gunn, *The Little Black Princess: A True Tale of Life in the Never-Never Land* [London, 1905], Melville & Mullen, Melbourne, 1906, p. 30.
15. Jeannie Gunn, 'A real story completed: Australia's little "Bett-Bett" is now a grandmother', *Age*, 15 January 1955.
16. Gunn, *The Little Black Princess*, p. 62.

17 Jeannie Gunn, *We of the Never-Never* [London 1908], Hutchinson, Melbourne, 1982, p. 63.
18 Ibid., p. 238.
19 Hodge and Mishra, *Dark Side of the Dream*, p. xiii.
20 Sally Morgan, *My Place*, Fremantle Arts Centre Press, Fremantle, 1987, p. 38.
21 Ibid., p. 98.
22 Ibid., p. 233.
23 Ibid., p. 349.
24 Ibid., p. 169.
25 Ibid., p. 340.
26 Ibid., p. 350.
27 Eric Michaels, 'Para-ethnology' [review of Bruce Chatwin, *The Songlines*, and Sally Morgan, *My Place*], *Art & Text*, no. 30, 1988, p. 44.
28 Ruby Langford, *Don't Take Your Love to Town*, Penguin, Ringwood, 1988.
29 Morgan, *My Place*, p. 351.
30 See Labumore: Elsie Roughsey, *An Aboriginal Mother Tells of the Old and the New*, McPhee Gribble, Ringwood, 1984. The editors of the book, Paul Memmott and Robyn Horsman, contribute 'A note on the editing process'.
31 Ibid., p. 350.
32 Sally Morgan, 'A fundamental question of identity', interview with Mary Wright, in *Aboriginal Culture Today*, ed. Anna Rutherford (special issue of *Kunapipi*, vol. 10, nos 1 & 2, 1988).
33 W.E.H. Stanner, 'The Dreaming', in *Australian Signpost* (ed. T.A.G. Hungerford), Melbourne, Cheshire, 1956, p. 52; reprinted in W.E.H. Stanner, *White Man got No Dreaming: Essays 1938–1973*, Canberra, ANU Press, 1979. Stanner's ABC Boyer Lectures, *After the Dreaming* (1968), contributed significantly to raising public awareness of the historical issues.
34 Ibid., p. 54.
35 Ibid., p. 51.
36 Langford, *Don't Take your Love to Town*, p. 262.
37 Cassandra Pybus, *Community of Thieves*, Port Melbourne, Heinemann, 1991, p. 4.
38 Ibid., p. 16.

3
MYTH

Bruce Bennett

Myth may be thought of as an invented story, arising from a collective belief, which gives events and actions a particular meaning. Among the many myths about myths is the one that 'truth' is an essential element in the invention. Another is that myths must have universal human significance. In this chapter I envisage a more humble use of the concept, which does not rely on mystical universality or on some fixed notion of human truthfulness. Rather, I want to suggest that a modern nation's 'civilisation' can be gauged in part by the stories its citizens tell about each other and the world they inhabit; and that the myths they generate sometimes run in tandem with history, sometimes counter to its perceived tendencies as communities reformulate their sense of themselves.

Australia's 'foundation myth' has been presented as the story of Anzac, or Gallipoli — a story that describes heroism achieved in defeat. The historical event from which the myth grew was a military landing at Anzac Cove, Gallipoli, Turkey on 25 April 1915. From a non-Australian perspective, the story doesn't always seem as important as it does to Australians, and its ingredients vary. An American perspective in the *Encyclopedia Britannica*, for example, presents the place and its significance in these terms: 'Gallipoli was the scene of determined Turkish resistance to the Allied forces during the Dardanelles Campaign of World War I, in which most of the town was destroyed.'[1] For Australians, the campaign was one in which eight thousand of their confrères were killed only fourteen years after the federation of the Australian colonies into a nation in 1901.

MYTH

The timing is significant. A story of ethical unity was required in order to give psychological force to the political reality of federation. Anzac provided the core of this story, although the New Zealand origins of the term have never received proper acknowledgement in Australia. As the inaugural Television Open Learning program in Australian studies[2] emphasises, the myth crystallised many aspects of assumed Australianness such as courage, patriotism, bush values and the mateship of Australian men in adversity. This Anzac story remains a potent source of imagery for the advertising industry.

Many Australians would testify to the persistence of the Anzac myth in the second half of the twentieth century. In my own family, for example, my father uses elements of this myth to present himself in a humorous light when he recounts stories of the action he did *not* see while allegedly 'pushing back the Japs' from the island of Morotai near Borneo in the latter phases of World War II. Popular discourse such as the Anzac story has produced sometimes enters a single literary text and finds a memorable distillation there. Such was the case with Alan Seymour's play, *The One Day of the Year* (1962), which dramatised in unforgettable fashion the questioning of the Anzac legend by university students of the relatively innocent pre-Vietnam years. The play does not resolve the generational conflicts of attitudes and values it exposes, but it shows dramatically how a powerful myth can interpenetrate the activities of ordinary suburban living, causing responses ranging from confrontation to pacification.

The representation of the wife and mother figure in the play as a supportive homemaker — the 1950s 'mum' who continually makes cups of tea — is essential to that generation's definitions of 'home'. If this mother figure is on the outer circles of the Anzac myth she is at the centre of another: the myth of the primacy of family. As master narratives, both Anzac and the family have been questioned most vigorously by members of the 'baby boom' generation who were children in the 1940s and 1950s and became writers, filmmakers or other contributors to mythmaking in the 1960s, 1970s and 1980s.

In spite of the proliferation of alternative stories, the Anzac complex retains some power as a 'core' story of nationhood.[3] John Romeril's play, *The Floating World* (1974), for example, has a protagonist, Les Harding, who still trades off the 'Anzac' aspects of his World War II experience as Alf Cook does in *The One Day of the*

Year, but in both cases a critique is implied. The essentially masculine orientation of most versions of the Anzac story and its tendency to exclude problems of ethnic or regional difference in the interests of a unifying story of mateship and national purpose have been questioned vigorously since the 1970s. Hence, for example, A. A. Phillips' assertively unifying title, *The Australian Tradition*, for his book of essays in 1958 has been complicated and pluralised in Laurie Hergenhan's *Penguin New Literary History of Australia* (1988). One of the factors in this generational change has been the professionalising of a literary culture in Australia, with the greater sophistication of inquiry that this has brought. Another factor has been the increasing political and social pressure exerted by minorities and perceived outsiders. The idea of a unitary Australian community has been more difficult for politicians and visionaries to maintain. Regionalists, ethnicists and feminists have all contributed to a multiplication of myths, all vying for authority within popular culture as well as in the burgeoning field of Australian studies.

Whose stories will circulate in contemporary Australia and be retold while others wither on the vine? Whose stories will be paramount? By focusing briefly on several perceived groups within the wider community, I will try to suggest how and why certain myths are promoted or contradicted and the ways they reflect on myth-making. The groups I have in mind are first, the Aboriginal population, and second, immigrants, both European and Asian. The underlying question is whether a new pluralist conception of Australia, associated with a multiplication of myths, is leading to a breakdown of a sense of community or a reformulation of it.

The question of the primacy of Aboriginal culture for all Australians is raised by Bob Hodge and Vijay Mishra in *Dark Side of the Dream*.[4] Hodge and Mishra present two main arguments: that the historical suppression of Aboriginal culture requires its reinstatement, and that, more controversially, as the repressed 'dark side' of the Australian consciousness, Aboriginal culture has the necessary authenticity to restore some sense of wholeness to the Australian psyche. According to Hodge and Mishra's account, Australia remains a 'neo-colonial' society. The tendency to binary categorisation (white/black, colonial/free, etc) gives Hodge and Mishra's book its fighting quality, but it has been attacked by the 'post-colonial' camp in academic criticism for oversimplifying the alternatives and not recognising the necessary 'hybridity' of racial and historical origins in settler societies such as Australia's.[5] If the latter tactic seems to represent a spiking of Aboriginal guns by a neo-Europeanist culture of complexity, it also makes the valid point that any mythology of 'pure' origins does not stand up to close examination.

Other books that closely examine literary texts by or about Aborigines, such as those by J.J. Healy, and especially Adam Shoemaker, provide more detailed and convincing sociohistorical contexts which satisfy the reader that culturally specific circumstances operate in the production and reception of Australian Aboriginal texts.[6] The Canadian-born Shoemaker convincingly concludes his study with the statement that 'three major elements coalesce in Black Australian literature — cultural nationalism, literary talent, and Aboriginal pride'.[7] Any Australian-based critique of modern Aboriginal literature must take proper account of all three elements and not resort to oversimplified international parameters applied to the Australian case.

The production and transmission of Aboriginal stories has changed radically since World War II. Whereas the principal mediators or translators of Aboriginal stories to a wider population in the 1940s and 1950s were European Australians — such as the anthropologists Strehlow, Elkin and Berndt — most Aboriginal stories of the 1980s and 1990s that have caught the literary and popular imagination have been written, or told fairly directly, by Aboriginal Australians. Appropriation of Aboriginal material by whites has been more closely interrogated than ever before.

The distinction between generations becomes evident in a consideration of Ronald Berndt's translation of the north-east Arnhem Land Aboriginal song-cycle, the Wonguri-Manjikai Moon-bone song, which in turn became the principal source for Les Murray's style and sentiments in 'The Buladelah-Taree holiday song cycle', a long poem celebrating this white Australian poet's own 'spirit country' of the Manning River area in northern New South Wales.[8] Berndt's translation was intended to replicate Aboriginal oral delivery but its phraseology, rhythms and repetitions are characteristic of the King James version of the Christian Bible:

> 'The evening song'
> from *Song Cycle of the Moon-bone*
>
> Up and up soars the Evening Star, hanging there in the sky

> Men watch it, at the place of the Dugong and of the Clouds, and of the Evening Star.
> A long way off, at the place of Mist, of Lilies and of the Dugong.
> The Lotus, the Evening Star, hangs there on its long stalk, held by the Spirits.[9]

Ronald Berndt's Anglophone background is evident, as this song-cycle proceeds, in echoes of the Song of Solomon and the Book of Job from the King James Bible. These books are, of course, themselves translations. The myth, as reproduced in these images of the Evening Star, is of the sacredness of place and an order of things controlled by the Spirits; its version of the lived-in environment is both physical and spiritual. But its principal filter is the archetypal literary and spiritual text of western civilisation. Clearly, the purity of vision that is implied emerges from very mixed sources.

A generation later than Berndt's collection of these songs, contemporary Aboriginal writer Mudrooroo Narogin (formerly Colin Johnson) writes his own versions of song-cycles in which the language more closely simulates the oral delivery of his Nyoongah people in the south-west of Western Australia and draws less on a high-brow British literary inheritance. The notion of a 'pure' literary inheritance (Anglicised) thus gives way to the more eclectic intertextuality of a post-modern age.

In *The Song Circle of Jacky* and especially *Dalwurra: The Black Bittern*,[10] Mudrooroo's language combines traditional Aboriginal rhythms and repetitions with eclectic international influences, including some myths of Asia. *Dalwurra* is the Aboriginal word for a black bird that used to inhabit the wetlands of Mudrooroo's native Avon Valley. Mudrooroo's allegorical protagonist is presented as a typically non-migratory bird that nevertheless migrates, travelling from Australia through Asia to Europe and back again. In this way, he partakes of the conditions of the traveller, one of the archetypal figures of Western literature; like Odysseus, he comprehends not only his own fate but also that of many people in the contemporary world. Whereas Ronald Berndt's translation of a traditional Aboriginal song-cycle had evoked a quasi-religious 'music of the spheres', Mudrooroo Narogin evokes the dislocation and disorientation of the post-1960s generation, which, in Australia as elsewhere, is culturally defined by its search for imaginary homelands.

The myth of home, of a place of belonging, is especially prevalent and poignant for Australia's Aboriginal people because they have so patently been displaced. The poetry of Oodgeroo Noonuccal (formerly Kath Walker), the autobiographical prose work, *My Place*, by Sally Morgan and the plays and poems of Jack Davis all dramatise this central loss — of places known and loved, of homes lost and the strategies to regain them in memory and imagination. In some respects, this mythic story is the master narrative of contemporary Australia.[11]

Whereas a recurrent note in much contemporary Aboriginal myth-making is of deprivation and loss (although, by Davis and Morgan especially, it is often dramatised humorously) a more optimistic note is injected by Aboriginal politician and songwriter Ernie Bridge. Politicians are, of course, professional optimists. As Minister for Agriculture, Water Resources and the North-West in the Western Australian Labor Government in the late 1980s and early 1990s, Ernie Bridge combined his political role with that of a country and western folksinger and evoked a jaunty myth of progress through the harnessing of natural resources and industrial development.

In an appropriation of leading myths of the white settler society — recalling Henry Lawson, Ned Kelly, Anzac-style patriotism and bush mateship — Bridge and his family produced a recording called *The Great Australian Dream*,[12] in which he sang of a visionary project to build a pipeline, which would carry fresh water from the sparsely populated north-west to the more densely populated south-west of Western Australia — a distance of some three thousand kilometres. In a style reminiscent of the American folksinger Woody Guthrie, Bridge was true to his name in linking a unique brand of environmental populism with a hint of the Aboriginal legend of the life-bringing Waugyl or Rainbow Serpent, thus refurbishing a dominant western myth of progress based on the growth of cities and industrial development.

The hope engendered by this version of a typically eclectic modern myth, which draws on the discourses of mystique and vision to fulfil the technological dream of progress through the exploitation of natural resources, seems to have been illusory. The opposition of those increasingly powerful modern mythmakers, the economists, the discovery of alternative water supplies and a change of government have combined to deflate increasing community fascination with the project, and it was shelved.

What remains is the song of a larger-than-life dream of an assimilated Aboriginal politician, combining pragmatic concerns and Dreamtime possibilities, which kept a dream alive in the popular mind, aided by press and television coverage. Of interest here is the mixed provenance of this dream and its almost mad clarity, which somehow floats beyond its material circumstances and enabled it to capture a community's imagination for a time. The conservative tendencies of this myth of hope are important — that it draws on local and national patriotism and established images and ideas in order to build faith in a 'new' vision. Also of importance is the overtly political motivation of Ernie Bridge's 'Great Australian Dream': the myths of contemporary Australia often have significant political contexts.

While Aborigines have contributed increasingly in recent decades to a wider understanding of the myths that might drive Australian civilisation, so too have immigrants from Europe and Asia. Some of their published work has been restricted to the minority language communities, but since the 1970s conscious policies and programs of multiculturalism have opened avenues towards a wider reading community. From an Aboriginal perspective, Mudrooroo Narogin has called this process 'centring the fringe'.[13] From the perspective of Australian writers born in other countries, the title of Sneja Gunew and Kateryna O. Longley's book of literary essays, *Striking Chords*,[14] indicates an aspiration (of the editors at least) towards engaging the attention of a wider community and thus contributing to national mythmaking.

The extent to which certain individuals or groups might inhabit a 'fringe' or contribute directly to national thinking is one of the vexing questions of contemporary cultural debate in Australia. The fringe, edge or margin has seemed a convenient metaphor to highlight the alleged position of regional, feminist, Aboriginal and immigrant writers and artists, and to some extent use of the metaphor has strengthened the political leverage of these groups in the cultural debate. They represent the outsider's claim to a voice on the national stage, and 'natural justice' seems to require scope for mobility and stronger transmission of views. Of course, there are some who argue that there is no such thing as a national culture — that the notion itself implies a false 'centrist model'.[15] But to change the metaphor from the spatial relations of centre-margins to the play of light, as in 'mutual illuminations', as Gunew proposes,[16] might not be a great alternative. There remain important differences among immigrants in terms of their view of the desirability as well as the achievability of integration to prevailing Australian myths and values; some will continue to propose a more separate cultural role in their adoptive country. These are important matters of emphasis in the debates about multiculturalism and nationality in Australia, and the ways of describing them need careful thought.

One of the post–World War II immigrant groups that receives little attention in *Striking Chords* is the Hungarians, who have had a disproportionately large influence on Australian intellectual and cultural life in these years. Like other political refugees from post-war communism in central and eastern Europe, the Hungarians settled in Australian cities and attempted to create new lives there. Usually well educated in their home country, they were often the sons and daughters of the managerial or land-owning classes. I have had the pleasure of knowing some of the Hungarians who came to Australia in the 1950s and will refer briefly to ways in which several of them have contributed to the reinforcement or adaptation of prevalent myths.

Consider the brothers Kovesi, Paul and Julius, who had lived in a town near Budapest until the Communist 'reforms' of the late 1940s made conditions impossible for them. After the usual immigrant hostels and menial jobs following their emigration to Australia in the early 1950s, Paul and Julius studied for university degrees in Australia and then England before being appointed to academic positions, in English and philosophy respectively, at the University of Western Australia. Paul recreated there his mythical golden age from the imaginative literature of Augustan England. King's College Chapel in Cambridge was a spiritual oasis, occasionally visited. Paul's outlook was cosmopolitan — he became an inveterate reader of the *New Yorker* and *Punch* — but London increasingly disappointed him as it became less 'English'. In a pilgrimage with him to Jane Austen's family home in Chawton, Hampshire, in the early 1970s, I observed that this was the civilisation in which Paul would have liked to have been at home. However, for all his gallantry of manner, and *noblesse oblige*, one felt that the break with Hungary in his early twenties had left him feeling forever adrift. It was left to his wife, Julia, to play the alternative role of the integrated immigrant. Although Julia, too, earned an Australian university degree (in dentistry) she gained her sustenance from the physical earth and a myth of the land, grafting her invented role of peasant and homemaker on to notions of the Australian pioneer settler. She developed a fruitful suburban garden and was fabled as one of Perth's best cooks. While observing all this from an ironically humorous distance, Paul retained the manner of a person whose soul was elsewhere. Husband and wife together played out the antinomic roles of European Australian mythology — those of exile and settler.

The commonly persisting assumption of the 1950s and 1960s that Australia could be an extension of Europe in the southern hemisphere affected Paul Kovesi's brother, Julius, in somewhat different ways, in the ideological sphere. Busy and bustling, and a witty worrier of ideas, Julius Kovesi developed philosophical skills to dismantle what he knew with absolute certainty was the false ideology of Marxism, from whose practices he had escaped. By the early 1960s he was countering the idea of a socialist Australia held by an increasing number of left–liberal Australian intellectuals. Julius Kovesi argued that the tendency to romanticise and generalise the notion of alienation from Hegel and the early writings of Marx was dangerous, for it extrapolated too readily from particular experience to the 'Big Animal', society at large.[17] 'Nature' posed a special problem for Kovesi; language, he argued, was 'slanted against human achievement in spite of the fact that all our human life is a human achievement', and he was particularly critical of appeals to 'nature' and 'natural law' by Marx and many others. 'Progress', he asserted, was not a bad ideal, especially in the face of a civilisation under attack by 'knockers and levellers'.[18] The myth of progress was well suited to the development at all costs approach of the conservative political parties in Australia at this time.

Another Hungarian émigré of this time, librarian and novelist Andrew Domahidy, expressed a view common among his confrères of Liberal Party Prime Minister R.G. Menzies as a hero:

> We applauded everything that Mr Menzies did and said. Menzies was strongly against the communists. At that time [the Cold War] we were so polarised that only black and white existed. That was the main reason we supported Menzies. And secondly, because he opened up many things. He did a lot for the universities, which again appealed to us. He was an inspiration to us and, I think, to the whole country.[19]

The idea of Menzies as hero is anathema to many Australian intellectuals, but his vision of an Anglo-Australia in the southern seas clearly appealed not just to Domahidy and his friends but also to many other European immigrants, many of whom would object strenuously to the official policies of multiculturalism of the 1970s and later as reducing the chances of the children of immigrants to 'find their own identity as Australians'.[20]

As a novelist, though, Domahidy's political concerns were overtaken by other interests, summed up in his alternating images of nature in his home country of Transylvania and his adoptive Western Australia. Domahidy's only novel so far translated into English, *Shadows and Women* (*Arnyak és asszonyok*), is dominated by the experience of expatriation. After his arrival in Western Australia, the novel's protagonist muses on his condition: 'You become an émigré in your own land; all of us have become émigrés on this earth. Some are local foreigners, others are foreign locals.'[21]

The site on which these transformations are inscribed in the novel is landscape — principally, the loved and remembered landscapes of Transylvania and then the new landscapes of southwestern Australia. The generic myth drawn on is that of the pastoral tradition in literature and painting. Domahidy's remembered country is the rural County Szatmar on the borders of prewar Hungary and Romania. Like other mythic regionalists, Thomas Hardy, William Faulkner or Randolph Stow, Domahidy recreates his country of childhood and youth with loving attention to sensuous detail. The counterpart to this mythic world is the author's 'second love' registered in the landscapes of south-western Australia. Of this adaptation, Domahidy has commented:

> The most difficult thing for me was to come to terms with the trees. They are so different. This pale, almost greyish green after the lush European greens was at first difficult. But somehow it happened, I came to love it and that is why I am still here.[22]

Inevitably, when one myth is overlaid on another and differences are observed, they become a focus of attention. But the registering of detail tends to occur within conventional limits. For example, Domahidy's Hungarian émigrés see Australia as a potential extension of the European imagination and thus without a history of its own. Moreover, 'nature', which philosopher Julius Kovesi had analysed in a sceptical, anti-romantic light, is presented by Domahidy in a much more romantic way. South-western Australia, for example, is perceived by Domahidy in gendered terms that recall D.H. Lawrence and Molly Skinner's image of this country in *The Boy in the Bush* as 'so big, so soft, so ancient in its virginity'. By contrast, Domahidy's view of the north-west, like Xavier Herbert's, is clearly a 'man's world'. The north-west landscape, in Domahidy's eyes (recalling, to some extent, Peter Cowan in this) is 'masculine': 'It is very cruel and beautiful in its cruelty. It has no femininity'.[23]

The myth of Australia as a cultural extension of Europe has been countered most powerfully in the 1980s and 1990s by the view that 'we are part of Asia'. Whereas official versions of the view abound, as part of an attempt to encourage economic and trading links in what is now called the 'Asia–Pacific region', cultural mythology has typically been slower to respond, both to economic changes and to the increasing Asian element in the Australian population.[24] Nevertheless, the early stages of a readjustment of perspectives is occurring and is evident in some parts of literary culture. Career diplomat Alison Broinowski's survey of Australian impressions of Asia, *The Yellow Lady*,[25] is also a critique of the 'tenaciously Eurocentric' outlook of Australians and itself contributes to the officially prescribed encouragement of changed perspectives.

A psychological analysis of the ambivalence of Australians towards Asia has been ventured by the cultural anthropologist Annette Hamilton in terms of fear and desire. Australian cultural representations of Aborigines and Asians, according to Hamilton, stem from their positions at the 'empty heart' and 'fragile boundaries', respectively, of the Australian consciousness.[26] Although Hamilton's assumption here of a 'national imagery', deriving from Durkheim and Lacan, might not be sufficiently sensitive to regional or intercommunal differences, it provides a basis for reconsideration of Australian myths of Asia. What is needed, in addition, is the kind of theorising that might facilitate a consideration of interactive mythologies within the still-open concept of the 'Asia–Pacific region'.

One place to begin is with the protagonist figures, the heroes and anti-heroes of myths. A series of papers in the recent book *Myths, Heroes and Anti-Heroes*[27] opens up this area, raising questions about the purpose, function and construction of myths of different societies in countries of the Asia–Pacific region. Myths range from the journalistic construction of Don Bradman as an Australian sporting hero to the uses of the Mahabharata in societies outside India, including Fiji. It is even suggested in one playfully intertextual chapter, by an Indian-born Australian from Fiji, that the Mahabharata provides the perfect mythic structure for international cricket.[28] There is no sense here of Commonwealth countries still straining under the yoke of a British empire; rather, old cultural icons are being reinvented and reassimilated in new ways according to changing conditions.

Among the issues provoked by myths of heroism or anti-heroism are questions of authority. Thus, for example, Sharifah Omah shows how the myth of divine kingship in Malay history, with its lessons about the sanctity of the ruler, has been a useful political tool in recent times. Japanese scholar Orie Muta also reveals how the state manipulation of hero worship has operated in Japan, both in the literary culture and beyond, but she also points to the emergence of anti-heroism in tandem with literary modernism in that country. Filipino novelist F. Sionil Jose tells of the writing of his novel *Po-On* in which he lays down his definition of the hero as a peasant revolutionary 'at a time when heroes in my country are movie stars and socialites turned politicians, soldiers who have betrayed the constitution, and even returning widows with three thousand pairs of shoes'.[29] Images such as these from the literary and social cultures of 'our region' provide important new contexts for Australian writers and readers against which to test their own myths of egalitarian democracy, mateship and the 'fair go' principle. At the same time, internal revisions are occurring, for example in the increasing status and authority of women, both in the literary culture and beyond, and in the serious attention given to Aboriginal mythology.[30] Increasing attention to the rights of women and of native peoples are, of course, part of an international (partly United Nations-inspired) movement in the Asia–Pacific, as elsewhere.

Perhaps the most important convergence of myths among countries of the Asia–Pacific occurs in their preoccupation with notions of home, belonging and exile. Myths of the land, and particular landscapes, occur as constellations within these stories. In another book arising from an international conference on literature of the Asia–Pacific region, *A Sense of Exile*,[31] Australian myths are explored and criticised alongside those from China, Fiji, India, Korea, Malaysia, New Zealand, Papua New Guinea, the Philippines, Singapore, Sri Lanka and Thailand. What emerges is a number of culturally specific but interestingly convergent stories about displacement and dispossession, caused by invasion and forced or voluntary migration. Certain primal oppositions recur, for example, in versions of 'paradise' and 'hell'; and, as the Indian literary historian Meenakshi Mukherjee points out, a state of 'exile of the mind' has had important linguistic and literary ramifications in India and throughout the region.[32]

The territorial impulse is not necessarily aggressive and can express itself in a variety of mythic formations. Singaporean critic Kirpal Singh has explored this aspect of the Malaysian–Australian poet Ee Tiang Hong's life and work. Ee left Malaysia for Australia in 1975 when he 'could no longer accept, intellectually or emotionally, the official and Malay definition of the Malaysian nation and culture'.[33] As a fifth-generation person of the Baba culture in Malacca, with its unique fusion of Chinese and Malay elements, Ee thought of Malacca as 'home'. In his collection *Tranquerah*[34] Ee was, as Kirpal Singh remarks, 'bodily in Perth but spiritually in Malaysia — more profoundly in Malacca'.[35] The stories he tells in verse, then, are principally of the lost, remembered home, the place of childhood and family history, of cultural continuity. Streets, shops, houses and the sea are its visible elements but memory, imagination and feeling are its real driving forces. Kirpal Singh remarks that: 'If the exile leaves home because of a sense of marginality within his community, the price of exile is yet a further marginalisation.'[36] However, this can be a fruitful writing position for some authors, and in a later poem 'Coming to', Ee Tiang Hong tells a personal story of migration, which strikes a chord with many contemporary Australians:

> *On terra firma, Australis*
>
> don't ask me how I got out, Eddy,
> and, Bruce, this isn't a suicide note,
> Heaven forbid! No sailing
> to Byzantium, either. Indeed,
> thankful just to have survived then —
> around an edge of consciousness,
> new faces, fellow Australian.[37]

I have argued elsewhere that the lost Australian is such a recurrent figure in Australian literature that it indicates a deep national anxiety, and that, in order to better understand this condition, more attention should be focused on constructions and deconstructions of place, region and community in the literary culture.[38]

In an age of increasing human and material mobility, the psychology of homelessness and its consequences is in urgent need of re-examination, and the myths of writers and artists might be helpful. Similarly, myths of heroism and anti-heroism seen as culturally specific formations but, with important comparative dimensions, could be examined for the light they throw on different societies' constructions of status and authority.

But myths can be enjoyed in their own right, too, for the pleasure they give through linguistic, visual or musical play. These elements of play and pleasure in mythmaking are too often forgotten by critics and cultural commentators, yet they are the very elements that have the capacity to rebuild the common understandings of communities, to give them, within the context of a proliferating pluralism, the human basis for their continuance as communities.

NOTES

1. *New Encyclopaedia Britannica*, University of Chicago, Chicago, 1982, Micropaedia, vol. 4, p. 394.
2. The Australian Studies course in the TV Open Learning program was produced by Griffith University and ABC Television in 1992.
3. See Robin Gerster, *Big-noting: The Heroic Theme in Australian War Writing*, Melbourne University Press, Melbourne, 1987. Alan Seymour and Richard Nile (eds), *Anzac: Meaning, Memory and Myth*, Sir Robert Menzies Centre for Australian Studies, University of London, 1991.
4. Bob Hodge and Vijay Mishra, *The Dark Side of the Dream: Australian Literature and the Postcolonial Mind*, Allen & Unwin, Sydney, 1991.
5. For example, Gareth Griffiths, 'The dark side of the Dreaming: Aboriginality & Australian culture', *Australian Literary Studies*, vol. 15, no. 4, 1992, pp. 328–33.
6. J. J. Healy, *Literature and the Aborigine in Australia*, University of Queensland Press, St Lucia, 1978. Adam Shoemaker, *Black Words, White Page: Aboriginal Literature 1929–1988*, University of Queensland Press, St Lucia, 1989.
7. Shoemaker, *Black Words, White Page*, p. 279.
8. Peter Pierce (ed.), *The Oxford Literary Guide to Australia*, Oxford University Press, Melbourne, 1987, p. 99.
9. Les Murray (ed.), *The New Oxford Book of Australian Verse*, Oxford University Press, Melbourne, 1987, p. 245.
10. Colin Johnson, *The Song Circle of Jacky and Selected Poems*, Hyland House, Melbourne, 1986. Colin Johnson (Mudrooroo Narogin), *Dalwurra: The Black Bittern*, Centre for Studies in Australian Literature, University of Western Australia, Nedlands, 1988.

11 See Kath Walker, *My People: A Kath Walker Collection*, Jacaranda Press, Brisbane, 1970; Sally Morgan, *My Place*, Fremantle Arts Centre Press, Fremantle, 1987; Jack Davis, *The First-born and Other Poems*, J.M. Dent, Melbourne, 1983, and *Kullark (Home) and The Dreamers*, Currency Press, Sydney, 1982.
12 Ernie Bridge, *The Great Australian Dream*, cassette tape-recording arranged and directed by Ernie Bridge, DR 9001, Perth (1990).
13 Mudrooroo Narogin, *Writing from the Fringe: A Study of Modern Aboriginal Literature*, Hyland House, Melbourne, 1990, pp. 179–94.
14 Sneja Gunew and Kateryna O. Longley (eds), *Striking Chords: Multicultural Literary Interpretations*, Allen & Unwin, Sydney, 1992.
15 See Gunew, *Striking Chords*, pp. 44–6.
16 Ibid., p. 45.
17 Julius Kovesi, 'The alienated big animal', *Westerly*, No. 2, 1962, pp. 119–122. See also Julius Kovesi, *Moral Notions*, Routledge & Kegan Paul, London, 1967.
18 Julius Kovesi, 'Nature and convention'. Proceedings of the First New Norcia Humanities Symposium, Perth, 1985.
19 Bruce Bennett, 'An interview with András Domahidy', *Westerly*, vol. 37, no. 2, 1992, pp. 40–1.
20 Ibid., pp. 36–7.
21 András Domahidy, *Shadows and Women*, Aeolian Press, Claremont, WA, 1989 (trans. Elizabeth Windsor), pp. 79–80.
22 Bennett, 'An interview with András Domahidy', pp. 38–9.
23 Ibid., p. 39.
24 If present immigrant proportions are maintained the present proportion of Asians in the Australian population (2–3 per cent) will grow to around 10–15 per cent by 2030. Department of Immigration, Local Government and Ethnic Affairs, *Australian Population Trends and Prospects*, Australian Government Publishing Service, Canberra, 1988, p. 102.
25 Alison Broinowski, *The Yellow Lady: Australian Impressions of Asia*, Oxford University Press, Melbourne, 1992.
26 Annette Hamilton, 'Fear and desire: Aborigines, Asians and the national imagery', in *Australian Cultural History*, vol. 9, 1990 (special issue: *Australian Perceptions of Asia*, ed. David Walker et al.), p. 16.
27 Bruce Bennett and Dennis Haskell (eds), *Myths, Heroes and Anti-heroes: Essays on the Literature of the Asia–Pacific Region*, Centre for Studies in Australian Literature, University of Western Australia, Nedlands, 1992.
28 Satendra Nandan, 'The Mahabharata in modern fiction', in Bennett and Haskell, *Myths, Heroes and Anti-Heroes*, pp. 201–9.
29 Sharifah Maznah Syed Omar, 'The myth of divine kingship in Malay history', in Bennett and Haskell, *Myths, Heroes and Anti-Heroes*, pp. 28–35. Orie Muta, 'Myths, heroes and anti-heroes in Japanese culture',

ibid., pp. 36–46. F. Sionil Jose, 'Notes on the writing of *Po-On*', ibid., p. 169.
30 See, for example, Richard Rossiter, '"Heroines" in Australian fiction', Suzette Henke, 'Constructing the female hero', Sue Hosking, 'Two corroborees' and Veronica Brady, 'Heroes against empire' in Bennett and Haskell, *Myths, Heroes and Anti-heroes*. See also Hodge and Mishra, *The Dark Side of the Dream*, and Shoemaker, *Black Words, White Page*.
31 Bruce Bennett and Susan Miller (eds), *A Sense of Exile: Essays in the Literature of the Asia–Pacific Region*, Centre for Studies in Australian Literature, University of Western Australia, Nedlands, 1988.
32 Meenakshi Mukherjee, 'The exile of the mind', in Bennett and Miller, *A Sense of Exile*, pp. 7–14.
33 Kirpal Singh, 'The only way out: Sense of exile in the poetry of Ee Tiang Hong' in Bennett and Miller, *A Sense of Exile*, pp. 33–42.
34 Ee Tiang Hong, *Tranquerah*, Department of English Language and Literature, National University of Singapore, Singapore, 1985.
35 Singh, 'The only way out', p. 37.
36 Ibid., p. 47.
37 Ee Tiang Hong, 'Coming to', *Westerly*, 3, 1986, pp. 56–7.
38 See 'Place region and community: An introduction' in Bruce Bennett, *An Australian Compass: Essays on Place and Direction in Australian Literature*, Fremantle Arts Centre Press, Fremantle, 1991, pp. 11–23.

4
IDENTITY

James Jupp

The search for an Australian national identity goes on remorselessly. Yet few ask why we need such an identity or what we would do with it if we had one. Were Australians emerging from oppressive colonialism there would be the same need to assert nationalism that has faced the whole of the Third World since the end of World War II, as it once faced the United States, Ireland or Poland. Yet British Australia was never oppressed once the convict phase was over. It developed self-governing institutions based on manhood suffrage at a remarkably early date. Its economy remained tied to Britain and its upper classes looked to London society. It was peopled through United Kingdom emigration, assisted by British and colonial governments with the aim of establishing a new Britannia.

The oppressed in Australian society, as we hardly need reminding, were the Aborigines, not the colonists. Unlike those of North and South America or of South Africa, the colonial elite felt no need to revolt against the homeland. Many remained almost pathetically loyal to it until the fall of Singapore in 1942 and even beyond. Theirs was a voluntary act of submission. Australian Anglophiles oppressed themselves and denied their own originality. The British at home scarcely cared what the 'overseas Britons' felt or did so long as the open spaces were available for immigrants, the profits flowed back to the City of London and the colonials flocked to the colours in time of war, as they did in large numbers.

Much radical historiography has tried to reassert that a sense of national identity did, indeed, exist — that it was directed against British cultural and economic domination and that it had its origins in the 1890s. The national identity issue became a football between the radical and conservative sides of Australian politics. The radicals, with a strong Communist input in the 1940s and 1950s, stressed Eureka, the trade union and labour movements, republicanism, British exploitation, the *Bulletin* and the legend of the nineties. They were sometimes embarrassed by the racism and crudity of their heroes, such as William Lane, Henry Lawson or Jack Lang. They posited a struggle between the Australian common man (feminism came later) and the English and their local upper-class sycophants. On the conservative side, the struggle was seen in terms of British Protestant Australians remaining loyal to the empire against the attacks of Communists and Catholics, many of them of Irish origin.

But if Australia has lacked a deep sense of national identity, what then are we to make of the endless repetition of the word *Australian* in advertising or of the undoubted sense that many Australians have that they differ markedly from other English-speakers? Is the Australian sense of national identity weaker than that of, for example, Belgians or Canadians, who do not share a common language? Is it any more confused than that of New Zealanders or South Africans? Could a sense of common identity be more clearly lacking than among the nationalities that, for more than seventy years, inhabited a political unit called Yugoslavia? The repeated claim that a sense of national identity is lacking suggests that once some common link was there which is no longer shared and which has not been replaced by other common links. The only strong common link that has so disappeared was racial and cultural descent from the inhabitants of the British Isles. The British are themselves a varied and culturally diverse people, who have less sense of national identity than they possessed when Britain ruled the largest empire in world history under one of the world's longest reigning monarchs.

The idea that all Australians once shared a sense of national identity, which they subsequently lost, must be seriously questioned. In many respects, as in the United States or in Britain itself, there were common attitudes and symbols unique to Australia and shared by most, if not all, Australians. These included populist egalitarianism, a resistance to affectation and snobbery, the much-vaunted sense of mateship that bonded male fellow workers, a contempt for politicians and intellectuals and some very conventional social attitudes, including sabbatarianism, dislike of homosexuals and support for the nuclear family with the wife and mother kept at home. Many of these common values were those of the respectable English working classes of the nineteenth century, reinforced in many cases by Catholic, Methodist or Calvinist beliefs from the Celtic fringe.

However, there were some beliefs that fit very uncertainly into a radical view of the Australian identity. Australian self-definition was racist towards immigrants and Aborigines. Racism was quite explicit in ostensibly radical publications such as the *Bulletin*, with its masthead 'Australia for the White Man' only removed in 1961 by its editor Donald Horne. It was openly stated in the platforms of the Australian Labor Party and the Australian Workers Union as well as by more obviously conservative organisations such as the Returned Services League. The forced assimilation policies of state Labor governments in Queensland and Western Australia towards Aborigines were even more draconian than those of their conservative counterparts.

Right at the end of his life, in the early 1970s, former federal Labor leader Arthur Calwell could write that a 'combined homogeneous and multi-racial Australia is impossible. Australia must be one thing or the other; we can never be both'. He also believed that 'Our so-called democratic society panders to the selfish, the licentious and the avaricious; it glorifies crime, exploits sex and encourages violence'. Yet at the same time Calwell remained an unregenerate socialist, despairing only that the 'great majority of Australians are too smug, too greedy, too slothful to care about the benefits of socialism'.[1] These views were perhaps exceptionally ideological, reflecting Calwell's devout Catholicism and his disappointments in politics. But the idea that Labor was a radical force in Australia, challenging all conservative ideas, is very hard to sustain, at least until the advent of the Dunstan and Whitlam governments in the 1970s.

There were obviously quite serious contradictions and tensions within the broadly egalitarian ethos that is often held to define the Australian national identity between the 1890s and the 1950s. 'Typical' Australians did not believe in the equality of women or of races and ethnic groups. They resented social inequality but equally resented intellectuals who criticised such inequalities and sought social liberalisation. They believed in democratic processes but not in the freedom of expression necessary to move beyond formal democracy to effective citizenship. They believed that the state was the major agency for protecting and advancing living standards but overlooked the extent to which public bureaucracies and employees were self-interested. Trade unionism, the most effective mass movement for sustaining Australian egalitarianism, did very little for women or immigrants and nothing at all for Aborigines. Ironically, the most important challenge to fossilised labour movement attitudes came in the 1940s and 1950s from the rigidly Stalinist Communist Party, which believed itself to be the inheritor of the Lawson tradition.

Part of the sense of national identity that had become widely accepted by the 1940s was the belief that Australians were both of British stock and superior to the British. In pre-1950s Australia most trade and investment was with Britain, most immigrants came from Britain, most Australian tourists went to Britain, intellectuals looked to (and often fled to) Britain and the media were dominated by British models. Yet many Australians regarded the native English as dirty, servile, unhealthy and altogether inferior. As late as 1965 British immigrants complained that Australians thought they all came from the slums of Coronation Street, site of the long-running English soap opera set in and around a Manchester pub.[2]

Just as Australian egalitarianism was flawed by racism, bigotry and rigid conventions, so the attitudes towards Britain were also contradictory. Local social establishments, especially in Victoria and South Australia, looked to 'home' with as much nostalgia as Anglo-Indians or Anglo-Argentinians. The families of such important Australian writers as Martin Boyd or Patrick White lived in two worlds, with London as their point of reference. It was this aspect of the British inheritance to which radicals objected, especially if they were of Irish Catholic descent.

A central identity problem almost uniquely faced by Australians is to disentangle their strong British inheritance from what is distinctively Australian. Even after two hundred years this problem has yet to be resolved, as the controversies about the monarchy and the flag underline. With a million British immigrants currently living in Australia, there is always a silent reserve of those likely to be annoyed by Australian nationalism. The common notion that no one objects to being called a 'Pom' has never been tested on this large element of the nation. It is not true! Any reaffirmation of Australian identity that is critical of the British connection will inevitably be less welcome by many of the silent million than by the more vocal minorities that seek to define themselves as different from and better than their British ancestors. Surveys conducted by myself and Professor McAllister (1986) in Adelaide and Perth (the two strongholds of British immigrants) showed that those born in England were much more likely to support the monarchy and the flag and to defend the British connection than were those born in Australia. They were also more tolerant of immigration![3] This is not to argue that British immigrants are strongly distinct from Australians. But they are not indistinguishable and cannot be presumed to have identical attitudes and beliefs.

Another two million Australians come from outside the British Isles and have no reason to support the British connection at all. Ironically, those least likely to take out Australian citizenship are the British, New Zealanders and other English-speakers. The contradiction is that those most assimilable to the British Australian norm seem least likely to see any need to abandon former national loyalties. Yet the debate over citizenship is always conducted as though the reverse were the case. It is the 'foreign' immigrants who are usually assumed to have ambivalent attitudes towards adopting citizenship, although this is not supported by any available statistics on naturalisation.

Essentially, Australian society comprises three major elements likely to have different orientations towards the British connection: British immigrants and native Anglophiles; native-born Australian identifiers, often of Irish descent; and non-British immigrants. A vocal but small element of Aborigines sees the British colonisation as a disaster. These elements interact with each other, and it would be wrong to assume that immigrants are ambivalent about their Australian identity or that the Australian-born are uniform and united. Nevertheless, it would be utopian and naive to imagine that all inhabitants of Australia do or can share in a common national identity. Indeed, some might argue that such an expectation is conservative and reactionary and ought not to be encouraged. It marks a return to the strong assimilationism that characterised official and popular expectations into the 1960s.

Australians have always known that they live on the edge of Asia but much effort has gone into denying the significance of this location. The White Australia policy, which effectively determined immigration between 1880 and 1970, simply insulated Australia from its neighbours altogether. Under this policy the

Asian presence in Australia declined to negligible proportions, as it was intended to do. The chances of meeting an Asian in suburban streets was no greater than it would have been in the British motherland. They could be sought in the small and decaying Chinatowns, just as they could in Limehouse (London) or Tiger Bay (Cardiff).

Today the Chinatowns are much bigger and far more prosperous. The only mainland capital without one is Adelaide. But there are now major Chinatowns in the suburbs as well — in Cabramatta, Springvale, North Richmond and Darra — based on Indochinese refugees. Of the two million tourists coming to Australia, half are from Asia, mainly from Japan, China, Singapore, Malaysia and Taiwan. The Japanese constitute the largest tourist element and dominate tourist facilities in Sydney and the Gold Coast. There are 250,000 Australians of Chinese origin. Even in remote mining towns there are noticeable numbers of Filipina women. Some Australians express alarm at these inevitable developments, fearing that the national unity created by White Australia will be fractured by 'Asianisation'. Many of these fears are so irrational as to suggest that collective insecurity is central to the Australian sense of identity.

Official policies, in contrast, often bend in the opposite direction from public prejudice. A Commonwealth premiers' conference in December 1992 considered it desirable that an Asian language be taught in all schools and only reluctantly avoided stipulating that such a language should be compulsory. Despite acute shortages of Japanese and Chinese teachers and a virtual absence of teachers in Korean or Thai, official language policy gives a high priority to 'languages of commerce', which are defined mainly in terms of their use in rapidly expanding east Asian economies. There is far less recognition than seems sensible that European languages, including English, are still the major media for world trade. There is also a reluctance to utilise the language skills of those already in Australia, including 260,000 speakers of Chinese, 160,000 of Arabic or 90,000 of Spanish. Non-English-speakers are still seen as deficient in English, rather than as a resource capable of training and utilisation. One of the basic dilemmas in developing a national policy on language has been the tension between the interests of established language teachers (often of French or German), of community languages (such as Italian or Greek) and of languages of commerce (such as Japanese).[4]

The focus on Asian influence masks the reality that the core component of Australia's multicultural society still consists of non-English-speaking-background (NESB) European immigrants and their children. It is they who constitute most of the so-called ethnic lobby through organisations like the Federation of Ethnic Communities' Councils of Australia, the leadership of which has come overwhelmingly from eastern and central Europe. It is Greeks who have made the greatest inroads into elected representation of any non-British immigrant group. It is Italians who still constitute the largest NESB element. It is those from Yugoslavia who have been most directly involved in the public displays of ethnic loyalty that annoy so many native Australians. Institutionalised multiculturalism rests on the fact that one in five Australians are descended from continental Europeans, most of whom arrived in the immigrant waves that began in the late 1940s.

In spite of all the changes since 1947, Australia is still not so obviously multicultural as Canada, the United States, Russia or the United Kingdom, not to mention most countries of the Third World. It has only one official language, English, which is the sole language of three-quarters of the population. Similarly, three-quarters of Australians are derived from the British Isles, although there are important cultural differences still between Irish Catholics and British Protestants and between the native-born and the million British immigrants. Still today, despite the fears of Asianisation, only five per cent are of non-European origin, including Aborigines. Three major cities, Sydney, Melbourne and Adelaide, are visibly multicultural and multiracial, while Brisbane and Perth contain substantial ethnic and racial minorities, as do Wollongong, Darwin, Newcastle and Geelong. Yet vast swathes of the countryside are still peopled by those of British descent, as are quite important cities such as Toowoomba, Bendigo or Ballarat. The great majority of elected politicians are native-born Australians of British or Irish descent, and the typical Australian is always assumed to be of similar origins. Australia might be close to Asia in geographical and economic terms, but it is nowhere near being an Asian country.

The dilemma that emerges is that Australia has traditionally defined itself as not being Asian and as desirably insulated from Asian influences. Yet it now finds itself economically dependent on Asian trade, tourism and investment to a degree unpredicted at the end of World War II. This has led to wide oscillations in public policy, especially in terms of language training, cross-cultural training or familiarisation with Asian history, politics or culture. There is an official reluctance to acknowledge that Australia can still continue as a predominantly European and English-speaking society without necessarily missing out on available opportunities in east Asia. The success of Canada in its dealings with Hong Kong, or of the United States in dealing with Japan or Korea, suggest that it is not necessary to modify indigenous cultures of European origin too dramatically. Yet Australia has some peculiar historic difficulties in adjusting to the region, not least of which is its lingering reputation as a white country. The notions that Asia is poor and backward, or that the Japanese should still be apologising for the war, or that hordes of Asian refugees are streaming towards Australia in small boats, have coloured much public debate and been very inadequately countered at the official level or by the media.

Australia has a traditional identity that is of little continuing utility or relevance, because it does not take ethnic variety or the shift in focus towards Asia into account. This has led some to argue that what is distinct about Australia is its successful multiculturalism. In contrast to many other societies, Australia has been able to accommodate a large number of differing cultures without overt conflict. It has given opportunities to many new arrivals without measurable discrimination other than that arising from poor English. It allows a far wider range of religious and moral alternatives than would have been thought feasible or desirable in the traditional past. Governments have made public and serious efforts to compensate for the disadvantages of Aboriginal peoples, which everyone acknowledges to be the most serious limitation on the concept of Australian multiculturalism. However, large numbers (and in some surveys a majority) of Australians are uncomfortable with the idea of multiculturalism, which is regularly attacked by public figures and by sections of the media.

What worries many Australians about multiculturalism is that ethnic variety might fragment national unity and a sense of identity. As Australia was exceptionally homogeneous before 1945 (outside Aboriginal areas), this reaction is hardly surprising. The 1947 Census showed Australians to be more than 90 per cent locally born and 99 per cent European (white). Had the question been officially asked, they would also have been described as 95 per cent of British and Irish descent. About 98 per cent spoke only

English. The only important measurable difference was that 19 per cent were Catholics. But Australian Catholics had followed Cardinal Moran's injunction in the previous century to become wholly Australian. Many, indeed, found it easier to be Australian nationalists than did Anglophile Protestants. At least 75 per cent of Catholics, as the earliest opinion polls of 1947 attest, supported the nationalist Australian Labor Party. There had been almost no Catholics in the leadership of the conservative parties, apart from Joe Lyons who had defected from Labor in 1931.

Although Australian society was remarkably uniform in 1947 on the surface, it was scarcely harmonious. A major fallacy in current debates about identity and multiculturalism is that ethnic diversity uniquely threatens social harmony. The homogeneous Australia of the 1940s was riven with social conflict. Many major trade unions were under Communist control. Industrial disputes reached their height in 1949 when the Chifley Labor Government ordered troops into the coalfields. The outlawing of the Communist Party became a major issue in 1950, deeply dividing society and leading eventually to a massive disruption of the Labor Party and the loss of many of its Catholic members and supporters. Religious and secular ideology proved far more disruptive than ethnicity has since. The class struggle was also waged with some determination, until it became increasingly irrelevant in the affluent 1950s.

Contemporary Australian society also has its problems. Unemployment has been consistently high. Interest rates have fluctuated and pushed home purchase out of the reach of many young couples. There is considerable crime, congestion and pollution in some large cities. Many conservationists seek to persuade Australians that there are too many of them and that a viable ecology can only be attained by rigorous population limitation. It is hard to see that any of these problems could be solved by developing a stronger sense of national identity. None are traceable to multiculturalism. Certainly none could be solved by becoming a republic.

The search for national identity appeals to various social interests. Many intellectuals, especially historians, feel responsible for interpreting the nation to itself. Many conservatives believe that discipline can only be maintained if there are common goals and attitudes. Out of such attitudes have come the noblest of nationalisms and the foulest of racisms in this century. One obvious function of a sense of national identity has been to persuade the country to go to war. One reason for being wary of the advocates of national identity and harmony is that, in Australia's past, homogeneity has always rested on racial hierarchies. Today such approaches are largely discredited. But many liberal intellectuals are very suspicious of Muslims, just as until recently they were suspicious of Catholics. Muslims constitute 1 per cent of the population and are a beleaguered working-class minority. In the past similar fears were often expressed about southern European 'peasants'. Some feminists are highly suspicious of their ethnic sisters and almost paranoic about ethnic patriarchy. One of the central arguments against multiculturalism is that there is even worse racism and sexism in the ethnic communities than among the worst of ockers.

Many of these fears and suspicions rest on the perception of immigrants as more 'backward' than Australians. Certainly many of the southern Europeans who came to Australia in the past were poorly educated and came from conservative and patriarchal societies. So do many of the Asian refugees who have arrived since the fall of Saigon in 1975. But lack of education has never been closely related to lack of intelligence in societies where mass education is not yet institutionalised. The chair of modern Greek at Sydney University was funded by an elderly, almost illiterate Greek who had made his fortune without much formal education but who wanted it spent on something of lasting value. A rather different approach from that of many of the high-flying Australian entrepreneurs of the 1980s! There is insufficient evidence to suggest that immigrants are more conservative than native Australians. Indeed, what little survey data exists suggests that they are less so on a range of issues.[5]

An immigrant society faces several dilemmas. When it actively sought immigrants, Australia had to grapple with the reality that strongly assimilationist attitudes were alienating large numbers of its new settlers. They resented the suggestion that their culture was inferior to the local brand, especially if they came from the better-educated classes of Europe, as did many refugees between 1938 and 1952 (the main period of educated Jewish refugee emigration to Australia). They found local attitudes towards family life and the relationships of the generations and the sexes disturbing and unacceptable. They saw their homelands becoming more prosperous and stable, and so many chose to return that an official enquiry was held in the early 1970s. Abandoning assimilationism recognised that you could not settle large numbers of people and expect them willingly to become 'real Australians' in a hurry.

Australia, then, became officially multicultural in the early 1970s, just at the point where the emphasis in immigration began to shift from Europe to Asia with the parallel ending of the White Australia policy. The new approach was enthusiastically endorsed by the Whitlam, Hawke and Keating Labor Governments and by the Fraser Liberal Government. It was taken up by Labor Premier Neville Wran in Sydney and by his Liberal successor, Nick Greiner. By 1990 every government in Australia officially endorsed multiculturalism and had created institutions to advocate and advance it. But what was it? Critics throughout the 1980s argued both that multiculturalism was divisive and that it was not defined.

The dilemma of assimilationism in an immigrant society is that many new settlers resent it and many more ignore it. People become assimilated at their own pace in a democracy, especially as that democracy becomes more tolerant and liberal. The dilemma of multiculturalism in a society with strong monocultural traditions is that the majority fears and resents concessions made to minorities. A major survey of their supporters conducted by the Liberal Party in 1991 found that 'more than 40 per cent of written responses raised issues connected with multiculturalism and immigration, and the theme permeating these responses is that Australia is overdue for a rational debate about the concept of multiculturalism'. Although there is no indication of the size and reliability of the Liberal sample, the opinions expressed are probably typical of widespread feeling among Anglo-Australians. Among commonly expressed concerns was that 'cultural or religious values brought into Australia by migrants would create unwanted divisions . . . and that some racial or religious groups continue to perceive that their first loyalty is to a culture, or a country, rather than to Australia'. The underlying theme was that 'Australia is now running the risk of encouraging cultural "ghettoism", and that Australia should exercise its right to determine its own cultural direction'. Somewhat ironically, those most critical of divisiveness are those most anxious for a debate, which many others see as potentially divisive.[6]

Despite nearly twenty years of official multiculturalism, it seems probable that the majority of native-born Australians are still assimilationists. They have been encouraged in this stance by the breaking of bipartisanship on multiculturalism, which began with comments by the then Liberal leader, John Howard, in 1988. In the past the division on national identity lay between conservatives who stressed the British connection and radicals who preferred to be 'offensively Australian'. Today the conservative/radical dichotomy is less meaningful. A division between the native-born and immigrants of non-English-speaking background might now be more important, as official formulations suggest in creating the NESB category. The majority wants an overt commitment to the Australia in which they were born and raised. The minority prefers a multicultural society in which the contribution of all Australians is duly recognised.

In a populist democracy politicians find it uncomfortable to espouse a cause that many people do not like or understand. Yet many have done so on both sides of politics in the past twenty years. This is often lampooned as 'seeking the ethnic vote' — as though that were a crime in a democracy! Yet few critics have ever suggested an alternative approach to integrating millions of immigrants from hundreds of cultures into a functioning and harmonious society — which is precisely what Australia has achieved over the past forty years. Multiculturalism essentially says (whether in Australia or Canada) that everyone legally accepted for permanent residence has the right to be treated equally, to exercise their own culture (including their own religion) to the point where it conflicts with the law, and to have pride in their origins elsewhere and to attempt to pass that pride on to their children.[7] What multiculturalism does not say is that Australia has no identity of its own, no culture of its own or no legitimate expectations of loyalty. It does not argue that distinctive ethnic groups need distinctive political or legal institutions, which is advocated by radical Aboriginal activists, drawing their inspiration from North America. But immigrants have never sought separatism, nor is it likely that they will.

It is more difficult to explain the rather complex ideas behind multiculturalism than the simplistic belief that all Australians are alike and believe in the same things. Australia is a prime example of a mass society. Public debate is conducted largely through the mass media, which naturally seeks to simplify issues to reach the widest audience. Many intellectuals are ashamed to be described as such, cringing to vulgar populism as befits their allegiance to outdated concepts of Australian culture. Many in the older generation still subscribe to the legend of the nineties. Some are simply conservatives, affected by the onslaught on multiculturalism recently launched in the United States (but referring to ethnic separatism and affirmative action rather than to the Australian situation of mild tolerance and modest subsidy). Many focus on racism as the major issue. Others argue that the age of nationalism is over and that multiculturalism simply ossifies in Australia cultural forms that have no place in the modern world of transnational companies and common markets. Politicians, with a few exceptions, prefer not to identify with ethnic minorities who can rarely determine election outcomes.

In times of economic depression immigration and immigrants become unpopular. Part of the national myth has been 'Australia for Australians'. This has always applied to jobs, which are currently scarce. Opposition to immigration and multiculturalism are inextricably joined. Despite official efforts to separate the two, the average Australian does not do so and with much reason. Government itself distinguishes between multicultural and Aboriginal policies, which is quite illogical but politically and administratively unavoidable. Although the Office of Multicultural Affairs is located in the Prime Minister's portfolio, the 'minister assisting' the Prime Minister on multicultural affairs is still the Minister for Immigration. The Department of Immigration still retains an 'ethnic affairs' branch, the functions of which are hard to distinguish from those of agencies officially concerned with multiculturalism. The slogan 'multiculturalism is for all Australians', coined in the early 1980s, has never convinced anyone that multicultural policies are not directed towards Australians of non-English-speaking background, the most active of whom are immigrants. This is a different situation from that of Canada, where long-established ethnic minorities have sustained multiculturalism and where there are two 'founding nations' tracing their origins back to the seventeenth century.

Official multiculturalism is, then, essentially an attempt to integrate immigrants (and their children) into an effectively harmonious society without alienating them by assimilationist expectations. This is a rather mundane objective, and government reports, written in very mundane officialese, constitute most of the literature of Australian multiculturalism. The combination of multicultural and social justice objectives, while it currently preoccupies the Labor Commonwealth and State Governments, is often nullified by the contradiction of seeking social justice in a society with high levels of unemployment. With rare exceptions such as Professors Zubrzycki and Smolicz (both, not coincidentally, Poles), academics and intellectuals have not been very interested. A growing number of creative writers are, and the Australia Council and the museums profession are now stirring themselves.

Still lacking is a coherent multicultural vision to juxtapose against the influential though very jaded bush image of the Australian identity or the black/white dichotomy of two nations, which is increasingly appealing to Aboriginal activists and those who seek a treaty between these two 'nations'. Multiculturalism is essentially liberal and suffers from the vagueness and lack of bite of many liberal formulations. It has been maliciously misinterpreted by many influential mainstream publicists who see ethnic diversity as necessarily undermining society. Marxists (of whom a few remain) do not like a creed that denies the class struggle. Conservatives cannot tolerate the ambiguities inherent in accepting different cultures. Nationalists rarely see that successful multiculturalism makes Australia more unique than the colonial hangover or the bush legend.

The FitzGerald Report on immigration policy[8] raised the issue of immigrant commitment to Australia. This theme has been taken up by supporters and opponents of official multicultural policies. But the idea of commitment means something different to those born in Australia, who are its most insistent advocates, and those coming from elsewhere who are expected to abandon much of the heritage in which they were raised. The ALP candidate for Bob Hawke's former seat of Wills, Greek-born Bill Kardamitsis, put the basic issue very well in March 1992: 'It's annoying, sometimes, because we always get thrown at us: "You're Greek", "you're Italian", you're never an Australian. You only had to visit the cemeteries to discover how committed ethnic communities are to Australia. We come here, we die and we are buried here. What more commitment does one want?'[9]

Unfortunately for Kardamitsis he lost a previously safe Labor seat to an Anglo-Celtic independent and football coach, Phil Cleary. Cleary went on to be disqualified in a case that revealed that neither Kardamitsis nor his Liberal opponent would have been qualified to sit either. Under a High Court decision both were judged to owe allegiance to a foreign power in contravention of section 44(i) of the Constitution, despite being Australian citizens. This raised a serious question mark over the equality of rights of perhaps one-and-a-half million Australians with dual citizenship who were still not completely equal in multicultural Australia. The British hangover lingered on in the wording of the Constitution, even though most of those with dual citizenship are, quite ironically, British.

Before Australians can resolve their dilemmas over national identity they need to face various issues much more clearly and sharply than hitherto. First, and belatedly, they must recognise that the British Empire no longer exists. This implies a move towards some variety of republic and a severance from the monarchic connection, which is mainly manifested today through the offices of governor-general and state governor. This will offend and disturb an older and conservative generation of Australians and a proportion of British immigrants. It has already progressed substantially with the ending of expatriate appointments to headships of state, the more recent termination of the imperial honours system and the much more recent announcement that no more Queen's counsels will be appointed. The major point at issue for all but convinced monarchists will be the powers and method of appointment of heads of state. This point can only finally be resolved through constitutional amendment, requiring the support of a majority of voters in a majority of states.

The second issue to be resolved in forging a new identity is that Australians are no longer drawn predominantly from the British Isles and never will be again in the proportions common before 1947. This is a cultural rather than a racial question. To divide Australians into those of non-English-speaking background and the Anglophone majority might not be entirely satisfactory. But it makes more sense than talking about 'white' and 'non-white' or (in the language of the police) 'Caucasian' or 'Asian'. Nor, despite the good intentions of those involved, is it very sensible to divide the population between Aborigines (less than 2 per cent) and 'settlers or invaders' (the other 98 per cent). This suggests that an English-speaking, thoroughly Australian Aborigine living in Blacktown is in some way more legitimately distinctive than a Macedonian living in Thomastown or a Vietnamese living in Cabramatta. To divide Australians in this simplistic way devalues the significance of a wide variety of cultures. Yet some form of reconciliation with Aboriginal Australia inevitably will need to be made and (as Henry Reynolds pointed out in chapter 1, 'History') Australian identity has only slowly confronted the lie of its foundation — *terra nullius*.

The third issue is that Australia cannot escape its location and need not fear its proximity to Asia. The very concept of 'Asia' needs to be queried, as there is less in common between urban Japanese and rural Bangladeshis than between suburbanised Anglo-Australians and suburbanised Asian immigrants. Whatever happens in the world's most densely populated region, there is little doubt that several Asian societies will become completely modern and affluent, possibly richer than Australia, and certainly very profitable areas for the sale of Australian goods and services. This is already happening and is essential if Australia is to survive the demise of its traditional British and European sources of immigrants, trade and investment. But this need not mean that Australia should turn its back on all parts of the world except its region. Once the centrality of the region is accepted, the next step will be to utilise Australia's wide and varied cultural and economic resources to reach out to those parts of the world likely to be of continuing relevance, including especially Europe and North America.

The fourth issue to be faced is that the nineteenth century is over and that the Australian of the twenty-first century will have no more in common with the bush Australian than the Americans have with Davy Crockett. While there is nothing wrong in having such heroes as Ned Kelly or the Man from Snowy River, there is something wrong in erecting them as symbols to emulate in the present. The great majority of Australians live in comfortable suburbs and work in white-collar jobs requiring high levels of education. This was not true a century ago but will be even more true in the future than at present. Nostalgia is superfluous but understandable. It might well be that the society of the past was more egalitarian and comradely than today's society but this could be questioned. It was certainly much less well educated and much narrower in many respects. It was male-dominated, and men were actually in a majority, which is no longer the case. Most employed Australians in the past were manual workers, which is never likely to be the case again. What is more, the worship of a rural manual past is counterproductive in that it belittles intelligence and expertise, which our Asian neighbours have in great abundance. The value of the past is in giving Australians a sense of belonging to this place rather than to anywhere else. But it should not mean worshipping values and attitudes that have no modern relevance.

So what should be the components from which a worthwhile sense of national identity might be built, and how can this be achieved? The debate over the oath of allegiance has already touched on some useful ideas. Australia is one of the world's oldest democracies based on manhood, and then universal, suffrage. In most states, adult males got the vote sixty years before, and adult females thirty years before, the British. The secret ballot was used earlier than in Britain or America, where it was called the 'Australian ballot'. Compulsory voting and registration, proportional representation and equal electorates were all pioneered in Australia in accordance with the Chartist principles of 'one man, one vote, one value', which were already known to the Ballarat miners at the Eureka stockade in 1854.

One important component of the Australian national identity is, then, acceptance of democratic procedures and institutions without challenge. This has not always meant acceptance of liberal norms or of free expression, although the situation has improved markedly since the 1960s. At no time for more than a century have democratic practices been departed from, despite being bent and battered in 1975 and from time to time in Queensland.

While egalitarianism has traditionally been an Australian value, its definition was previously narrow and encouraged mediocrity, authoritarianism, behavioural uniformity and conformity. It did not apply to women, ethnic minorities or Aborigines. But since the 1970s egalitarian principles have been extended as a basis for multiculturalism, equal employment opportunity and access and equity in public services. Australians are no longer, officially, regarded as inferior because of their racial, religious or cultural background. Women are, officially, regarded as legally equal to men and entitled to equal treatment. Clients are served, officially, in a sensitive and sensible manner, even if they cannot use the language of the majority. Minority groups are given such special facilities as might be needed to equalise their opportunities while also enjoying facilities open to all. The reality is still not the same as the official intention. But it is closer than ever before to genuine egalitarianism aimed at equalising life chances.

Democracy and equality must, then, be the essential ingredients in developing a sense of Australian national identity on already existing values. But existing values are not always very useful in developing appropriate attitudes for the future. Opposition to elitism or intellectual activity is not going to be very helpful when competing, cooperating and doing business with many Asian or European societies. That part of the Australian identity that emphasises sport, leisure and relaxation might be very attractive but is also potentially damaging to that other characteristic of the Australian experience, an affluent lifestyle. It is arguable that many immigrants, as in North America and elsewhere, have introduced values that will modify the centrality of leisure. The ending of shop hour and restaurant licensing restrictions can largely be traced to such immigrant influences. The aspirations of immigrant parents for their children are also slowly changing the ethnic background of Australian élites, and many parents resent education systems which are still wedded to equality of outcomes, basic proficiency and 'education for life'.

It is highly unlikely, and doubtless undesirable, that the kind of uniform national character cherished by past generations of Australians can be reproduced in modern conditions of ethnic, intellectual and lifestyle variety. Australia has four times as many people as at federation, and they are much better educated. The mass media, which are a major influence in shaping concepts of the nation, are torn between Americanisation and nostalgia and act as a brake on positive rethinking. But it does not have an altogether negative record on issues such as Australia's role in Asia, multiculturalism, Aborigines, the environment or tolerance of diversity. As in other, larger and more complex societies, Australia now has a quality media as well as a popular press and television, which are not nearly as racist and intolerant as their counterparts in England. The role of government remains important, although official exhortation will not change attitudes if other factors are not also at work, such as rising educational levels, greater employment of women and continuing immigration.

The battle over the Australian identity will continue in the media, in politics and in the education systems. The most desirable national identities will be the ones that combine democratic and egalitarian principles with multicultural and cosmopolitan outlooks. They will be conscious of the unique and fragile physical environment, unlike previous generations of Australians. They will accept the equality of races and nationalities, unlike previous generations. They will preserve and develop the British and European inheritance without excluding an understanding of Asian cultures, languages and economies. Then we really will have a Lucky Country with a worthwhile civilisation!

Notes

1. A.A. Calwell, *Be Just and Fear Not*, Lloyd O'Neil, Melbourne, 1972, pp. 127, 243, 249.
2. James Jupp, *Arrivals and Departures*, Cheshire-Lansdowne, Melbourne, 1966, p. 27.
3. James Jupp (ed.), *The Australian People*, Angus & Robertson, Sydney, 1988, pp. 429–34.
4. Uldis Ozolins, *The Politics of Language in Australia*, Cambridge University Press, Melbourne, 1993.
5. See, for example, J. Jupp, 'The defused issues: Ethnic and Aboriginal affairs' in I. McAllister and J. Warhurst (eds), *Australia Votes*, Longman Cheshire, Melbourne, 1988, pp. 162–95.
6. Liberal Party of Australia, *Australia 2000*, Liberal Party of Australia, Canberra, 1991, pp. 57, 59.
7. Office of Multicultural Affairs, *National Agenda for a Multicultural Australia*, AGPS, Canberra, 1989.
8. FitzGerald, S. (chair) (1988), *Immigration: A Commitment to Australia*, AGPS, Canberra.
9. *Age*, 11 March 1992.

5

CITIZENS

Laksiri Jayasuriya

It is commonly agreed that one of the essential features of citizenship is the right to be able to criticise one's country. But the actual qualities of citizenship are less clearly defined in Australia, which has no bill of rights and few other legal and formal mechanisms embracing and guaranteeing the rights of citizens, except through the common law. Citizenship has been one of those 'democratic truths' taken for granted by Australians without full knowledge or public debate on what it means[1] — its rights and obligations. Yet the example of too many places in the world is that citizens often tragically don't know or appreciate exactly what citizenship is until it is taken away. Only then do citizens know truly what they are fighting for.

Citizens are a principal unit of society, but it was not until 1949 that there was any such thing as an Australian citizen. To this time Australians were either British subjects — and subjects and citizens are quite different things — or they were aliens. The indigenous Australians, the first Australians, stopped being subjects and became citizens of Australia in 1967. In 1993 the oath of allegiance for permanent residents not born in Australia — the mechanism by which non-Australians, known earlier as 'aliens', become Australian citizens — changed its wording so that citizenship stressed loyalty to Australia, not the British monarch. From the point of view of citizenship, then, it might be argued that Australian civilisation did not begin until 1949 or 1967 or 1993. Perhaps Australian civilisation will not be properly constituted until Australia has become a republic.

To be a subject is to be subjected to authority — subjected to particular rules, laws and obligations imposed by the state. Citizenship derives from a different source. It is rooted in the principle of equality. As a moral principle and justification of policy in a liberal democratic society like Australia, equality is also applicable to the provision of well-being, of looking after one another. Citizenship, properly constituted, involves rights, participation, solidarity and integration. It enshrines the principles of justice, rights and equality within a participatory framework and is attuned to the needs of minorities and, equally, the wider society.

In his chapter 'The state of liberty' in Coleman's *Australian Civilization* (1962), Douglas McCallum argued: 'It is a great pity that La Perouse rather than Captain Phillip did not establish the first settlement in Australia.' A French colonial background would have guaranteed 'Liberté, égalité, fraternité' as a matter of course before the convicts, the Chartists, the gold prospectors and pastoral and rural labourers 'established the peculiarly parochial mould of our native tradition in struggles for freedom'.[2] The implication is that citizenship would have been more clearly defined — although McCallum does not mention citizenship at all. The historical process of citizenship has been one of gradual extrication from law and custom made in London. Citizenship devolved on to Australians. It has not been established as a birthright — and in consequence there are few guarantees.

Yet citizenship provides an attractive and powerful base for constructing a 'democratic pluralism' to enshrine the social values and moral ideals of contemporary Australia. On the one hand citizenship is the achievement of equality and social justice for all minority groups, indigenous as well as non-indigenous; that is, for Australians and ethnic communities. On the other is the attainment of a process of integrative nation-building. The conceptualisation moves us towards a more democratic form of pluralism built around identity, social justice, minority group rights and enhanced social participation — all of which are firmly anchored in the idea of citizenship.

British social theorist T.H. Marshall has defined *citizenship* as a 'status bestowed on those who are full members of a community. All who possess the status are equal with respect to rights and duties with which the status is evidence'.[3] This account of the essence of citizenship has two important aspects. The first is that citizenship is both a status and a set of rights and, importantly, there is a strong undertone of achieving a 'measure of equality'. Citizenship rights operate on the principle of equality. Second, the historical emergence of citizenship rights and principles has been pitted against market forces and social structures, especially class factors. The market, operating through its system of monetary exchanges and distribution of goods, creates class inequalities. The conflict between these two tendencies of the democratic polity and the capitalist market is central to the mediation (or compromise) of citizens' rights and obligations.

The links between three subsystems — polity, market and welfare — highlight the critical relationship between citizenship and social stratification and create the hyphenated society of democratic-welfare-capitalism — the social democratic state. It is this structural mechanism that permits equal status as a citizen to be compatible with inequality in the market operations of the capitalist economy. This is because citizenship provides the 'foundation of equality on which the structure inequality is built';[4] that is, the rights and duties people — in our case Australians — share by virtue of their citizenship. Clearly the principle of equality is central because it is the equal status of citizenship that 'bestows upon individuals *equal* rights and duties, liberties and constraints, powers and responsibilities'.[5] Herein lies the crucial significance of the welfare state in a democratic system, which was to make inequality more acceptable and legitimate.

Equality can relate to an 'equal start in life and career open to talents'. It can also mean 'fair shares' in the sense that there are legitimate and defensible inequalities. T.H. Marshall's contention that 'some inequalities are fair and defensible, and others are not'[6] might be defended by the argument that inequalities would be tolerated if they benefit the worse-off members of society.[7] Marshall's strong belief in this principle of equality convinced him that the capitalist system could be made more equal by democratic reforms in civil, political and social domains. Hence the classic statement that 'equality of status is more important than equality of income' and his faith that equality will enrich people's life chances in the long run.

The equality principle is applicable not just in determining who is entitled to rights — that is, equity issues (procedural equality) — but also in ensuring that there would be a fair and just distribution (substantive equality) of scarce resources in meeting needs implicit in fulfilling rights. Thus, the needed reforms of the polity were to be built around rights, but the exact nature and form, their range and precise number and their classification have been matters of controversy. Basic to this particular idea of citizenship is the notion that there are a range or 'bundle' of rights associated with being a citizen, namely civil, political and social rights. While the scope and specific entitlements of some of these rights, in particular social rights, might be questioned in modern democratic societies, the status of civil and political rights is fairly unproblematic.

In western industrial democracies, civil and political rights were achieved in the eighteenth and nineteenth centuries. They granted individuals rights of liberty and equality before the law. These basic rights were regarded as 'negative rights' because the freedoms they granted implied a corresponding obligation on others to refrain from interference or obstruction in the enjoyment of these rights. These 'negative rights', identified in freedom of speech, movement, association and assembly, are basically about the liberty of the individual. The 'free and equal' status conferred by these civil rights often enabled the achievement of political rights, which in turn were granted to all citizens without distinction. These encompassed the right to 'full and equal membership' of the political community and exercising a degree of autonomous control and choice in matters of government. Thus one set of rights is concerned with liberty, as seen in the classical liberal manner, and the other with democracy.

Social rights range from the right to a 'modicum of economic welfare and security to the right to share to the full in the social heritage and to live the life of a civilised human being according to the standards prevailing in society'.[8] These social rights forming the basis of social citizenry are regarded as 'positive rights'.[9] They include such rights as the right of access to resources, income, health care, education and welfare, all of which are measures of social protection and involve a 'claim to the resources of others, including the tax system'.[10]

Whatever the specific sequence of development of these rights of citizenship — and this is in dispute — it is generally agreed that a foundation in civil and political rights is more conducive to the development of social rights. The primacy of the former in granting the status of citizenship is the norm in the liberal democratic state of Australia. Consequently the grant of citizenship has meant conferring full membership of a modern community and affording the protection of the state by means of civil and political rights, the specific nature and form of encroachment of which varies from society to society.

The achievement of 'political citizenship' is essentially a matter of enjoying individual and political rights and, in the more conventional liberal approach to citizenship, its limits and boundaries refer narrowly only to legal membership of a social collectivity such as the nation state. Thus, to be granted citizenship in Australia has meant little more than the entitlement to the legal protection of the state via civil and political rights. The achievement of these rights is of critical importance for individual well-being because their denial means exclusion, oppression and exploitation by other groups. In many parts of the world, ethnic minorities have experienced almost complete denial of fundamental rights on the grounds of ethnicity. These groups are not deemed to be 'legal citizens of the state'; for instance, the Indians of Fiji have restricted rights. However, the immigrant settler society of Australia has, as a rule, refused to discriminate between immigrants and others with regard to civil and political rights and has been more liberal in granting political citizenship status.

One of the outcomes of the Whitlam reforms (1972–75) relating to ethnic minorities was to remove distinctions and anomalies in the political citizenship status of immigrants, especially between 'British subjects' and 'aliens'. Following the recommendations of the Lippman Committee, these differentiations between immigrant settlers were eliminated and all new settlers were thereafter regarded as 'permanent residents', thereby entitled to civil and political rights without formal requirements of citizenship.[11]

In the 1980s and 1990s this conventional thinking about migration and citizenship has been challenged and appears to be under review. For example, there are restrictions on permanency of tenure in the public service. The trend has been given added credence by the FitzGerald Report on immigration (1988), which advocated a restriction of access to certain rights (for instance, welfare) and benefits to those who are not formally regarded as 'Australian citizens'.[12] This proposal, recommended as an exercise in nation building, represents more a concession to a growing sense of Australian nationalism rather than the development of a well-formulated concept of citizenship intended to give meaning to a new philosophy of settlement. Whatever the limitations of this formulation, its fundamental weakness is twofold. First, the notion has been loosely and erroneously characterised in terms of obligations and duties of citizens — a feeling of *noblesse oblige* — and second, citizenship is limited to negative rights, guaranteeing rights to freedom and protection of liberty.

In the light of this poorly conceived proposal, it might be instructive to consider briefly how civil and political rights have been dealt with in relation to immigrants and new settlers. The qualifications of Australian citizenship for new settlers now are among the most liberal in the world. What is most significant, however, is that little or no attempt has been made to secure for ethnic minorities the conditions necessary for the achievement of civil and political rights. For example, workers from non-English-speaking backgrounds are poorly represented in trade unions and play virtually no leadership role.

In brief there is no guarantee for minority groups in matters of these rights unlike, for example, Canada where minority groups have built-in constitutional safeguards to redress any violations of their civil and political rights. Since there is nothing in Australia comparable to a bill of rights or a charter of freedom of rights such as exists in Canada, Australia is able to provide rights only through the rule of law and the jurisdiction of the law courts. And except for some anti-discrimination legislation, most of which is gender-related, as well as human rights legislation, there are no legal or constitutional safeguards specifically applicable to citizenship, which is left to the common law and the political and social institutions created by and accountable to a democratic parliamentary system.

In part this reflects the overwhelming influence of British constitutional and jurisprudence traditions in Australian political life and an implicit faith placed in the supremacy of parliamentary and legal institutions as a basis for safeguarding the basic political rights of citizenship. A distinctive feature of this distinctly Anglo-Saxon tradition of jurisprudence is the view that common and similar human needs require common and similar treatment. An important consequence of this conservative legal tradition is that Australian political and social institutions have been reluctant to concede 'group rights' to ethnic minorities or, for that matter, any minority group, and there is a general unwillingness (except for women and the disabled) to recognise the need for differential treatment in catering for the special needs of various groups of citizens. Sometimes this is defended on the hollow ground of avoiding stigmatising and marginalising these groups, but the fact is that these groups are already stigmatised and marginalised as minorities.

Clearly there is an unavoidable ethical dilemma where individual rights and the equality principle are put at risk in the interests of disadvantaged groups. Yet equality does not mean absolute equality;[13] rather, in special circumstances, such as in the interests of the wider society and the common good, this principle can be modified as positive discrimination. The paradigm of cultural pluralism is restricted when dealing with matters of differences among ethnic groups. An exception to this was the 1986 Department of Community Services report on the ethnic aged, *Strategies for Change*, which specifically targeted differential treatment for ethnic groups.[14]

Commenting on the political and social scene in Britain, Jenkins and Solomos have noted that the prevailing orthodoxy of 'British individualism militates against a group perspective'.[15] This is equally true of Australia where there is a denial of minority group rights and a resistance to viewing a person as having greater or lesser rights by virtue of belonging to a group. The 'language of rights applies to activities and claims of individuals rather than groups as categories of people'.[16] Yet the growing politicisation of ethnicity, partly enabled by state intervention, has resulted in various forms of ethnic mobilisation and thereby provided acceptable ways of defining ethnicity and minority status, usually in terms of identifiable categories, such as language groups. For these reasons Australia has resisted a group-based approach to the question of equality, the only exceptions being affirmative action legislation for the disabled, women and recent anti-racist legislation in New South Wales and Western Australia.[17]

What is probably most distinctive about the Australian scene is the nature and extent of industrial citizenship rights — the right to strike, bargain collectively, form trade unions and so on — enjoyed by all resident Australians, including those who are immigrants and who have not taken out 'Australian citizenship'. As dissension in Victoria, following the radical industrial reform programs of the Kennett Government (elected in 1992), and the rejection of the Howard 'Jobsback' policy in the re-election of the Keating Federal Government in 1993, make clear, industrial citizenship is a powerful self-conceptualisation in Australia. Industrial citizenship has played a major role in the development of the Australian welfare state.

There is a long tradition in Australia of interpreting social rights as economic rights, the latter privileging the industrial activity of men, rather than advocating the 'political citizenship for men and women alike'.[18] This tradition of labourism created a welfare state dominated by the market as the 'proper provider of welfare, employment and services'[19] and in keeping the rights of citizenship and participation at a minimum. Because 'migrants' and ethnic minorities are readily accorded industrial rights, their social rights, along with those of others similarly placed, have been heavily circumscribed. In brief the Australian notion of industrial citizenship is based on compensation through the industrial system and not on the broader social rights of citizenship. It thereby weakens the minority groups, more than other groups, because their bargaining position in the market place is always vulnerable. Therefore, critical for the welfare of all minority groups (ethnic, aged, disabled, etc) in terms of their disadvantaged status is the question of social rights. Admittedly, an extended view of citizenship that includes a complex of social rights is inherently problematic. Furthermore, in particular, the position of ethnic minority groups in a context of citizenship warrants special attention and is a critical issue for the future state of multiculturalism in Australian public policy.

Underlying the general conception of social rights and citizenship is the philosophical view that rights are about needs not wants. Furthermore, what must be justified prescriptively are the grounds on which our needs ought to be collectively met. That is, through some form of state intervention as institutional welfare, citizens have a right to welfare. This justification for meeting needs through whatever welfare mechanism (for instance, state welfare or mixed economy welfare) is an essential first step in defending guaranteed welfare. It is this logical rationale and moral stance that underpins the defence of the social rights and welfare rights of minority groups such as ethnic minorities in terms of common citizens' rights and not in the partial terms of the industrial citizen. Granted the logic of this argument in matters of public policy, we are able to insist not only on equal treatment on the grounds of citizenship rights but also, more importantly, in special circumstances, to make claims for 'differential treatment' such as for ethnic groups, the disabled or the aged.

This mode of reasoning is significant for policy development because it suggests one effective way of dealing with the paradox of having to reconcile universalist and particularist demands in matters of equity relating to minorities. The adoption of this rationale permits us to defend the vital principle of 'equal but different'. The principle of equality requires differential treatment to remove inequalities and handicaps that debar people from achieving equality through resort to equal opportunities. Differential treatment can be defended by the argument that it is essential for the claim of full citizenship rights.

In arguing for the defence of welfare rights as an essential component of social citizenship and its provisions collectively, two critical issues are implied. One is the centrality of need in claiming rights. The distinction between needs and wants, as previously observed, is generally accepted as being integral to arguments about welfare, welfare provisions and, in particular, the defence of the welfare state. Indeed, if the welfare state is to have any credibility, there have to be some limits on what can be provided collectively by state intervention.

One way of specifying the boundaries of the welfare state is to argue that the 'satisfaction of wants falls outside the public domain to be left to the private sector'.[20] This distinction, which warrants specification in terms of how one distinguishes needs from wants (compare arguments about absolute/relative poverty), is particularly relevant because it is coterminous with the public/private distinction in feminist theorising and multiculturalist policies. Thus, for example, if multiculturalism is to be sustained and funded out of public funds, it should be clearly recognised that the responsibility of the state is the 'public domain' and directed to meeting identifiable needs, seen as part of citizens' rights, so long as the 'public' sphere includes gender and ethnic-related needs, hitherto confined to the 'private' domain.

This necessitates a clarification of the boundaries between public and private in that certain needs are placed outside the public domain and hence become depoliticised. The 'democratic idea of citizenship must find a way of constructing the public and private that does not relegate all differences, diversity and plurality to the private'. Mouffe (1988) adds that a post-modern concept of citizenship has to acknowledge rights that cannot be universalised and that particular communities have specific needs. Clearly, according to this perspective, 'democratic politics has to make room for peculiarity and difference'.[21]

Moreover, 'citizenship rights are essentially concerned with the notion of social participation of persons within the community as fully recognised legal members'.[22] According to Marshall, what is fundamental about the idea of citizenship is that it confers 'full membership of a community where membership entails participation by individuals in the determination of the conditions of their association'.[23] Participation is circumscribed by the nation state and the requirements imposed by the legal status of being a citizen. In this sense, participation is largely a matter of political rights and political participation. Yet political rights and social rights, while interconnected on many levels, are none the less identifiably distinct entities. Political and social participation are similarly associated but different. While economic security and social well-being are regarded as being necessary for effective political participation, it is also true that civil and political rights, being a form of power, are a precondition for demanding other rights, such as welfare rights, and claiming benefits guaranteed by the state. Although effective participation necessitates both aspects, the exercise of power derived from political citizenship is essential to social participation.

The question of participation brings to the fore an important feature of the principle of equality, which is not a matter of the formal recognition of rights alone but also of enforcing them and thereby achieving the equity inherent in rights. Disadvantaged and powerless groups need to be able to exercise their civil rights in order to create the conditions that would enable them to claim their entitlement to 'social rights', such as education and health services. The minimal notion of equality of opportunity is even less than minimal as far as these groups are concerned because they merely affirm the existence of 'equality of opportunity' without enabling basic conditions necessary for its effective realisation. It is in this sense that strengthening political citizenship through full and effective participation is a necessary condition for the struggle of 'social rights'. For this reason much of the discussion of citizen participation has centred on the achievement of political participation. Inevitably, the nature and extent of participation has been confined for many minority groups to political participation.

As James Jupp has observed in chapter 4, 'Identity', and elsewhere, generally ethnic minorities have low rates of political participation and are 'weakly represented among the political élites and rate poorly on other available indicators such as participation in formal organisations'.[24] Where there is political participation, it is usually limited to community power brokers and ethnic élites who have more often than not been co-opted by the political and administrative structures of society. These élites are empowered by multiculturalism — multiculturalism is mediated through them — but their involvement is minimalised to the extent that major social and political institutions remain largely inaccessible. The imperatives of participation clearly require the recognition and involvement of minority groups within the structures of civil society. It is a matter not merely of equality of treatment but also of acceptance and ability to perform within all the structures of civil society.

The application of the concept of citizen rights to the domain of ethnic minorities is itself of considerable significance, particularly in relation to class analysis. Increasingly we are looking at the expansion of citizenship without reference to class conflict. Questions are rather more related to pluralism, such as race and ethnicity, human rights and social ecology, all of which are associated with new social movements or social forces demanding changes in the achievement and expansion of citizens' rights. Indeed, without identifying the concerns and pressures of these groups, it is not possible to understand what is properly meant by citizenship and the rights of citizenship in modern societies: 'the outcome of social movements which aim either to expand or defend the definition of social membership . . . The boundaries which define citizenship . . . ultimately define membership of a social group or collectivity'.[25]

Social movements such as land rights movements, environmental movements and women's movements, when expressing the aspirations, interests, values and norms of social collectives and other social changes, like those arising from war and migration, have significantly contributed to the development of an expanded notion of citizenship. And different social movements have raised different questions about the meaning, significance and form of citizenship itself. The demand for citizenship is essentially one of redefining the boundaries of the spheres of justice.

This raises the prospect of treating cultural pluralism as a new social movement based on ethnicity, the sense of ethnic identities and the cultural aspirations of new groups of citizens. It represents, in a relatively loose form, the collective aspirations and sentiments of diverse groups, most of which are on the periphery of society and claiming for their members a greater degree of participation and the rights and entitlements of citizenship to which they feel denied. In this sense, the growth of multiculturalism may be rightly seen as a 'precondition for an increased participation in citizenship through change in the culturally perceived criteria of social membership'.[26] The movement towards interest group politics, most evident in the green movement and Women's Electoral Lobby, is an expression of this growing trend in Australia, which can no longer be resisted by formal political and social structures.

Yet the sociopolitical changes being demanded by these movements might not be for an expansion of rights, perhaps with the exception of cultural rights for some groups, but an affirmation that the rights granted formally by the state are guaranteed through special mechanisms, giving recognition to all identity and minority groups in the public domain via legal and constitutional means. It is these guarantees, the rights of enabling participation in citizenship, that are most deficient in Australia. Thus, with respect to ethnic minorities, the agenda for 'democratic pluralism', leading to a minority group rights model of multiculturalism, grounded in the idea of citizenship, would have a two-fold purpose: to achieve the maximum degree of political participation and to guarantee equal civil, political and social rights.

What is fundamental to the idea of citizenship is the involvement of people in the communities in which they live; that is, the struggle for membership by various groups habitually excluded from full social membership (social closure) but who demand enjoyment of all social benefits. Thus, if citizenship is to provide a defensible intellectual and moral basis for multiculturalism, ethnic relations and ethnic affairs policies as democratic pluralism, it has to go beyond conventional understanding of rights. Put simply, citizenship is not about 'where people stand, but about what they do. It is about participation'.[27]

The meaning of citizenship as a normative principle of participation and community is perhaps the most valuable dimension for any form of democratic pluralism. It is not just about the political community but about all aspects of what it means to be a member of a society. Participation in this broadest sense is clearly the most significant defining and central characteristic of citizenship. Citizenship is about the

> struggle for membership and participation in the community ... for different groups, classes and movements [who] struggle to gain degrees of autonomy and control over their lives in the face of various forms of stratification, hierarchy, and political oppression.[28]

Citizenship means membership of a community. The essential distinction is between rights *per se* and rights that provide conditions for effective participation. The process of achievement of citizenship status, as equal communal members with full rights of participation, is of foremost significance because it is in this context that the paradigm of cultural pluralism that has gained salience over the past few decades has singularly failed. Ethnic minorities, some groups more than others, are not merely victims of discrimination and prejudice. That is obvious enough. Their position has been structurally marginalised and isolated from the mainstream. On account of social exclusion, these groups have been denied opportunities for effective participation by virtue of their membership and belonging to a 'community'.

Political citizenship, as active involvement in the political structure and community, is an important feature of citizenship, especially for ethnic minorities, and is central to being in the public domain. The complete achievement of political citizenship is a matter of power relations among different social groups, a most neglected dimension in which discussions of citizenship have been focused more on class struggle. In whatever way we deal with the issue of power relations, the concept of citizenship needs to broaden the sphere of the public domain, to allow all ethnic minorities access to the main institutions of the state and of civil society. Participation in this broad public sphere is central to citizenship.

All industrial societies inevitably go through a degree of homogenising, a levelling, a degree of democratisation, due to the growth of a consumer-oriented mass society. Thus in the realisation of citizenship: 'Social integration spread from the sphere of sentiment and patriotism into that of material enjoyment'.[29] Social integration is likely to be a function of economic and social well-being achieved through social membership of a community and a common citizenship, based on equality inherent in such a notion of citizenship. In this context societal integration (system and institutional) is more fundamental than social integration. Critics, however, have pointed out that this point of view inadequately accounts for the integration problems of a culturally and socially diverse society such as Australia:

> it assumes that core assumptions of civilisation or culture are more or less stable and that integration is a process of historical expansion through the incorporation by different groups within a common national community.[30]

This interpretation is partly based on a failure to understand the alternative ways in which the notion of integration has been conceptualised. But it is also the case that this apparent inconsistency arises only when one adopts a particular view of civilisation, namely, a view stressing attitudinal and affective characteristics. The difficulty is avoided by adopting a more materialist interpretation of culture, such as that based on the work of Raymond Williams (as Andrew Milner argues in chapter 12, 'Culture'), and suggests an acceptable way of incorporating ethnic minority groups into the wider society.

This account of integration is important in two main respects. In the first place, the integrative function of citizenship arises primarily because the social policies that distribute and allocate the 'common goods' of citizenship are premised on a sense of mutual aid and altruism; that is, a mutual concern for others and a moral consensus about the desirability of welfare. The integrative function of citizenship, therefore, derives directly from welfare because this focus on need rather than market forces (e.g. the ability to pay) enforces a common standard, which serves as a levelling force. In this sense, welfare integrates.

Thus the universality of social rights as embodied in services, which are only contingent on the rights and entitlements of citizenship, reduces social distances and marginality. It is this commonality — 'When you are weighing a naked baby on a pair of scales, the idea of social class does not obtrude itself unduly'[31] — that leads to a diminution (not elimination) of class distinctions and, in a plural society, to other differentiations. This class fusion produces a new common experience, which is unifying and integrating. It is for this reason that 'universality', so essential to integration, is more likely to be achieved, irrespective of ethnicity, through the exercise of citizenship where equality of status is more important than equality of income. Put simply, a reduction in equality enhances integration and engenders stability: 'qualitative equalisation between persons . . . reduces the importance of class distinction and other social distinctions'.[32]

The other important feature relevant to the integrative function of citizenship is a strong insistence on reciprocity — that there are obligations closely associated with citizens' rights. There is no doubt about the primacy attached to rights and that the integrative function derives from citizens' rights not duties; however, the interplay between rights and duties remains one of the unresolved problems of social policy, the response to which depends on ideological grounds — whether one adopts a collectivist or individualist stance. Rights certainly more often are couched in the language of individualism, whereas duties are cast more in the collectivist strain. This, of course, could be argued differently, depending on how rights are justified prescriptively, as poet Les Murray argued so clearly in his initial wording of the Australian oath of allegiance, which not only specified the obligations of the individual to the collective but also of Australia to the individual. In the final drafting by the Attorney-General's Department, the obligations of the collective were dropped.[33]

For social integration, perhaps more important than citizens' rights is the status of citizenship and participation. This is based on loyalty to civilisation, which is a common possession, and a 'greater range and diversity of interests and values of citizenship can be accommodated by it'.[34] This conceptualisation, then, permits flexibility and a wider basis for social integration, which takes place through a process of socialisation into the values and interests of the 'common civilisation'. For Marshall this is a 'common material civilisation', not one of values and norms. The conditions under which this internalisation takes place are greatly dependent, among other factors, on the power relationship between groups and individuals. The participation in a 'common civilisation', interpreted as the existence of a 'common material culture', especially in a pluralistic community, arising from mass production and the growth of capitalism, avoids the particularism and value conflicts implied by normative integration.

It seems clear that only a pluralistic conception of citizenship can accommodate properly the proliferation of new political aspirations and with this the multiplicity of new democratic demands made on Australian society. Therefore, it must remain a prime task of policy-makers and the definers of policy to articulate clearly the goals and social purposes of citizenship as it relates to a new charter for Australian society based on democratic pluralism. The language of public discourse will need to change from identity politics to minority rights and to issues such as race and gender relations and, concurrently, the social and political landscape will need to incorporate the pluralism of society, especially within the whole spectrum of institutions, with new and different forms, images and styles of conduct.

NOTES

1. Although in 1993, the National Centre for Australian Studies at Monash University, in conjunction with 'Ideas for Australia' program, co-ordinated a series of symposia on citizenship.
2. Douglas McCallum, 'The state of liberty' in Peter Coleman (ed.), *Australian Civilization*, F.W. Cheshire, Melbourne, 1962, p. 27.
3. T.H. Marshall, *Citizenship and Social Class*, Cambridge, Cambridge University Press, 1950, p. 84. See Laksiri Jayasuriya, 'Citizenship, democratic pluralism and ethnic minorities in Australia' in Richard Nile and Alan Seymour (eds), *Immigration and the Politics of Ethnicity and Race in Australia and Britain*, Sir Robert Menzies Centre for Australian Studies, University of London/Bureau of Immigration Research, Melbourne, 1991, pp. 27–43.
4. See T.H. Marshall, 'Citizenship and social class' in T.H. Marshall (ed.), *Citizenship and Social Development*, Greenwood Press, Connecticut, 1973.
5. D. Held, *Political Theory and the Modern State*, Polity Press, Cambridge, 1989, p. 198.
6. T.H. Marshall, *Social Policy*, Heinemann, London, 1975, p. 111.
7. J. Rawls, *A Theory of Justice*, Oxford University Press, Oxford, 1972.
8. Marshall, 'Citizenship and social class', p. 16.
9. See Laksiri Jayasuriya, 'Citizenship and welfare: Rediscovering Marshall', in Peter Saunders and Sara Graham (eds), *Beyond Economic Rationalism: Alternative Futures for Social Justice*, Social Policy Research Centre Reports and Proceedings, no. 105 (University of NSW), 1993.
10. R. Plant, *Citizenship, Rights and Socialism*, Fabian Society Tract No. 531, Fabian Society, London, 1988, p. 10; also D. Copp, 'The right to an adequate standard of living: Justice, anatomy and the basic needs', *Social Philosophy and Research*, vol. 9, no. 1, pp. 231–61.
11. Department of Labour and Immigration, *Final Report of Committee on Community Relations* (Lippmann Committee), AGPS, Canberra, 1975.
12. FitzGerald, S. (chair), *Immigration: A Commitment to Australia*, AGPS, Canberra, 1988.
13. R. Dworkin, *Taking Rights Seriously*, Duckworth, London, 1978.
14. Department of Community Services, *Strategies for Change*. Report of the Ethnic Aged Working Party, AGPS, Canberra, 1986.
15. R. Jenkins and J. Solomos, *Racialism and Equal Opportunity Policies in the 1980s*, Cambridge, Cambridge University Press, 1987, p. 108. See also J. Solomos, 'Race, ethnicity and public policy in Britain', in Nile and Seymour, *Immigration and the Politics of Ethnicity and Race in Australia and Britain*, pp. 70–81.
16. A.H. Birch, 'The rights of man and the rights of ethnic minorities', unpublished paper, Research School of Social Sciences, Australian National University, Canberra, 1987.
17. See G. Pointer and S. Wills, *The Gift Horse: A Critical Look at Equal*

Employment Opportunity in Australia, Allen & Unwin, Sydney, 1991.
18 Jill Roe, 'Chivalry and social policy in the Antipodes', *Historical Studies*, vol. 22, no. 88, 1987, pp. 395–410.
19 P. Beilharz, 'Social democracy and social justice', *Australia and New Zealand Journal of Sociology*, vol. 25, no. 1, 1989, p. 91.
20 J. Edwards, 'Justice and the bounds of welfare', *Journal of Social Policy*, vol. 17, no. 2, 1988, pp. 127–52.
21 C. Mouffe, 'The civics lesson', *New Statesman*, 7 October 1988.
22 B.S. Turner, *Citizenship and Capitalism*, Allen & Unwin, London, 1986, p. 134.
23 Marshall, 'Citizenship and social class', p. 70.
24 James Jupp, *The Challenge of Diversity: Policy Options for a Multicultural Australia*, AGPS, Canberra, 1989, p. 7.
25 Turner, *Citizenship and Capitalism*, pp. 85–92.
26 J.M. Barbalet, *Citizenship*, Open University Press, Milton Keynes, 1988, p. 103.
27 R. Dahrendorf, *The New Liberty*, Routledge & Kegan Paul, London, 1975, p. 44.
28 D. Held, *Political Theory and the Modern State*, Cambridge University Press, Cambridge, 1989, p. 199.
29 Marshall, *Citizenship and Social Class*, p. 96.
30 Barbalet, *Citizenship*, p. 93.
31 T.H. Marshall, *Rights to Welfare and Other Essays*, London, Heinemann, 1981, p. 51. See also T.H. Marshall, *Citizenship and Social Class*, Pluto, London, 1992.
32 Barbalet, *Citizenship*, p. 50.
33 Reported on Australian Broadcasting Corporation, *AM*, 5 October 1993.
34 Barbalet, *Citizenship*, p. 88.

6

HOMOSEXUALITY

Dennis Altman

Citizenship has not always been applied equally nor has it yet (as Laksiri Jayasuriya has argued in chapter 5, 'Citizens') achieved the status of celebrating equality along with difference. Australia is in the process of becoming self-consciously a plural society — not simply multicultural — and sexuality is one area in which pluralism has acted as a positive force for the right to be different but equal. In the summer of 1984 I was employed to help write and narrate a television documentary on Sydney's Gay — now Lesbian and Gay — Mardi Gras, the largest community street festival in Australia, which draws up to a quarter of a million spectators. The film was commissioned by the Special Broadcasting Service, which had been established in the 1970s to provide radio and television programs in major 'community languages', and was to be screened as one of a series of 'community festivals'.

That a government instrumentality could imagine a gay event as one of such a series reveals a great deal about the ways in which Australia has conceptualised the development since the 1970s of a large and visible lesbian/gay community. The language of multiculturalism, with its emphasis on Australia as composed of a variety of diverse communities, each with its own 'culture', has provided space for the gay world, which has few counterparts elsewhere; although in some ways it is reminiscent of the argument that religious tolerance in the Netherlands created a political culture that has allowed greater acceptance of homosexuality than elsewhere in Europe.[1] The argument of this chapter is that the development of multiculturalism as a defining characteristic of Australian identity has allowed for a marked increase in tolerance for other groups, of which the lesbian/gay community is perhaps the most obvious, both because of its size and because its acceptance would seem to run counter to so many traditional Australian values.

Australia is constantly in the process of inventing and reinventing its identity, as is apparent from the heated debates about republicanism, which are more debates about national identity than about constitutional arrangements. The very fluidity of national identities (as James Jupp argues in chapter 4, 'Identity') tends to undermine fixed concepts of what is or is not acceptable. Australia today is very far removed from the sort of country that it was in the 1950s and early 1960s, an apparently conservative amalgam of English and Irish social, political and religious values and institutions. In a country where being Australian has so many meanings it is far easier to see lesbians and gay men as making up yet another community who should be accepted as part of the rich diversity of multiculturalism.

It was not always like this. Australia until the 1960s was particularly hostile to homosexuality, particularly male homosexuality. While it has become fashionable recently to point to the convict heritage of homosexuality, it seemed as if the most persistent part of the tradition was the very strong condemnation by state and church of homosexual behaviour. One of the most striking passages in the first great Australian novel, *For the Term of His Natural Life*, describes the flogging to death of a young convict guilty of such behaviour. Garry Wotherspoon devotes much of his account of Sydney gay history to detailing the homophobic traditions and the policing of homosexuality that persisted until the very recent past.[2] Unlike some countries of western Europe or even the United States, Australia had neither a significant gay subculture nor any sort of political movement until the end of the 1960s. Like numbers of other Australians who felt marginalised at home, many homosexuals went overseas; some, like Sumner Locke Elliott, only returned through their writings.

We can assume there has been a homosexual history in Australia since the arrival of the First Fleet — indeed since the arrival of Aborigines, as homosexuality certainly existed in most Aboriginal communities.[3] For a political movement to develop requires a certain concept of homosexual identity, and that was far slower to develop. Of Sydney between the two world wars Wotherspoon writes:

A homosexual world certainly existed, but it was secret, fragmented and tainted by its illegality. The dominant heterosexual culture set the rules, and there was little questioning, even by the majority of the persecuted themselves, of their designation or their place in society. Male homosexuals largely accepted the social stigma placed upon them, and so lived lives haunted by guilt ... They had to live with society's estimation of themselves as perverts — whether predatory or effeminate or both — who should be dealt with by the full force of the law.[4]

There were of course homosexuals, both men and women, with a sense of identity — 'they had words to identify themselves — "camp" and "queens"; they had milieux where they could live fairly openly'[5] — but by and large most people who experienced homosexual desire or practised homosexual sex did not see it as constituting a significant part of their social identity. It would take a number of social and cultural changes before what might be understood as the shift from a psychological truth — the homosexual potential of all humans — to a sociological untruth — a sense of lesbian or gay identity and community — could occur.

This shift was largely a product of the much larger shifts that took place across the western world in what is often called 'the sixties', although it was more accurately a period that began perhaps around 1963–64 and ended in the mid 1970s. In Australia the period Donald Horne refers to as a 'time of hope'[6] saw a major challenge to the dominant sociocultural values and institutions of Anglo-Irish Australia. Between 1965, when Australian conscripts were first sent to take part in the combat in Indo-China, and 1972, when Gough Whitlam led the Labor Party to its first victory in twenty-three years, virtually no aspect of Australian social life remained unchanged. The old dichotomies between a (male) public sphere and a (female) private sphere, which had made Australia seem so emotionally impoverished, began to break down as a new generation undermined its certainties.[7]

The combination of a libertarian attack from the counterculture on conservative assumptions and the rebirth of a feminist critique of the dominant gender order provided a social space within which a lesbian/gay movement became imaginable in Australia. While its birth was considerably influenced by events overseas, especially in the United States, it took root because of Australian conditions, which meant that a lesbian/gay identity became a possible way for at least a minority to live publically.[8] The first generation who 'came out' and declared their homosexuality as a political act discovered that by so doing they created a new space, larger than that of the then small commercial homosexual world, which made it possible to begin to conceive of homosexuals as another minority group, deserving all the protection and support offered by the new ethos of multiculturalism (which began under Whitlam, although it was officially named by his conservative successors).

It is hard to remember that any sort of acknowledged homosexual world is only two decades old in Australia and that it was not until the early 1970s — beginning in South Australia and the ACT — that homosexual acts were decriminalised, a process that continued until 1990. By 1992 only Tasmania had retained the old British laws against (male) homosexual behaviour. There are many explanations offered for Tasmania's obdurance but probably the single most important fact is its unreconstructed upper house, which is elected on a remarkably unrepresentative set of boundaries. During those two decades all the institutions of a large community have come into being, with a lesbian/gay world large enough to produce its own press, business, religious, social and sporting institutions. By the 1990s politicians of all major parties assumed that the lesbian/gay community was large enough to spend some resources on courting its vote in both state and federal elections, and several politicians — for instance, the Independent NSW MLA Clover Moore, whose seat is based in inner Sydney — regarded the community as a major constituency.

Of course the development of a visible lesbian/gay world was not always smooth. I am deliberately using the term *world* as it embraces the idea of a multiplicity of communities and of people who might in some ways interrelate with that world without necessarily identifying as part of an organised community. The question of how far female and male homosexuals have anything in common besides (some) common enemies has been a constant one in all western countries, and in the 1970s Australia saw a more marked separatism than was true of most countries. A number of women who had been active in the early days of CAMP (the Campaign Against Moral Persecution) left, feeling that the sexism of gay men was too entrenched to battle against, and most lesbian feminists seemed to feel more commonality with heterosexual feminists than with homosexual men.[9] This attitude began to break down in the 1980s, particularly in Sydney, and this particular trajectory can be traced through the evolution of the lesbian/

gay press: Melbourne's co-sexual *Gay Community News* gave way in 1983 to the male-oriented *Outrage* magazine, but by the beginning of the 1990s the publishers of *Outrage* launched a newspaper in Sydney, *Capital Q*, with a female editor and clearly directed at attracting a co-sexual audience. Generational changes have produced lesbians who are far more assertive and at least some gay men who are more able to accept feminist positions, which are themselves shifting rapidly.

In that particular trajectory other changes reveal themselves. *Gay Community News* was, as its name suggests, a self-consciously political publication that began as the newsletter of the 1978 National Homosexual Conference in Melbourne. The shift to *Outrage* was accompanied by a shift from a volunteer collective to a professional business, which has remained as one of the more successful examples of gay capitalism. Although *Capital Q* brought a return to some of the co-sexual politics of the 1970s, it was also a product of a much larger commercial lesbian/gay world, with enough businesses catering for that market to support two national monthlies for men, half a dozen or so regular give-away gay papers and a smaller number aimed primarily at lesbians. As a reflection of the smaller economic power of lesbians the latter are less expensively produced and rely on a smaller advertising base. At the same time it is probably true that lesbians have been more interested in alternative economic ventures: there are numerous lesbian-run alternative health centres, for example. The expansion of the gay market is worth more analysis than it has yet received in Australia. As one example of its importance, by the early 1990 several car companies had begun specific sales campaigns aimed at the 'upwardly mobile gay market'.[10]

The post-Whitlam period is usually perceived as bringing a decline in radicalism in Australia, but the lesbian/gay movement continued to grow, less marked by the development of middle-class institutions and co-option into the system than was true of the United States. By 1981 the American lesbian/gay movement had largely lost whatever ties to the left it once had, symbolised by the name of its major institution, the 'Lesbian and Gay Task Force'.[11] In Australia the movement either remained true to its radical roots or failed to break out of a left-wing ghetto, depending on your perspective, while the great majority of lesbians and especially gay men who were flocking to the new commercial institutions catering to them ignored the movement almost entirely.[12]

Mardi Gras, which began as an Australian commemoration of the riots at New York's Stonewall Inn in 1969 said to mark the beginning of gay liberation, was soon switched to the end of the summer and became a popular and seemingly apolitical event.

Except that, first, *any* public celebration of homosexuality by its very nature is political and, second, the onset of the AIDS epidemic changed the meanings of all gay activities. Even before the AIDS epidemic, however, it was clear that things had changed radically in Australia. When the Wran Government temporised over decriminalisation of homosexuality in New South Wales for a number of years after their election in 1976 they helped to create a new gay militancy, which enjoyed considerable popular support. Somewhere in the past decade attitudes had changed to the point that regarding homosexuals as either criminal or sick seemed strangely old-fashioned and unacceptable. So much so that I remember debates in which it was very difficult to persuade some liberals that there was an issue at all — this at a time when legal prohibitions remained in four states. It was not just that public opinion polls supported decriminalisation of homosexuality, it was more that a sea change in attitudes changed the very tenor of debate, so that those who argued for the moral assumptions of the past — most notoriously the Reverend Fred Nile's Festival of Light — seemed both old-fashioned and bigoted. And in the post-modern world the former was even more damaging to their cause than the latter.

In 1992, with only three opponents, federal Cabinet voted to remove the ban on homosexuality within the armed forces. What was most interesting about this decision — which followed months of public debate and lobbying, particularly by the forces themselves — was that it was widely approved and that the government felt able to take it in the period leading up to an election. In a period of two decades homosexuals had been repositioned from perverts to citizens: in as far as there is an official discourse, as reflected in the editorial pages of the quality press, equal rights for lesbians and gays — and this was an issue that affected both women and men — had become part of it.

This might seem surprising in view of the enormous attention paid to homosexuality as a result of HIV/AIDS and the tendency for homosexuals to be blamed for the epidemic. Certainly when the epidemic first emerged in the early 1980s it seemed as if it would open the way for a re-energised hostility to homosexuals and the possible loss of all that had been gained in the previous fifteen years.[13] Like a number of other western industrialised countries, AIDS in Australia was at the outset — and has remained — largely confined to spread through male homosexual contact. This could have become the basis for scapegoating and attacking homosexuals. Instead Australia developed a response to the AIDS epidemic that saw the recognition by government of the legitimacy and importance of the gay community and thus strengthened the institutions of that community considerably.

The basis of what was to become known as a 'partnership' approach to AIDS policy-making was a decision by then Health Minister Neal Blewett that an adequate response to HIV/AIDS would require the cooperation of those most affected.[14] Following his visit to San Francisco in early 1985 Blewett established a National Council on AIDS (NACAIDS), the membership of which included two representatives of the gay community, the first time in our history that the Federal Government had publically recognised the community. Subsequent HIV/AIDS policy, both federal and state — although with some exceptions, most notably the Bjelke-Petersen Government in Queensland — was to continue a policy of supporting and recognising the special stake of the gay community in all aspects of the epidemic.

Partly because of generous government funding, partly because of considerable community response, Australia has some of the largest volunteer AIDS organisations in the world and, although the AIDS councils are not exclusively gay, those in the larger states particularly are strongly influenced by the special relationship between the epidemic and homosexual men. Services are provided to the full range of people infected, and many of the volunteers are not gay men; home care and personal support services, such as those offered by the Community Support Network and Ankali in Sydney, or the Support Program of the Victorian AIDS Council, attract considerable numbers of middle-aged women as volunteers. But the driving force behind almost all the AIDS councils is gay men, and in the eastern states at least they are de facto gay organisations. (Other community organisations also received government support and to some extent recognition; most clearly the Hemophilia Society, but also groups representing sex workers and drug users, who were even more stigmatised. Partly because of this, partly also because of a lack of self-assertion comparable with that of gay men, these organisations have been far less successful in large-scale community development.)

In some ways AIDS reinforced the divisions between gay men and lesbians as the new resources and attention brought by the epidemic inevitably focused almost exclusively on men. Unlike the United States, lesbians have not played a prominent role in AIDS politics in Australia, and certainly some quite consciously disassociated themselves from the issue. Yet, as already mentioned, the 1980s and 1990s have seen an erosion of the separatism between lesbians and gay men so that increasing numbers of political, cultural and social activities are now consciously co-sexual. This trend is most pronounced in Sydney where many of the features identified with gay men in the late 1970s — dance parties, Mardi Gras, sexual experimentation — have been embraced enthusiastically by at least some lesbians. There remain, of course, a number of lesbians who eschew too close ties with men and insist on a lesbian feminism that stresses a woman-centred culture and sexuality very different in its emphases from, say, the Ms Wicked competitions, which have entertained both women and men in the last few years.

While Australia saw very close cooperation between government and organisations based in the affected communities, and while the extent of alienation from the state experienced by the AIDS organisations of the United States has little resonance here, the epidemic has produced a certain radicalisation that has primarily impacted on the gay world. The driving force comes from People with AIDS (PWAs) themselves, who have articulated an anger at both government and, sometimes, the community-based AIDS organisations. The central issue has been that of approvals of therapeutic drugs, and as a result of both careful lobbying by groups like the AIDS Council of NSW and more direct action by groups such as ACT UP (AIDS Coalition to Unleash Power), major changes were made by the Commonwealth Government to government procedures for drug approvals.

ACT UP seemed to many Australians an unnecessary American import, particularly as some of its most prominent spokespeople were themselves American immigrants. More generally, however, this reflects the reality that many of the institutions and values of the lesbian/gay world have come from the United States, which has tended to shape contemporary homosexual culture to an even greater extent than other aspects of Australian life. In his survey of global lesbian/gay communities the American writer Neil Miller commented on the lack on an Australian gay literature:

> I met any number of gay men in Australia, New Zealand and South Africa who had come out after reading gay American novelists like Edmund White and David Leavitt, but had virtually no one to chronicle their experiences.[15]

This is a slight exaggeration. There is more of an indigenous lesbian/gay literature than Miller suggests,[16] and the signs are that it is rapidly increasing. But with the striking exception of Patrick White, a number of major Australian writers have been remarkably closeted about their lives. It is hard to dispute the assertion that cultural references to homosexuality are overwhelmingly external. Other than the film *The Clinic*, the much-touted Australian film industry has not produced a film in which a lesbian or gay character is central.

There is little doubt that American lesbian/gay assertion has been the dominant influence on Australian developments, but this does not mean that we should deny the extent to which developments here have arisen out of particularly Australian conditions. The first homosexual rights organisation, CAMP, did not owe much to American influences. Rather, I would argue, it came into being as a result of certain shifts in the social, political and cultural climate, which paralleled similar shifts taking place at the same time in the United States.[17] The history of the two movements diverged in the different sociopolitical conditions of the two countries; notably, Australia saw a much milder version of the politicised fundamentalism associated with frequent anti-gay political campaigns from the late 1970s on.[18] Throughout the 1980s and 1990s there has barely been an election year in the United States that has not seen an attempt somewhere to limit homosexual rights through some sort of citizen-initiated referendum.

American ideas continue to influence the rhetoric of the Australian lesbian/gay movement, most recently in the adoption by some Australians (almost always in their twenties) of the American term *queer* as an alternative to *lesbian* and *gay*. *Queer* is used to signify an unwillingness to accept either the political correctness associated with lesbian feminism or the 'clone' identity of gay men, and an embracing of all those who differ from the 'norm'. Thus queers can include trans-sexuals, sex workers, heterosexuals who practise sado-masochism; anyone, that is, who is regarded by the larger world as 'perverse'. Clearly there is at work here something of a repudiation of the respectability that the older lesbian/gay world is seen as having achieved. This divide was epitomised in a split in the Melbourne community around the candidature of drag queen Barbra Quicksand in the Victorian state elections in October 1992. When a number of prominent 'community leaders' endorsed the ALP candidate rather than Barbra they were attacked by a younger and more militant generation as 'ALP Daddies'.

But it would be misleading to depict 'queer Australia' as no more than a cultural offshoot of the United States. It seems more accurate to argue that ours is an increasingly global culture, in which style, music, fashion and ideas constantly circulate and are enriched by numerous national sources. Thus in response to the lack of much Australian lesbian/gay writing one could point to a number of Australian authors who have published overseas or to the significant contributions of Australians to the creation of an international lesbian/gay culture. Equally, the great increase of interest in lesbian/gay/queer studies in the 1990s, with university courses acknowledging the area in departments including English, history, politics and cinema, has its base both in overseas cultural influences and in the concern of Australians to make sense of the ways in which this society has sought to conceptualise and control homosexuality.

On the cusp of the twenty-first century can we assume that an identity and community based on homosexuality will remain a part of the social fabric of Australian life? The answer is probably yes for the foreseeable future. Even as a new generation claim to be less comfortable with 'traditional' terminology, they act in ways that reinforce the idea of a separate community, even if its boundaries are rather different from those established in the current lesbian/gay worlds. Those worlds will be reshaped by a new generation, but I suspect we are a long way from seeing them dissolved.

The new lesbian/gay generation is emerging in a very different social environment from that which shaped the founders of the movement. While social attitudes towards homosexuality remain ambivalent — acceptance is certainly far from universal — there is an available space to live as a homosexual that was unimaginable in the early 1960s. This is most obvious in the inner areas of our large cities; the Darlinghurst and Newtown areas of Sydney, the Valley in Brisbane, St Kilda/Prahran in Melbourne and Northbridge in Perth are widely regarded as gay centres, as are Northcote (Melbourne) and Leichhardt (Sydney) for women. But even outside these concentrations the existence of a visible lesbian/gay world remains a reference point for homosexuals who are able to take advantage of a more widespread social tolerance to live in suburban or rural Australia.[19] The remarkable growth of a lesbian/gay movement in Tasmania in the last few years — and Tasmania has been the state in which the legitimacy of homosexuality has been most bitterly contested in the political arena — owes something to a determination by local homosexuals not to accept the idea that gay life can only exist in metropolitan centres.

What does seem clear is that the trajectory of lesbian/gay life in Australia since the early 1970s throws into question some of the assumptions we have made about the nature of Australian society. It could be argued that I have taken too sanguine a view of the homosexual condition in Australia. Discrimination, persecution and even direct violence remains a fact of life, and certainly significant elements of opinion-makers in this country, particularly those with strong fundamentalist religious views, remain unconvinced that homosexuality should be accorded any sort of recognition as legitimate. The extent of violence against those perceived as gay has reached alarming heights, not only in Sydney — where the police have made some attempt to increase security in the Oxford Street area — but also in country towns such as Rockhampton. Between 1990 and 1993 in New South Wales there were at least eleven deaths resulting from gay bashings.[20] While government and police have to some extent recognised the problem, it would be absurd to suggest that there is not considerable discrimination within the legal system. As late as 1992 a Victorian jury released a youth of 23 who had killed a 65-year-old man by cutting off his head with a kitchen knife and then set fire to his flat because of sexual advances made to him.

Yet since the early 1970s Australia has seen changes that bring the social recognition of equality for lesbians and gay men close to that achieved in what are generally regarded as the most tolerant societies such as Denmark and the Netherlands. For anyone who can remember the dominant attitudes of the 1960s this is quite remarkable, and demands explanation.

At the outset of this chapter I suggested that apart from the sort of social changes common to most western countries, the ideology of multiculturalism has played a particular role. By emphasising tolerance and diversity as central ingredients of the national ideology multiculturalism has helped broaden the range of what is regarded as acceptable, even 'Australian'. It is not surprising that

Tasmania, the most decentralised state as well as the one least affected by diverse immigration, has emerged as the most hostile to acceptance of homosexuality, a theme I have explored elsewhere.[21]

While multiculturalism recognises the importance of religious traditions, the very fact that it requires some acceptance of religious diversity helps to limit the power of organised churches. Australia has always been a far more secular society than, say, the United States, and groups like the Festival of Light have had relatively little political impact compared with the success of the organised religious right in that country. Equally the strength of the women's movement in Australia, which some observers have compared very favourably with the United States,[22] has helped to create an environment in which gay/lesbian worlds could develop. (Margaret Reynolds explores the achievements of the women's movement in chapter 7, 'Women'.)

Both queer radicals and religious conservatives agree that there is something intrinsically subversive about homosexuality. It is perceived as challenging both gender regimes and the organisation of society around the heterosexual family. Even limited shifts towards accepting homosexuality, such as decriminalisation or the banning of discrimination in employment, are therefore regarded by both sides as signalling a shift in social values. Yet the rise of an interest in Australia in human and minority rights — not traditionally part of our dominant political culture — since the 1970s has coincided with the growth of lesbian/gay self-assertion.[23] It is striking that the shift to the right on economic policies that has characterised both major parties in the 1980s and 1990s has by no means been matched — as it was in Britain and the United States — by an increase in right-wing moralism. Indeed attitudes towards homosexuality seem less the product of party politics than of response to lesbian/gay visibility. The Liberal New South Wales Government has a better record than the Burke/Dowding/Lawrence Labor Governments of Western Australia, and Liberal candidates in inner-city seats campaigned for the gay vote in the 1992 Victorian and the 1993 federal elections.

The most difficult question posed by multiculturalism is the extent to which we should or could grant recognition to groups whose values and behaviour mean intolerance of and discrimination against others. The most strikingly example is that many traditional cultures are based on a systematic denial of the equal rights of women. When church groups — including some of the longest-established ones in white Australia, such as the Sydney Anglican diocese — support discrimination against homosexuals, should they thereby forfeit their right to participate fully in a multicultural society? Do we not need to conceptualise multiculturalism to mean an appreciation of diversity, which requires an insistence on both mutual acceptance of different cultures and a respect for individual liberties if it is to be consistent with larger liberal democratic values?

There will always be a problem in balancing individual rights — which are the basis of most theories of liberal democracy — with those attributed in multicultural discourse to groups or communities. Political sensitivities have made it very difficult to ask questions about the compatibility of democracy and multiculturalism without being accused of racism or of giving ammunition to overtly racist groups. Yet there needs to be a more vigorous interrogation than has occurred so far of the connection between multiculturalism and democracy, in particular of the compatibility between the rights of the individual citizen and the rights of communities.

There is certainly a strong argument for the proposition that a democratic society has the right to maintain certain basic rules which apply to all, irrespective of their religious or ethnic status. We do not allow polygamy or clitorectomies — indeed, we use the legal system to prohibit them — even though many ethnic groups claim that these practices are part of their traditional culture. In the case of lesbians and gay men, conservatives argue that they are claiming rights that undermine those of the larger society. As the right-wing Catholic B.A. Santamaria put it:

> If the homosexual lobby insists on claiming the titles of 'marriage' and 'family' for its relationships, it should be firmly told that while its members may be free to follow their own choice, the community is equally free to protect the most basic social institutions and not to weaken them by lying about their nature.[24]

I would argue that Santamaria does not demonstrate how respect for homosexual relationships weakens heterosexual ones, although I would note that the tone of his comments is already more liberal than those of the Vatican or his own writings in the 1970s and 1980s. A genuinely multicultural society is surely one that can allow a wide range of social institutions and behaviour, provided that they do not impinge on the rights of others. Homosexual marriage — not yet a major demand of the lesbian/gay movement in Australia — does not deprive anyone else of their rights while lack of equal police protection or differing criteria for child custody clearly do. In this sense, the ability of Australia to protect the safety and basic human rights of its lesbian and gay citizens becomes a test of its democratic character.

NOTES

1 See R. Teilman, *Homoseksualiteit in Nederland*, Bonn Meppe, Amsterdam, 1982, which includes a summary in English.
2 See Garry Wotherspoon, *City of the Plain*, Hale & Iremonger, Sydney, 1991.
3 See R. Brain, *Rites Black and White*, Penguin, Ringwood, 1979.
4 Wotherspoon, *City of the Plain*, p. 78.
5 Ibid., pp. 78–9.
6 Donald Horne, *Time of Hope*, Sydney, Angus & Robertson, 1980.
7 Here critics from the right and left can sometimes agree. Compare, for example, Miriam Dixon, *The Real Matilda*, Penguin, Ringwood, 1974, and Ronald Conway, *The Great Australian Stupor*, Sun Books, Melbourne, 1971.
8 See Dennis Altman, 'The creation of sexual politics in Australia', *Journal of Australian Studies*, no. 20, 1987, pp. 76–82.
9 This is discussed by both Denise Thompson, *Flaws in the Social Fabric*, Allen & Unwin, Sydney, 1985, pp. 55–71, and Verity Burgmann, *Power and Protest*, Allen & Unwin, Sydney, 1993, chapter 3.
10 V. Trioli, 'Hyundai makes a pitch for the gays', *Age*, 17 December 1992.
11 See Dennis Altman, *The Homosexualization of America*, Beacon, Boston, 1983, chapter 4.
12 See C. Johnston, 'From gay "movement" to gay "community" ', *Gay Information*, no. 5, 1985.
13 See Dennis Altman, *AIDS and the New Puritanism*, Pluto, Sydney, 1986, for examples of some of the early debates.
14 For accounts of the Australian response see J. Ballard, 'The politics of AIDS' in H. Gardner, *The Politics of Health*, Churchill Livingstone, Melbourne, 1989, and Dennis Altman, 'The most political of diseases' in V. Minichiello, D. Plummer and E. Tinewell (eds), *AIDS in Context*, Prentice Hall, Sydney, 1992.
15 N. Miller, *Out in the World*, Random House, New York, 1992, p. 360.
16 See Dennis Altman, 'A closet of one's own', *Island*, no. 48, 1991, pp. 30–2, and Robert Dessaix (ed.), *Australian Lesbian and Gay Writing*, Oxford University Press, Melbourne, 1993.
17 See Wotherspoon, *City of the Plain*, chapter 5 and Thompson, *Flaws in the Social Fabric*.
18 See Altman, *The Homosexualization of America*, chapter 4.
19 On gay life in rural Australia see P. Oswald, 'Living on the land', *Campaign*, October 1992.

20 See R. Hill, 'Still in the closet', *Bulletin*, 13 October 1992, p. 31.
21 See Dennis Altman, *The Comfort of Men*, Heinemann, Melbourne, 1993.
22 For example Anne Summers, 'Sisters out of step', *Independent Monthly*, July 1990.
23 For a discussion of shifts in Australian political culture see Dennis Altman, *A Politics of Poetry*, Pluto Press, Sydney, 1988.
24 B.A. Santamaria, 'Gays must admit that AIDS discriminates', *Weekend Australian*, 23–24 January 1993.

7
WOMEN

Margaret Reynolds

Australian feminists are justified in claiming considerable credit for major change in attitudes and policies relating to women since the 1970s. The second wave of feminism early in the 1970s coincided with a general call for social change, which led to the election of the Whitlam Labor Government in 1972. This period provided both the foundation and the incentive for developing policies that would change the rigid gender role divisions of Australian society and start to create a recognition of the need for greater equality between women and men. Whitlam recognised the new mood of Australian women and initiated key reforms in employment and childcare. He appointed the first women's adviser, Elizabeth Reid, to head the new Women's Affairs Section of his department. His administration implemented equal pay for work of equal value in the Australian Public Service, recognised equal employment opportunity through the ratification of International Labor Organisation Convention 111 and introduced maternity leave.

Three major influences can be identified as being critical in shaping these reforms. First, Australian women themselves were affected by European and North American feminist movements and began to organise at a local level seeking basic change. As a result a range of women's organisations developed or expanded their commitment, with some, like the Women's Electoral Lobby, taking direct action in the political process. Women were seeking alternatives in the home, the workplace and their communities and were actively questioning their lack of power within male-dominated Australia.

The beginnings of the feminist movement led to the second

major influence as individual women sought to challenge male monopoly of power by entering the non-traditional domains of parliament, the judiciary, trade unions, business and universities. Finally, Australian political change occurred at a time when the United Nations had set a very determined timetable for reform, so further incentive was given women in setting their demands in an international context.

Australian women have a strong activist tradition, which can be traced from the colonial era of Caroline Chisholm to the suffrage movement of the 1880s and 1890s.[1] Australian was the first country in the world to give women both the right to vote and the right to stand for parliament. But it would be inaccurate to interpret this initiative as reflecting the enlightenment of that era. Women themselves made strenuous efforts through a variety of organisations to focus attention on their right to vote, and this struggle lasted more than two decades. Women throughout the country campaigned for the franchise at state and federal levels and eventually persuaded enough male parliamentarians to vote in support of women's equal franchise.

Audrey Oldfield reminds us that the campaign for the vote in the late nineteenth century occurred at a time when Australian women were moving out of domestic service and taking places in the workplace previously occupied by men.[2] Therefore the ideas and organisation of the Australian labour movement coincided with the debate about women's working conditions and wages, further strengthening the arguments for women's suffrage.

When in 1902 federal parliament passed the Commonwealth Franchise Act, women were accused of being 'social despots' who advocated a society of polyandry, free love and lease marriages.[3] Furthermore, it was argued that the women's vote would 'sap the very foundation of a nation' and granting women's suffrage would lower the status of women and give married men a double vote!derpresses[4] One speaker even predicted that 'by passing measures of this kind we shall be training women to become masculine creatures and entirely unfitting them to discharge the functions which properly belong to their sex'.[5]

From the beginning of federation women were determined to enter federal parliament. The first occasion on which women nominated for any national parliament in the British Empire occurred in 1903 when three Australian women nominated for the Senate. One of these was Vida Goldstein, a feminist and suffragist, who had taken over the organisation of the United Council for Women's Suffrage in 1899. The two other women who also made unsuccessful attempts to enter the Senate in 1903 were Mrs Nellie Martel, an elocutionist, and Mrs Mary Ann Moore Bentley, a journalist, both of New South Wales.[6] Vida Goldstein ran three times for the Senate, in 1903, 1910 and 1917. She was also a candidate for the House of Representatives in 1913 and again in 1914. While she was not successful in winning a seat in either house she made a highly significant contribution to political and social reform. She campaigned for the right to vote and to stand for parliament; equal pay for equal work; the recognition of a basic wage; protection for neglected and homeless children and the abolition of child labour; equal property rights for spouses; equal parental rights; and the establishment of a women's hospital and of children's courts.[7]

Vida Goldstein was a controversial figure. Many objected to her radical views about the rights of married women and her challenge to male dominance of the political system. The press lampooned the Women's Federal Political Association, later the Women's Political Association (WPA), of which she became president in 1903 and which had proposed and assisted her candidature for the Senate. Nevertheless, the likelihood of defeat did not dampen her enthusiasm for political campaigning. She later wrote:

> I accepted nomination because I saw what a splendid educational value the campaign would have. I knew I would attract much larger audiences as a candidate than if I were advertised to give a lecture on women's part in the federal elections, or some such subject. I believed that people would come to my meetings out of curiosity to see the wild woman who sought to enter Parliament.[8]

In 1984 her contribution to the women's movement was recognised by the naming of the federal electoral division of Goldstein in Victoria in her honour.

Despite the fact that Australia was one of the first countries in the world to grant votes to women, it was forty-one years after the passing of the Commonwealth Franchise Act before women were elected to federal parliament. After such a promising start it is ironic that this time lag, between the right to stand and the achievement of parliamentary representation, was the longest in the western world. Why, then, did it take so long for women to be elected to federal parliament? The most obvious reason is to be found in the position of women in Australian society. As in many other countries, it was not usually acceptable for women to work outside the home. The exceptions were single women, who promptly gave up their jobs on marrying, or women who were forced by financial hardship to provide for their families. In an age when a woman's role in society was more restricted, many women were encouraged to believe that paid employment would occupy only a short part of their lives. Women who pursued professional careers were in the minority and did so with the expectation of not marrying.[9] World War II changed many attitudes and practices. In 1943 two women were finally elected to federal parliament, Dorothy Tangney, Senator for Western Australia, and Dame Enid Lyons, a widow who followed her husband, the Hon. Joseph Lyons (Prime Minister 1932–39), as representative for Braddon in Tasmania.

From 1950 to 1965 there were five women in federal parliament but for a period of more than twenty years until 1975 not one woman occupied a seat in the House of Representatives.[10] Since then there has been a marked increase in women's representation in both the Senate and House of Representatives with 19 female Senators being elected out of a total of 76 between 1975 and 1991 and 10 female Members out of a total of 147.[11] It is salutary to consider that between 1901 and 1991 430 individuals have been elected to the Senate and only 34 of them have been women. The record for the same period in the House of Representatives is even worse with 849 elected, 16 of whom have been women.

From the 1960s the women's movement was influenced by writers like the American Betty Friedan and the Australian Germaine Greer who were challenging the stereotypes of women and their very limited role in society. The counterculture of student politics in the late 1960s had created fertile ground for questioning many aspects of the status quo, so women's reading and discussion was quickly translated into action. Consciousness-raising groups were established on campuses and in suburban living rooms, but the debate soon resulted in activist groups and more formal organisations demanding change in abortion laws and recognition of women's health and safety, equal opportunity and childcare. The Women's Electoral Lobby (WEL) was established as a political lobby group for the 1972 elections when radical change seemed possible with the election of the first socialist government for a quarter of a century.

Beatrice Faust, a well-known feminist, was impressed by an article by Gloria Steinem in the new US magazine, *Ms*, which rated the attitudes of presidential candidates on issues of special interest to women. She established a small group in Melbourne to consider using a similar strategy in the 1972 federal election. Faust, an abortion law reform campaigner, was able to use this network to establish a similar group in Sydney, and the concept quickly spread so that Women's Electoral Lobby groups of more than two thousand members were soon operating in all states and territories.

The Women's Electoral Lobby focused on six major areas of reform: equal pay, equal employment opportunity, free contraception services, abortion on demand and free twenty-four-hour childcare.[12] Early submissions made by WEL concerned the luxury tax on contraceptives (to the Tariff Board Inquiry, July 1972) and childcare provision the 1972 Federal Budget. None of the parties had any clear policies on childcare, but the initial lobbying efforts were rewarded when the McMahon Liberal Government included a childcare option in the August Budget and related legislation was introduced in October 1972.

To assess the attitudes of parliamentarians and candidates to major issues of concern to women a questionnaire had to be posted to them, but the response rate was so poor that an alternative approach was adopted. WEL introduced more structured personal interviews with candidates and published the responses.

> The survey was a resounding success. In the context of political uncertainty and the probability of a change of government, few candidates felt sufficiently confident to ignore this apparently powerful new lobby group. There was a very good response rate and the form guide was given wide publicity by newspapers such as the *Sunday Telegraph*, the *National Times* and the *Sun-Herald*, and the *Age* printed it as a lift-out supplement. Local newspapers ran material based on the form guide relating to local candidates. WEL also undertook leafletting of some electorates, produced posters and distributed how-to-vote cards and copies of the form guide at polling booths. The *National Times* in a front cover headline called WEL 'the rising new force in Australian politics' (20.11.72) and Nancy Dexter wrote in the *Age* that: 'The 1972 federal election must go down in history as the first in which the average woman is really interested. Much of this interest is due to WEL . . .' (23.11.72). Robert Turnbull in the *New York Times* described WEL as 'an organised and formidable factor in the election campaign'. (26.11.72)[13]

This strategy was further enhanced by 'Meet the Candidate' forums, hosted by WEL to encourage candidates for election to do their homework on women's issues. Such an event was held in north Queensland during the 1974 state election campaign.

> we embarked on a novel approach to lobbying — a cocktail party to be followed by a public forum! There was an air of triumph as we hand-printed gilt-edged invitation cards — WEL Townsville cordially invites you to attend a Cocktail Party on the occasion of debating Women's Issues prior to the forth-coming State Election.
>
> Many of us wondered if the invitation would have the desired effect. Would the all male contingent really front up for sherry and olives and then be prepared to be grilled by a female audience? It was a daunting prospect in 1974!
>
> Fortunately, aspiring politicians realised they had nothing to lose and responded willingly. Sitting parliamentarians were more reluctant but were swept along by the example of their opponents and a little curiosity![14]

Writing in 1977, Iola Mathews summed up the gains of the Whitlam era as follows:

> In the next three years practically every reform asked for by WEL in its original questionnaire was acted on by the new Labor Government. Women gained equal pay and the male minimum wage. Committees were set up to look into discrimination in employment and a Working Women's Centre started in Melbourne.
>
> The Federal Government for the first time put funds into family planning clinics, made contraceptives cheaper, and channelled some funds into sex education. Family Law Courts were set up to make divorce speedier and more humane and federal funds helped set up women's health centres, refuges, rape counselling centres, drop-in centres, learning centres and playgroups.
>
> Pensions for widows, single mothers and deserted wives were increased and a supporting mother's benefit introduced and federal funds for child care increased dramatically.[15]

After the dismissal of the Whitlam Government the women's program of reform stalled. Funding was cut back, and paternity leave and the Children's Commission, which was to have been the body responsible for community-controlled childcare throughout Australia, were abolished. However, the Liberal Prime Minister, Malcolm Fraser (1975–82) did initiate the appointment of a Minister Assisting the Prime Minister on Women's Affairs, the first time such a portfolio responsibility had been allocated.[16]

Furthermore, during the years of the Fraser Government there were improvements in childcare, refuge funding and the beginnings of women's health services. During these years women's programs were particularly vulnerable in states where ultra-conservative governments resented such social change.[17] For example, in Queensland the Bjelke-Petersen National Party Government refused to pass on funding for women's refuges, and women's policy development in that state did not begin comprehensively until after the election of a reformist Labor Government in 1990. In contrast some other state governments were ahead of the Federal Government in implementing legislative reform and social policy to address discrimination against women. Hence in New South Wales between 1976 and 1986 there was major progress in changing the structures that had limited women's full participation in all areas of community life.[18] Other Labor state governments in Victoria, South Australia and Western Australia both initiated and complemented reform at the national level.[19]

While the 1970s remained a period of vocal activism for Australian women, it was not until the return of a federal Labor Government in 1983 that women's issues were adopted as part of the national political agenda. The influence of the WEL in setting the pace for reform should not be underestimated. Not only did it establish the key issues firmly in minds of the electorate, it also politicised thousands of women, ensuring that a new generation of political activists would dominate the debate on behalf of women for at least two decades. WEL was a springboard for the entry of large numbers of women into public life. Three successive Labor Ministers Assisting the Prime Minister on the Status of Women, former Senator the Hon. Susan Ryan (1983–87), myself (1987–90) and the Hon. Wendy Fatin (1990–93) were active members of Women's Electoral Lobby. A founding member of WEL in Melbourne, Carmen Lawrence, became Premier of Western Australia in 1990. Two of her Cabinet colleagues, Kay Hallahan and Yvonne Henderson, shared a WEL background in Western Australia. Similarly in South Australia, Anne Levy, a founding member of WEL in South Australia, became president of the Legislative Council and then Cabinet minister. Another WEL member, Virginia Chadwick, became Liberal Minister for Family and Community Services in New South Wales.

Several other female parliamentarians were instrumental in establishing WEL groups in their states, and many others who acquired their lobbying techniques and practical political knowledge are now in influential positions in the bureaucracy, statutory authorities, political parties and trade union movement. WEL members have also assumed significant positions of authority as women's advisers to premiers and prime ministers, as directors of equal opportunity and as commissioners and consultants responsible for top-level policy advice. The first sex discrimination commissioner, Quentin Bryce, was a founding member of WEL in Brisbane.

After the 1977 election Senator Susan Ryan (ACT 1975–87) carried out research into some of the causes of Labor's particularly devastating defeat and discovered what was to become known as the 'gender gap'.[20] She discovered that traditionally fewer women voted Labor than men and that this pattern had only been broken in 1972. Furthermore, Ryan alerted her male colleagues to the fact that if women had voted Labor in the same proportion as men, the ALP would have won every federal election since World War II except 1977. This advice resulted in a serious examination of the status of women both in the party structure and, to a lesser extent, in the trade union movement. For the first time in its history the ALP formally acknowledged the male-dominated image of the party and its failure to attract women's votes.[21] In the following years leading up to the re-election of a Labor Government in 1983 Ryan was able to exert considerable influence in advocating change within the party as well as developing specific policy initiatives that reflected the concerns of Australia women. Labor's ability to maintain its share of women's votes in successive elections in the 1980s and 1990s delivered it an unprecedented term in office.

A national committee of inquiry into the operations of the ALP recommended in 1979 that affirmative action was the only way to break down gender imbalance within the party. Ann Forward was appointed convenor of a national working party charged with drawing up a set of guidelines for implementation, which were endorsed at the 1981 National Conference of the ALP. A National Status of Women Policy Committee was established to examine the work of all other national policy committees for their impact on women. In 1983 a second social democratic government, under the leadership of Bob Hawke, was elected. This national election was significant in that for the first time the women's vote was acknowledged as having been influential in determining the outcome. The ALP had campaigned strongly, promising a range of reforms that would radically reform the status of women. At the same time a number of women were elected to both houses of parliament, so that, when a new government was formed, there was a determined women's lobby within and outside the government ready to oversee the implementation of a women's reform agenda. In the wake of the 1993 election the defeated Liberal–National Opposition reshaped its front bench to include more women as a consequence of the coalition's realisation that links exist between women in parliament, women's issues and women's votes in elections.

The establishment of an Office of the Status of Women in the Department of Prime Minister and Cabinet was an important signal that women's policy development was to be a prime focus for the new government, recognising that the gender gap had been narrowed and that female voters expected promised reforms to be processed promptly. Susan Ryan, who for five years in opposition had worked to channel women's aspirations into a realistic set of policy reforms, was the first woman appointed to a Labor Cabinet. As Education Minister she was also given the additional responsibility of Minister Assisting the Prime Minister on the Status of Women. The introduction of this new position provided women with a key figure to act as a catalyst in monitoring the new government's program. Not only did the position offer additional resources within the bureaucracy, but also the role itself increased the focus on the government's intention to address status of women issues across all departments.

The positioning of the Minister Assisting and the OSW in the Prime Minister's Department was both of symbolic and practical benefit. First, the profile of the status of women generally was raised, giving it the imprimatur of the prime minister. Second, the opportunity for a close association with the Cabinet process enabled new policy proposals to be monitored for their impact on women.

The influence of a caucus Status of Women Committee, comprising up to twelve female members and senators, further strengthened the new administrative structures. The committee met weekly when parliament was in session and had the authority to ask ministers and senior departmental staff to explain the progress of policy development and implementation. It was a powerful ally for the Minister Assisting the Prime Minister who could rely on her female colleagues when there were differences about policy direction or resource allocation.

However, the newly elected government remained committed to legislative measures to outlaw discrimination and to give women fresh opportunities in the workforce. In its first two years it implemented three key legislative reforms. The *Sex Discrimination Act 1984* detailed its objectives as being:

- to give effect to certain provisions of the *Convention on the Elimination of All Forms of Discrimination Against Women.*
- to eliminate so far as possible discrimination against persons on the grounds of sex, marital status or pregnancy in the areas of work, accommodation, education, the provision of goods and services, the disposal of land, the activities of clubs and the administration of Commonwealth laws and programs.
- to eliminate so far as possible discrimination involving sexual harassment in the workplace and in educational institutions.
- to promote recognition and acceptance within the community of the principle of equality of men and women.[22]

A sex discrimination commissioner working in the Human Rights and Equal Opportunity Commission became responsible for administering the legislation and exercises certain statutory powers of inquiry, conciliation and settlement of sex discrimination complaints.

Since the implementation of the Sex Discrimination Act women have utilised this procedure to draw attention to discriminatory practices particularly in the workplace, and the majority of cases have been successfully conciliated. Perhaps the greatest impact of the legislation has been its educative effect, ensuring that people are more likely to be aware of what constitutes discrimination. Nevertheless the increased awareness does not appear to have reduced the complaint rate. In 1990–91 803 complaints were lodged officially, representing a 35 per cent increase over the previous year. The largest proportion, 36.3 per cent, were lodged on the grounds of sexual harassment in employment, and 19 per cent related to discrimination on the grounds of pregnancy.

In 1984 the *Public Service Reform Act* was passed. It required all federal government agencies to produce equal employment opportunity programs for four target groups: women, Aborigines and Torres Strait Islanders, people with disabilities and people of non-English-speaking background. The *Affirmative Action (Equal Employment Opportunity for Women) Act 1986* embodied further legislative reform. It required all employers with a hundred or more employees to develop affirmative action programs and established the

Affirmative Action Agency. These two measures aimed to break down the barriers that had limited women's promotion in both the public and private sectors.

The Affirmative Action Agency introduced and monitored a program of action requiring private companies to report annually by submitting details of progress in implementing workplace reform in giving greater recognition and opportunity to female employees. Affirmative action legislation also applies to universities, which as independent institutions are not covered by public service requirements. Affirmative action was strongly resisted by the private sector when it was initially debated. However, there is now a high level of conformity with the annual reporting procedures, and companies are acknowledging the benefits of utilising the skills of the whole of their workforce. Companies are expected to report on their selection and promotion procedures as well as reforms that recognise maternity and childcare provision. There is criticism that the Affirmative Action Agency is unable to enforce the implementation of reports as detailed, the only penalty for negligent companies being to be named in parliament. Nevertheless, the overall educative role of this agency is important in changing attitudes to women in the workforce.

While legislative reform has been significant in setting a clear framework for abolition of gender-based discrimination, specific policy measures and program initiatives have been equally important in changing the social climate in which women live. Perhaps the most important strategy to influence government policy is the introduction of an annual Women's Budget Statement issued by the Department of Prime Minister and Cabinet as part of the federal Budget each August. This initiative focuses the minds of public servants and government ministers alike and thus helps to ensure continued commitment to new policy programs that address the needs of women and their families. Furthermore, as part of the Women's Budget strategy the public service is required to report progress on the implementation of reforms aimed at gender equality. The Women's Budget process has been strengthened by the adoption of 'gender equality' indicators, utilising information drawn from the Australian Bureau of Statistics, to reflect changes in the role and status of women and illustrate the impact of policy reform. In each policy area a number of programs are each budgeted for in the relevant government department.

Programs are monitored by the Office of the Status of Women.

'Women's units' in several departments provide specific responsibility for planning and coordination, thus enhancing the general level of understanding of women's issues. This approach has successfully combined mainstreaming of women's programs with separate responsibility of an office and minister to scrutinise implementation by government departments. While there remain areas of frustration and neglect, the overall strategy appears to suit the Australian system of public administration.

In 1986 the Federal Government began developing its response to the United Nations document, *Forward Looking Strategies*, which required governments to develop comprehensive national policies to abolish obstacles to the full and equal participation of women in society by the year 2000. The *National Agenda for Women*[23] was the result of extensive consultations with more than 25,000 women around Australia from diverse backgrounds and a wide range of organisations or interest groups. By 1988 the agenda was formally launched as the blueprint for continuing reform in those key areas of concerns raised by Australian women. The agenda listed as areas of specific policy concern: consultation and participation in decision-making, education, women at home and families, employment and training, childcare, leisure care, sexual discrimination, the portrayal of women in the media, social security, income security, superannuation, housing, violence against women and children, women with special needs, and international cooperation.[23]

Throughout the 1980s and 1990s there has been a dramatic escalation of program developments, which have established key milestones for women. In assessing the influence of the feminist movement on public policy it is essential to acknowledge the role played by a number of key female leaders, most of whom were young activists in the late 1960s and 1970s who learned the ways of the political process through Women's Electoral Lobby and who went on to put their new skills into practice in parliament.

It is also important to mention the unique role played by the two women, Joan Kirner and Carmen Lawrence, selected by their respective parliamentary parties to become Australia's first female premiers. It is ironic that both women became leaders at a time when their governments were unpopular because of serious allegations of economic mismanagement.

Around Australia, as Kirner and Lawrence took control, both media and community debate focused on the homely imagery of the women being brought in to clean up the mess. But both Kirner and Lawrence quickly established their own style of leadership in the Victorian and Western Australian parliaments and gained considerable personal public support. However, neither was able to turn back the tide of resentment and disapproval of their governments, which had both allowed a serious decline in standards of public accountability. Their governments were defeated in 1992 and 1993, yet there remains tremendous admiration for Kirner and Lawrence as leaders who had shown courage and determination in challenging the male stereotypes of political leadership.

Participation in the Australian political process has increased nationally with more than a hundred women in state and federal parliaments; that is, 13 per cent of elected representatives. In most governments there is now usually at least one female minister in Cabinet, except in Tasmania and the Northern Territory.

In 1987 Prime Minister Hawke made a public commitment to a minimum of three women in his ministry and had to negotiate with the three factions that control selection of ministers to ensure that his goal was attained. While three women were appointed in July 1987 — Susan Ryan, myself and Ros Kelly — this situation only lasted six months when Ryan's retirement both reduced the number of ministers and left Cabinet without a female member for more than two years. While Ros Kelly entered Cabinet in 1990 the number of female ministers remained at two until 1992 when Jeanette McHugh filled a vacancy.

The Prime Minister had recognised the necessity for a women's adviser and invited Anne Summers to join his personal staff early in 1992. Summers has an impressive background as an activist with Women's Electoral Lobby, as head of the Office of the Status of Women and editor of *Ms* magazine. Her work as adviser was significant in educating the new prime minister about women's policy developments in areas not personally known to Keating. While Keating was particularly supportive of overhauling family payments and recognition of sole parents' retraining needs, he was less familiar with issues like violence against women.

Summers provided both the philosophical and practical knowledge for updating policy advice to prepare the government for appealing to female voters in 1993. She oversaw market research to define the priority issues, and she developed subtle strategies to guarantee that the prime minister understood those issues. The Women's Electoral Lobby, still influential in 1993, issued a 'report card' summarising the record of both major parties in regard to their status of women policies:

> We have prepared reports on the careers and characters of two teams, the Australian Labor Party and the Liberal/National Party Coalition, who are competing for the position of running your enterprise. We have voluminous files on both contenders as we have been following their progress for many years . . . Unfortunately, although both teams have shown flashes of interest and co-operation, in the main they have been far from model pupils, being slow to learn and too easily persuaded to join the big boys for a smoke at the back of the bicycle sheds. During their years here both teams also displayed a distressing tendency to hog the lion's share of the food in the dining room, to stake claims to the largest part of the playgrounds and to continually interrupt and shout over the girls in debating sessions.
>
> Nevertheless, as you will see when you study the accompanying Report Cards, one of the boys has shown rather more promise than the others in regard to those matters which lie closest to the heart of this school — matters that concern equity of opportunity for women, the well-being of their families and social justice for all — but not forgetting prosperity and productivity.[24]

Throughout the election both Labor and Liberal leaders targeted female voters with policies and speeches about childcare, superannuation, women's health and violence. But ultimately the Labor record of extensive social reform and commitment to a fairer society was a decisive factor in returning the Keating Government with an increased majority. At his victory speech the Prime Minister acknowledged the women's vote of confidence with a special mention: 'And let me thank the women of Australia.'[25]

After the 1993 election there was again public debate about the number of women to be appointed to Prime Minister Keating's new ministry. Rumour spread that only two female ministers had any chance of being returned as the male majority jockeyed for positions for themselves. Media speculation highlighted a range of men who were described as obviously talented and eligible for appointment. Yet again the women would have been left behind had the Prime Minister not personally negotiated to ensure the final representation of three female ministers and one parliamentary secretary, just four of the forty prize positions!

While most Australian women would concede the shift in public opinion in relation to greater recognition of women's contribution to society, there remains much more work to be done to overcome the disadvantages of women built up over several generations. It is true that younger women are accepting the changed environment as a fundamental right, yet some entrenched chauvinism remains in the system. The need for continuing reform was highlighted in a recent House of Representatives report, *Half Way to Equal*,[26] which acknowledged extensive change in societal values but recommended further action, particularly in regard to sexual harassment, workers with family responsibilities, and an official recognition of women's contribution.

The reform agenda is gradually changing attitudes and practices in the relationships between men and women. The traditional male-dominated image of Australia is slowly fading as women assert their place and present a more balanced view of the nation. As a result Australia is becoming a more genuinely egalitarian society that seeks to value the talents of both women and men.

NOTES

1 Portia Robinson, *The Women of Botany Bay*, Penguin, Ringwood, 1993.
2 Audrey Oldfield, *Woman Suffrage in Australia: A Gift or a Struggle?* Cambridge University Press, Melbourne, 1992, p. 18.
3 Extracts from Commonwealth of Australia Parliamentary Debates Session 1901–02 (House of Representatives, 23 April 1902).
4 Ibid.
5 Ibid.
6 Extracts from *Women in the Senate: A History*, Senate Brief, June 1991.
7 Ibid.
8 Kerryn L. Arnery, 'Hidden woman: Locating information on significant Australian women', unpublished paper, Melbourne CAE, 1991.
9 Oldfield, *Woman Suffrage in Australia*, p. 18.
10 *Recognition for Women in Australia: A Discussion Paper*, prepared for the House of Representatives Standing Committee on Legal and Constitutional Affairs for the Inquiry into Equal Opportunity and Equal Status for Australian Women, December 1991.
11 Ibid.
12 Elsbeth Preddey, *Women's Electoral Lobby*, WEL Australia and WEL New Zealand, 1985, p. 3.
13 Ibid., p. 8.
14 Ibid., p. 18.
15 Ibid., p. 41.
16 Marian Sawer, *Sisters in Suits: Women and Public Policy in Australia*, Allen & Unwin, Sydney, 1990, p. 7.
17 Ibid., p. 8.

18 NSW Advisory Council to the Premier, *A Decade of Women in New South Wales 1976–1986*, Allen & Unwin, Sydney, 1987.
19 South Australia, *Sex Discrimination Act 1975, Equal Opportunity Act 1984*; New South Wales, *Anti-discrimination Act 1977*; Victoria, *Equal Opportunity Act 1977, Equal Opportunity Act 1984*; Western Australia, *Equal Opportunity Act 1984*.
20 Address by Senator Susan Ryan to Political Directors of Key Women's Organisations, Washington, November 1987, p. 4.
21 Marian Sawer and Marian Simms, *A Woman's Place: Women and Politics in Australia*, Allen & Unwin, Sydney, 1984, p. 141.
22 *Sex Discrimination Act 1984* (Cwlth).
23 *Forward Looking Strategies*, United Nations Organisation, Geneva, 1986; *National Agenda for Women*, AGPS, Canberra, 1988.
24 WEL National Office, WEL Report Card, press release, Canberra, 20 February 1993.
25 Paul Keating, 'Federal election victory speech', Bankstown, 13 March 1993.
26 *Half Way to Equal*, Report of the Inquiry into Equal Opportunity and Equal Status for Women in Australia, House of Representatives Standing Committee on Legal and Constitutional Affairs, AGPS, Canberra, 1992.

8
POLITICIANS

Sol Encel

The concept of political culture, once reserved for specialists, has become a commonplace of public discourse. The notion is associated particularly with the names of two American political scientists, Gabriel Almond and Lucian Pye, who began using it in the 1950s. Almond used the term to distinguish between political science and political sociology. The former was concerned mainly with the study of institutions, while the latter dealt with the 'social environment of the political system'. Political institutions can only be understood within a cultural (i.e. symbolic) context, which he described as political culture.[1] Pye argued that political culture denotes the psychological and subjective dimensions of politics, and defined it as 'the set of attitudes, beliefs and sentiments which give order and meaning to a political process and which provide the underlying assumptions of rules that govern behaviour in the political system'.[2]

Political culture is not an uncontroversial concept. Tim Rowse, writing from a neo-Marxist standpoint, criticises it as an ideological construct that imposes a false unity on the political system and on society as a whole. Political culture, according to Rowse, is a 'hegemonic' concept reflecting conservative politics and conservative social theory, which emphasise individual predisposition as the origin of social reality. It is ahistorical because it invokes the existence of an immutable national character or essence and negates the struggles and conflicts that underlie the superficial impression of continuity. Thus, conventional notions about the continuing importance of egalitarianism and state interventionism are idealist illusions.[3]

Rowse's view is not shared by the majority of writers on Australian politics, as he himself concedes. A more representative view is that of Hugh Emy, who argues that the study of political culture exposes people's expectations about the system, which in turn affect the actual conduct of politics. Political culture thus enlarges the scope of political science from the study of power and control to the role of the political system in maintaining social cohesion.[4]

The connection between popular culture and political culture in Australia can be expressed in terms of a number of conceptions about politics and politicians. Some of these are of popular origin, although they are often shared by intellectuals. Other conceptions derive from the work of political commentators, although in some cases they have become incorporated into popular discourse. In the early years of the twentieth century Australia was visited by a number of British and French literary and social critics whose writings exercised much influence on accepted views about Australian political culture over a long period. These writers were themselves inspired by the example of Alexis de Tocqueville, whose classic work on *Democracy in America*, first published in 1835, retains some influence to the present day. They included the Frenchmen Pierre Leroy-Beaulieu, Albert Métin and André Siegfried, and from Britain, Sidney and Beatrice Webb and James Bryce. Bryce, a prominent jurist and political scientist, had previously written another classic book on the United States, *The American Commonwealth*, which was in large part a rejoinder to Tocqueville.[5]

Like Tocqueville, these writers were struck by the low level of political debate in Australia and the minor role played by ideology in the political process. Métin, a French socialist, expressed this reaction clearly in the title of his book, *Le Socialisme sans Doctrines*, first published in 1901. He observed that the Australian Labor Party had no interest in theoretical arguments. Although it appeared to be a class party, carrying on a struggle against the bourgeoisie, its concern was not to achieve socialism but to obtain better working conditions within the existing capitalist system. 'Socialism,' he declared, 'the philosophy of which appeals to many European reformers, does not attract the Australian workers and actually disturbs them by the breadth of its ideas.' On the employers' side, he noted, there was a corresponding absence of argument, merely an intransigent opposition based on the defence of their profits. 'The publicists who uphold the capitalist cause restrict themselves to practical matters, and reveal that they are on unfamiliar ground as soon as they venture upon intellectual questions.'[6] This observation is a clear echo of Tocqueville's complaint about the tyranny of the majority and its pernicious effects on the level of political debate:

> I know of no country in which there is so little true independence of mind and freedom of discussion as in America. In any constitutional state in Europe every sort of religious and political theory may be advocated and propagated abroad [but] in America, the majority raises very formidable barriers to the liberty of opinion.[7]

Tocqueville, of course, was concerned with the negative effects of democracy in France as much as in America, and he makes little allowance for the fact that the United States in the 1830s was still largely a colonial society in which there was no established intellectual culture.

Bryce, in his own magnum opus written fifty years after Tocqueville, remarks on this colonial crudity. He also argued that the lack of interest in theoretical debate, which Tocqueville had described, was typical of politics in all Anglo-Saxon countries and that the Americans were merely conforming to this general pattern. Bryce, who was British ambassador to the United States for several years, had a much more intimate knowledge of American politics and society than Tocqueville, and his interpretation is in many ways more accurate. We should note, however, that concern with theoretical or ideological questions has decreased even further in the United States, whereas it has increased significantly in Australia since the days of Métin and Siegfried, especially in the last thirty-five years or so.

In his search for the distinctive characteristics of Australian political culture, Emy takes a somewhat similar line. The state, he argues, is not regarded as the repository of any particular political ideals. He claims that political ideals exist only at a social level within the traditionally idealised patterns of mateship and egalitarianism. Consequently, political actors do not make distinctions between the purposes and values of public order, of the political realm or of the individual's private sphere. The general view of political authority is both 'pragmatic and disdainful'. He suggests that this view might be called 'epicurean' in that it exalts private satisfaction above any notion of the common good. It reflects a hope that society might be able to do without politics, which is an essentially demeaning activity that 'intrudes into and interferes with private lives'.[8] However, as Emy himself notes, that unspoken premise is contradicted by the expectation that the state should and could respond positively to the material demands of various interest groups, a point noted by numerous other writers including W.K. Hancock, Alan Davies and the present author.[9]

The epicurean conception of politics engenders a 'non-political' as distinct from an 'anti-political' stance. Hence the ambiguous attitude to authority noted by many observers. The exercise of political authority is taken as a necessity, and political leaders are always regarded with a degree of suspicion. Somewhat paradoxically, however, Emy concludes that there *is* a political consensus founded on the principle of 'equalisation' and that the great reliance on judicial and quasi-judicial institutions noted by other writers rests on an underlying commitment to equity.[10]

One of the major ideological issues in Australian politics throughout the twentieth century has been the role of state intervention in economic and social affairs. Métin noted that the labour movement was committed to a high level of state intervention to protect living standards and to provide essential services. André Siegfried suggested that the ideas of laissez-faire individualism brought to Australia by British settlers had been modified beyond recognition and, like Tocqueville, he believed this meant the curtailment of individual liberty:

> Up to our day, or nearly so, England has been regarded as the stronghold of doctrinaire individualism . . . Every day the English show themselves prepared to accept some new intervention of the public authority and, under the compulsion of self-interest, to sacrifice some part of their liberty. For long the colonials have led the way along this path, and it is a curious spectacle to see the sons of the men of the [laissez-faire] Manchester School becoming the most stalwart disciples of State intervention.[11]

Siegfried's words were a response to the enthusiastic espousal of state action by the Liberal and Labor politicians he met in both Australia and New Zealand. A striking statement of these beliefs was made by W.A. Holman, later Labor Premier of New South Wales, in 1905. Holman took part in a public debate against George Reid, the conservative Prime Minister, who attacked the Labor Party as the 'socialistic tiger', which was threatening individual liberty through state intervention. To this, Holman replied:

> We regard the State not as some malign power hostile and foreign to ourselves, outside our control and no part of our organized existence, but we recognize in the State, we recognize in the Government merely a committee to which is delegated the powers of the community . . . only by the power of the State can the workers hope to work out their emancipation from the bounds which private property is able to impose on them today.[12]

The classic account of state interventionism is, of course, Keith Hancock's book of 1930, *Australia*, which still provides a reference point for subsequent commentators. Writing in the Tocqueville tradition, he linked political institutions with the social order and with popular culture. To the average Australian citizen, he wrote, the state means

> collective power at the service of individualistic 'rights'. Therefore he sees no opposition between his individualism and his reliance upon government. Every citizen claims his rights — the right to work, the right to fair and reasonable conditions of living, the right to be happy — from the state and through the state.

And he concluded with a famous sentence in which he paraphrased the well-known formula of Jeremy Bentham: 'Australian democracy has come to look upon the state as a vast public utility, whose duty it is to provide the greatest happiness for the greatest number.'[13]

Hancock also argued that while these views were widespread throughout Australian society, they were particularly associated with the Labor movement, and he put forward a theory of political party differences that remained influential for many years. On this theory, the Labor Party was the party of initiative and the conservative parties were the parties of resistance whose main concern was that governments should interfere as little as possible with the accumulation of private wealth.

Hancock was not the first person to present this formulation. James Bryce, mentioned above, described Australian politics in similar terms in his book, *Modern Democracies*, published in 1921, in which he referred to the conservative parties as parties of resistance or caution.[14] Bryce himself picked up these ideas from popular sentiment when he visited Australia before World War I, just as Tocqueville borrowed heavily from the works of the American Justice Story (who complained bitterly about Tocqueville's failure to acknowledge the fact). Other commentators have used more dramatic imagery, one describing the Labor Party as the lodestar of Australian politics, and another as its magnetic pole.[15]

The initiative–resistance picture of Australian party politics was subjected to destructive criticism by Henry Mayer in 1956. According to Mayer, this picture was derived by treating Australian politics in terms of class struggle, and he denied the applicability of such a quasi-Marxist interpretation to Australian reality. In fact, he maintained, it was much more relevant to analyse Australian politics in terms of pressure-group activity, along the lines of most American political analysis since the 1920s. The activities of pressure groups (or interest groups) were the real engine of Australian politics. The parties were not self-sufficient and isolated entities, and the conflict between them was often more apparent than real.[16]

Thirty years after Hancock, Alan Davies addressed himself to the same questions. Although he accepted Mayer's critique of the initiative–resistance theory, he also argued that we should attach special importance to the role of the state bureaucracy as the major source of government policy, more important than either parties or interest groups. Davies' work is an outstanding example of the use of the concept of political culture to expose the social norms that affect the role of government in society and the way in which the interaction between social norms and political demands produces characteristic patterns of authority and political behaviour.

Davies observed, with typical irony, that one of the most widespread images of Australia was that of the anarchic, self-sufficient individual who is opposed to established authority, like bushrangers of the nineteenth-century. He suggested that, in reality, the 'characteristic talent of Australians . . . is for bureaucracy', but the tradition of anarchic individualism means a certain shamefacedness about this indisputable fact. 'People feel that being a good bureaucrat is a bit like being a good forger.'[17] Davies himself exhibited a degree of ambivalence on the subject since he evidently believed that bureaucrats had too much influence on politics. On the other hand, he also regarded bureaucrats as custodians of the national interest who were concerned to protect it from selfish interests, as represented by a variety of interest groups working through or alongside the political parties.[18]

Writing a few years after Davies, I extended his argument to describe a 'bureaucratic ascendency' that gives Australian politics some of its distinctive character and extends beyond the range of governmental institutions as such:

> The bureaucratic quality of social and political organisations in Australia colours the whole pattern of social relations. It arises partly from the special problems of settlement in a large, remote, and inhospitable country, and partly from the deliberate use of bureaucratic institutions to satisfy the social demands of an egalitarian society [i.e. Hancock's 'vast public utility whose duty it is to provide the greatest happiness for the greatest number']. The bureaucratic ascendency includes a characteristic style of decision making which rests on broad public willingness to delegate the power to deal with economic and social demands to rule-making bodies of an administrative or quasi-judicial nature. One area where this legal–bureaucratic system operates, with profound consequences for the whole pattern of social relations in Australia, is that of industrial arbitration, where the processes of collective bargaining and employer–employee confrontation over the distribution of rewards are replaced by a legal–bureaucratic hierarchy of industrial tribunals.[19]

The industrial arbitration system, set up soon after Federation, was particularly important as the instrument for introducing the principle of a national minimum wage. Events in Australia were influenced by the concept of the 'national minimum standard' put forward at the end of the nineteenth century by social–democratic and other radical groups in Britain. In Britain itself, this concept was never totally accepted. In particular, it never took the form of a national minimum wage. In Australia, however, the policy of a minimum or basic wage was established as early as 1907, not through parliamentary legislation but through a decision of the national industrial tribunal, the Court of Conciliation and Arbitration. The president of the court, Justice Higgins, who had previously been a radical member of parliament, agreed to fix a so-called fair and reasonable standard for a national basic wage. This standard, revised by the same court from time to time, remained the cornerstone of wage-fixing in Australia for the next sixty years.

A dramatic illustration of its role occurred in 1931, at the trough of the world depression, when the court imposed an all-round cut of 10 per cent in wage levels. This cut, although it was bitterly opposed by the labour movement at the time, was effectively enforced. It also illustrated the extraordinary strength and effectiveness of the bureaucratic ascendency and its ability to impose discipline in a situation that in many other countries led to political crisis, violence and Fascism.

Following the wage cut of 1931, the Arbitration Court was also responsible for restoring wages to their previous level in 1934, a moderate increase in real wages in 1937, the introduction of a forty-hour working week in 1948 and equal pay for women (at least in principle) in 1972. It is interesting to note that, by contrast, Australia did not ratify the United Nations convention on the elimination of discrimination against women until 1984.

It has been fashionable in recent years to compare Australia and Argentina, countries that faced similar problems as the result of the collapse of international commodity prices during the depression and have again faced them because of the decline in commodity prices since the 1970s. In reality, the political contrast between the two countries could hardly be more extreme. Whereas Argentine politics has been dominated by Fascism and militarism since 1930, democratic institutions in Australia have never been in serious danger.[20]

Bureaucracy and legalism have the effect of giving particular importance to the legal profession. Here again we may refer back to Tocqueville, who was struck by the great prestige and political predominance of lawyers in the United States. The government of democracy, he wrote, is favourable to the political power of lawyers. By contrast, the *ancien régime* in France had shut lawyers out of the possibility of gaining political power, thereby turning them into republican radicals like Robespierre. Lawyers, he remarked, belong to the people by birth and interest, to the aristocracy by habit and task, and they may be regarded as the natural bond and connecting link of the two great classes of society.[21] In a society without a monarchy or hereditary aristocracy, lawyers provide the nearest thing to an aristocratic class, and their natural conservatism is important in restraining the excesses of the majority, with which Tocqueville was so concerned.

Tocqueville's observations have considerable relevance to Australia, where the legal profession has played a major role in establishing and operating the structure of authority. As in the United States, the existence of a federal constitution subject to judicial interpretation has given enormous powers to the judges of the High Court of Australia to act as legislators. Although they have exercised these powers with restraint, following the general reluctance of judges to assume a legislative role, the history of the High

Court is studded with decisions that have decisively shifted the balance of the constitution. Apart from the High Court, the political importance of the legal profession has been greatly enhanced by the role of judges in the industrial arbitration system. Thirdly, judges are frequently called on to act as royal commissioners. Although the royal commission of inquiry is a nineteenth-century British invention, its role in Britain has become relatively insignificant since the 1960s. In Australia, by contrast, its popularity has never waned. At any one time, it is not unusual to find two or three royal commissions operating in various state and federal jurisdictions. In one thirty-year period (1930 to 1960) which I analysed some years ago, there was a total of seventy royal commissions or similar bodies, covering a wide range of political, economic, fiscal and other issues.[22] One particular subject that constantly generates royal commissions is that of corrupt behaviour by politicians and/or government officials. In recent years, there has been a tendency to convert these bodies into permanent tribunals inquiring into governmental corruption. This has happened in two states, Queensland and New South Wales, and could soon happen in others.

The collectivist element of Australian political culture came under sustained ideological attack during the 1980s. In the twelve to fifteen years that culminated in the federal election of 1993, there was a steady rise in the strength and sophistication of right-wing ideologies based on 'free market' economics and competitive individualism. Paul Kelly, in a detailed account of this period, remarks that 'Australia's political debate began to swing decisively as the forces for free market reform mobilised across a newly emerging agenda which would dominate the entire decade'.[23] Kelly went on to suggest that the historical significance of this right-wing ideological surge was that it was not confined to specific policy issues but was directed at the 'Australian settlement' which had underpinned our political culture since Federation. He identified five 'pillars' of this settlement: White Australia, wage arbitration, state paternalism, trade protection and imperial benevolence.

What is particularly interesting about this catalogue is that it crosses party lines. The right-wing ideological position focuses on three of the items in Kelly's list: arbitration, protection and state action. The most systematic and comprehensive statement of this position was published by the Liberal leader, John Hewson, under the title of *Fightback* at the end of 1991. This manifesto included a commitment to cut protective tariffs to negligible levels by the year 2000; a goods and services tax (GST) to replace many other direct and indirect taxes; and a transformation of industrial relations that would replace awards made by tribunals with individual contracts between employer and employee. It also included a commitment to 'small government'. In publishing this package of proposals, Dr Hewson, a former professor of economics, declared that he wanted a mandate to rebuild the Australian economy from top to bottom, brick by brick. He claimed that the Labor Government, which had been in office for nearly nine years, was reluctant to make the changes required to lift the country out of recessionary economic conditions, including the highest unemployment rate since the 1930s. The Labor Party, he said,

> had yet to present a convincing argument why we shouldn't put our house in order on the lines of rational economics first and then see whether we have the ability to compete internationally that they claim we should have.[24]

In reality, the labour movement had already moved in the direction of 'economic rationalism' by the time *Fightback* was published. The move towards lower tariffs had been initiated by the Whitlam Labor Government in 1973 and taken considerably further under the Hawke Government (1983–91). The Hawke Government, in consultation with the Australian Council of Trade Unions, also moved away from the award system towards a system of 'enterprise bargaining', which preserves the role of the unions as negotiators and maintains the final authority of industrial tribunals but shifts the emphasis away from centralised awards for entire industries or occupational groups. In addition, the Hawke Government, after a long period of conflict within the labour movement, accepted the argument for privatisation of some of the largest public enterprises controlled by the Commonwealth.

The Labor Party also addressed itself to the other two of Kelly's five 'pillars', which the conservative parties have been singularly reluctant to disturb. 'Imperial benevolence' was symbolically abandoned by the Labor Party in December 1941 when the wartime Prime Minister, John Curtin, delivered a Christmas Day address in which he declared that Australia had given up its traditional dependence on the British imperial connection 'without pangs'. At the time, Curtin's speech provoked great outrage in the press and among the conservative parties.

Although the imperial connection has in fact withered only gradually, a significantly different reaction greeted the speeches made by Prime Minister Paul Keating fifty years later, during a visit by the Queen, when he foresaw that Australia would become a republic by the end of the century and stressed the need for an independent national identity. These speeches were greeted with outrage by the conservative parties, but the public reaction was generally favourable, signalling a decisive shift in this aspect of the political culture.[25]

White Australia, the last of Kelly's pillars, was abandoned by the labour movement in the early 1970s together with its traditional hostility towards immigration, especially from non-British sources. The shift towards a non-discriminatory immigration policy was accompanied by the espousal of multiculturalism as a proper response to the growing numbers of first- and second-generation immigrants of non-English-speaking, including Asian, background. This is another matter on which the conservative parties have found it difficult to readjust their perspectives. Although successive party leaders, from Malcolm Fraser onwards, have reaffirmed their support for multiculturalism, the concept has never been accepted with enthusiasm inside the Liberal Party or its junior partner, the National Party. This suspicion about multiculturalism is linked with nostalgia for the British/imperial connection, dramatised in the sentence uttered by the late Liberal leader Sir Robert Menzies a generation ago, when he declared that he was 'British to his bootheels'. These attitudes have found their most sophisticated expression in the writings of the historian Geoffrey Blainey, who startled many of his academic colleagues in 1984 when he expressed his loyalty to the tradition of an 'Anglo-Saxon' Australia and has continued to do so since his original foray on the subject.[26] Many of his articles criticising multiculturalism have appeared in Liberal Party publications. The persistence of these attitudes was noted by a newspaper columnist after the spectacular defeat of the Liberal–National coalition in the federal election of March 1993. The coalition parties, he declared, would have to bury the Menzies tradition before they could win the electorate.[27]

Free market ideologies have been particularly influential in eroding support for the interventionist role of the state, as enunciated by Holman in 1905 and described at length by Hancock twenty-five years later. Writing in 1988, Wiltshire could still observe that the Labor Party had a 'binding commitment' to public ownership and that the conservative parties, 'whilst seemingly committed to private ownership, have only rarely been prepared to dismantle public bodies whilst in government'.[28] But he noted that the public sector was justified both by ideology and by pragmatism and that its retention was mainly due to the latter. Since the 1970s Labor Party pragmatism has increasingly pushed Labor governments towards a retreat from the binding commitment to public ownership. In the early years of the Hawke Government (1983–91) ministers argued for the adoption of some elements of privatisation, essentially in pragmatic terms aimed at the reduction of the budget deficit, overseas indebtedness and the capital needs of public sector enterprises. The government also justified its commitment to privatisation as a means of protecting welfare funding. In March 1988 Prime Minister Hawke warned his opponents in caucus that funding for education, health and social security would be in danger without the proceeds to be gained from privatisation.[29]

The shift in government policy under Hawke is well illustrated by its actions in relation to telecommunications. From federation onwards, telecommunications was a public monopoly under the control of the Postmaster-General's Department. In 1975 telecommunications was separated and placed in the hands of a public corporation, Telecom Australia. Under the Fraser Government (1975–83) various proposals for introducing private competition into the industry were considered, but the Hawke Government rejected them when it took office. By 1988, however, the government had accepted the need for competition in principle. Its policy statement was, none the less, couched in traditional terms, stressing the objective of providing 'universal access to standard telephone services on an equitable and affordable basis'. A further ministerial statement in November 1990, announcing the sale of the publicly owned satellite network (AUSSAT), signalled a radical shift towards competition as an end in itself and the virtual disappearance of the traditional rhetoric.[30] In 1992 Telecom's monopoly came to an end with the sale of AUSSAT to a private operator, Optus Ltd, which was also licensed to provide telephone services. The government also pressed ahead with the privatisation or partial privatisation of a number of public enterprises, including Australian Airlines, Qantas Airways and the Commonwealth Bank. Activity was also stepped up at the state government level, especially after the election of Liberal governments in New South Wales (1988) and Victoria (1992).

The effects of Hawke Government policy were clearly to tilt the balance of the system away from the traditional predominance of the public sector. Whether this can be ascribed to the baneful influence of 'economic rationalism', as Michael Pusey has argued with great passion, or whether the explanation is more complicated, as a number of his critics have maintained, will remain in dispute.[31] What is beyond dispute, however, is that the election victory of the Labor Government in 1993 represented a significant public vote against free market ideology, the effects of which are likely to be felt throughout the 1990s.

In the last section of this chapter, I propose to discuss the special relationship between political culture and political leadership. Political leaders are often said to 'represent' the societies they lead, and there is some truth in this folk wisdom. The advent of particular individuals to positions of power provides important insights into the society and culture that produce them. Hitler and Nazism were a distinctively German phenomenon, just as Stalin and Stalinism were unmistakably Russian. Likewise, only the United States could have produced a political leader like Ronald Reagan. Indeed, in his case the realistic and the symbolic aspects of his role were virtually identical, as though the seat of government were actually in Hollywood rather than Washington DC.

The relationship between political culture and political leadership is to be found not only in the character and attitudes of the leaders themselves but also in the attitudes of the population at large towards their leaders. Tocqueville, for one, detected a profound ambivalence towards political leaders in democratic societies. Democratic institutions, he alleged, 'awaken and foster a passion for equality which they can never entirely satisfy'. As a result, distinguished talents are not appreciated; democracy, he says, 'awards its approbation very sparingly'. Like Plato and Aristotle, Tocqueville believed that democracy encourages demagogues. Not only is it deficient in

> that soundness of judgement which is necessary to select men really deserving of its confidence but has neither the desire nor the inclination to find them out ... hence it often assents to the clamour of a mountebank who knows the secret of stimulating its tastes.[32]

Similar sentiments are to be found among Australian writers, although they alternate between deploring the inability of the public to choose capable leaders, on the one hand, and on the other blaming the leaders for being manipulators who are able, in the words of Abraham Lincoln, to fool most of the people most of the time. Donald Horne, who first became famous in the 1960s for describing Australia as the 'lucky country', has consistently decried the quality of political leaders. By calling it the lucky country, he meant that the quality of life was due to good luck rather than good management. This encouraged apathy and a lack of striving, which enabled incompetent people to gain favour. These second-raters are, in Horne's words, 'racketeers of the mediocre who have risen to authority in a non-competitive community'.[33] It is the misfortune of the ordinary people, whose potential for achievement is great, that their affairs are controlled by second-rate élites. Other Australian commentators have made similar observations. A well-known Australian biologist and science writer, the late Professor A.J. Marshall, wrote in 1942 that the incompetence of politicians in Australia was due to the fact that the public was 'conditioned to second-rate political representation'.[34] And a radical historian, Brian Fitzpatrick, lamented in 1955 that the Australian people had 'shown themselves singularly poor hands at furnishing from their number fit persons to rule'.[35]

Public antipathy to politicians manifests itself with particular strength whenever the payment of members of parliament is under review. Members' salaries are normally reviewed by a special tribunal, usually chaired by a judge, on which MPs are not represented. This first took place in 1951, when the Federal Government appointed a special ad hoc committee which made a thorough examination of the case for increasing the pay of MPs and invited public submissions. In its report, the committee remarked that it had been flooded with letters, overwhelmingly hostile to any salary increase on the ground that politicians were already overpaid and that in any case they were not worth the money. The report of a similar committee in 1959 led to an avalanche of letters to the newspapers, most of them attacking the proposed increases. Henry Mayer and two of his colleagues analysed more than seven hundred such letters, published in seventeen newspapers around the country, and commented that most of the writers seemed to regard the task of government as being similar to running a big business. Those who favoured pay increases justified them on these grounds. Ironically, those who opposed pay increases also took this 'managerial' view of politics and justified their opposition on the grounds that politicians were not capable managers. They also seemed to feel, in a self-contradictory way, that these same incompetent managers had usurped the authority of the people.[36]

The complaint of usurpation reflects a basically populist view of politics as an occupation for scoundrels. Such complaints are not, of course, unique to Australia. No country has a monopoly in this field. The old joke that 'in this country we have the best of everything, including the best politicians that money can buy' has universal appeal. However, one of the characteristic topics of public discussion in Australia is the attempt to link popular attitudes with the allegedly poor quality of local politicians. One common contention is that Australian egalitarianism manifests itself in a dislike of so-called 'tall poppies'. This was the view of Hancock and of others before him.

The actual term *tall poppy* was apparently introduced into public discourse by J.T. Lang, Premier of New South Wales 1930–32. As an economy measure during the world depression, Lang reduced the salaries of senior government officials and gained some popularity when he described this as 'cutting down the tall poppies'.

Whether Lang's actions did, in fact, make him more popular cannot be determined with any accuracy. Public attitudes to 'tall poppies' have been examined by an Australian psychologist, Norman Feather, over a period of twenty years. Feather prefers to call them 'high achievers'. The latter term is also favoured by the mass media, which might reflect changes of attitude since the 1930s. Generally speaking, Feather's work suggests that there is no particular antipathy towards high achievers in Australia, although sporting personalities and entertainers are more highly regarded than politicians. He did, however, find that political allegiance made a significant difference to these attitudes; predictably, Labor Party supporters were less sympathetic to high achievers than supporters of the conservative parties.[37]

The 'tall poppy' argument has also been examined by Hugh Mackay, who specialises in 'qualitative' research on social attitudes. Mackay believes that the supposed Australian aversion to tall poppies is a myth and that adulation of 'leaders and heroes' is just as common in Australia as elsewhere. The real objection, he maintains, is to arrogance: 'Australians are not uncomfortable with success, but the egalitarian ideal has made them very uncomfortable with the idea that success implies superiority or that success gives anyone the right to swagger.'[38]

Daniel, in an extensive study of occupational prestige, found that, contrary to popular mythology, both MPs and cabinet ministers were highly rated on occupational prestige scales, close to other highly rated groups: judges, medical specialists and university professors. She concluded that while distrust and cynicism are undoubtedly widespread, this 'does not intrude on a clear perception of the power of politicians, especially ministers', although this perception is coloured by a continuing suspicion of established authority.[39] In a study of the qualities that the public expects in an 'ideal' prime minister, Mayer concluded that the demand was for a strong and exceptional individual.[40] This is a far cry from a famous editorial in the *Worker* newspaper in 1914, which declared that the Labor Party was 'infinitely in advance of the days when the workers had to be "led". They have no use for leaders'.[41]

Egalitarian pressures do appear to have significant effects on the personality and behaviour of political leaders. Some years ago, I suggested that these pressures contributed to the emergence of two dominant types, the 'larrikin' and the 'prima donna', which have figured in both state and national politics at various times.[42] Although the typology is not exhaustive, I believe that more than half of prime ministers and party leaders since federation fit into one or other of these categories. In recent years Sir Robert Menzies, Gough Whitlam and Malcolm Fraser could all be described as prima donnas and Sir John Gorton as a larrikin. Another larrikin type was Arthur Calwell, leader of the Labor Party from 1960 to 1966. The pose of the larrikin is not difficult to understand in Australia where it clearly appeals to widespread social attitudes. Moreover, it is not confined to any one party as the type can be identified in all major parties. Nor does it necessarily indicate humble social origins. Some of the larrikins had a deprived childhood and had to struggle hard to achieve upward mobility, but others did not. Sir John Gorton, Liberal–Country Party Prime Minister 1967–71, was a particularly good example of the political larrikin, but he was the son of a landowner, attended one of the most exclusive private schools for boys and completed his education at Oxford University. Sir Robert Menzies, who was Liberal Prime Minister for a record period of more than eighteen years and could be described as the *prima donna assoluta* of Australian politics, came from a small country town and obtained his education by gaining scholarships to school and university.

The prima donna type could perhaps be explained as a reaction to a society where the possession of personal authority has always been treated with suspicion, despite the fact that people like strong leaders. A person who aspires to political power is under some compulsion to assert the right to exercise it. By contrast, the larrikin deals with the problem by treating authority with irreverence, as though being prime minister is a bit of a joke. Moreover, in a small country there is relatively little competition in an activity like politics and this can lead to a conviction of absolute superiority. In countries where the need for political leadership is less open to public question, and competition is also much sharper, a person who becomes prime minister is under much less pressure to assert a personal ascendency.

Sir Robert Menzies, throughout his long career, rarely concealed his contempt for lesser mortals. As a recent commentator has remarked, Menzies 'ran the national government like an indolent ringmaster'.[43] One of his successors, Gough Whitlam, was another outstanding example of the prima donna type; indeed, he applied the term to himself. One biographer, Graham Freudenberg, quotes him as saying, 'I don't care how many prima donnas there are in the Labor Party, so long as I'm the *prima donna assoluta*'.[44] Freudenberg also notes that Whitlam's exalted view of himself was apparent at an early age. When the young Whitlam graduated from the University of Sydney in 1939, a valedictory essay in his college magazine observed dryly that it was 'unfortunate that Gough could not claim direct descent from Olympus . . . A continuous and fairly successful attempt to conceal his real contempt for his fellows was Gough's constant practice'.[45] Years later, Whitlam was to demonstrate his contempt when he described the national executive of the ALP, with whom he was at loggerheads, as 'twelve witless men'. Another biographer refers to Whitlam as a 'Titan' and describes how he dominated the government to such an extent that it became *his* government.[46] A journalist once epitomised this dominance by describing Canberra as 'Whitlamabad'.

Concern with the personal qualities of prime ministers or aspiring prime ministers has clearly increased since the 1960s as the result of television, which greatly increases the exposure of political leaders and stimulates the public appetite for information about their individual peculiarities. This appetite also accounts for the increasing number of political biographies that have appeared in the last twenty-five years. Political biography is, in fact, becoming a significant branch of literature, written in an increasingly sophisticated manner. Three recent prime ministers — Whitlam, Fraser and Hawke — have each received substantial attention. Fraser, like Whitlam, also conforms largely to the prima donna type. Paul Kelly, writing about Fraser's term of office (1975–83), emphasises Fraser's dominance of his party and government, extracting respect from his senior colleagues and 'tutoring his junior colleagues like school boys'. He demanded responses with such ferocity that he frightened people into acquiescence. He was also one of the wealthiest men ever to sit in the federal parliament. Combined with his upbringing as the son and grandson of large landowners, his wealth endowed him with a 'patrician sense of superiority which pervaded his career and was the source of his strength'.[47]

Kelly makes a similar point about Bob Hawke, Fraser's successor, although in almost every other regard the two men were utterly different. Hawke also saw himself as a man of destiny but in his case the origin of his certainty was religious, deriving from his upbringing and especially the influence of his mother. Another biographer, Blanche d'Alpuget, has also emphasised the influence of Hawke's mother.[48] Hawke was supremely successful in using television to nurture his personal ascendency. He saw himself as 'holding a patent on his own telepathic bond with the community . . . he symbolised the new politics in which the people would be the direct source of a leader's authority and television the instrument of that authority'.[49]

We conclude with Hawke's successor, Paul Keating, who might be expected to make as great an impact on the political culture of Australia as any of his immediate predecessors, especially given his striking and unexpected success at the federal election of 1993. Keating, like Whitlam, Fraser and Hawke, sees himself as a man of destiny. Early in Keating's career, the journalist Craig McGregor noted his love of power and his willingness to 'grasp the naked flame'.[50] Michael Gordon, in the first substantial biography of Keating as prime minister, notes that he identifies himself with Winston Churchill, especially because of the latter's ability to make tough decisions. Keating, he adds, has a touch of hubris.[51]

It is particularly easy to attach the term *prima donna* to Keating since he conferred it on himself. In December 1990, in a remarkable speech widely regarded as a challenge to Hawke's leadership, Keating described himself in terms of a performer, walking on to the parliamentary stage and 'doing the Placido Domingo'. Not surprisingly, 'Placido Domingo' has become his regular nickname among political commentators.

It is ironic that we require a feminine term to describe political leaders who have all been men. In Britain, where the type has been much less common, Margaret Thatcher provided an unusual example of semantic correctness. Such a major step in the development of Australia's political culture still lies ahead. The aftermath of the 1993 election, in fact, suggests that it is already on the way. Senator Bronwyn Bishop, one of the best-known women in the Liberal Party, received considerable publicity when she refused to join Dr Hewson's shadow ministry in opposition. Senator Bishop has often been compared to Margaret Thatcher. It was evident at the time that Senator Bishop's obvious leadership ambitions were making her male colleagues uneasy. Perhaps she had discovered that, as one British commentator remarked about Mrs Thatcher, well brought-up Englishmen had no idea how to handle a strong, assertive woman.[52] Senator Bishop's colleagues were brought up rather differently, but they too might have similar problems when faced with a woman who, like Mrs Thatcher, is determined always to have her own way.

NOTES

1 Gabriel Almond, 'Political theory and political science', *American Political Science Review*, vol. 60, no. 4, 1966, pp. 869–79.
2 Quoted by Tim Rowse, 'Political culture', in Graeme Duncan (ed.), *Critical Essays in Australian Politics*, Edward Arnold, Melbourne, 1978, p. 8.
3 Ibid.
4 H.V. Emy, *The Politics of Australian Democracy*, Macmillan, Melbourne, 1974, p. 16.
5 James Bryce, *The American Commonwealth* (abridged edn), Macmillan, New York, 1896.
6 Albert Métin, *Le Socialisme sans Doctrines*, Alcan, Paris, 1901, p. 255.
7 Alexis de Tocqueville, *Democracy in America*, World's Classics, London, 1946, p. 192.
8 Emy, *The Politics of Australian Democracy*, p. 341.
9 W.K. Hancock, *Australia*, Benn, London, 1930; A.F. Davies, *Australian Democracy*, Melbourne, Longman, 1964; Sol Encel, 'The concept of the state in Australian politics', *Australian Journal of Politics and History*, vol. 5, no. 1, 1960, pp. 62–76, republished in C.A. Hughes (ed.), *Readings in Australian Government*, University of Queensland Press, Brisbane, 1968, pp. 34–50.
10 Emy, *The Politics of Australian Democracy*, p. 347.
11 André Siegfried, *Democracy in New Zealand*, Bell, London, 1919, p. 51.
12 *Socialism: Official Report of a Public Debate*, Sydney, 1905, pp. 62–3.
13 Hancock, *Australia*, pp. 61–5.

14 James Bryce, *Modern Democracies*, Macmillan, London, 1921, vol. 2, p. 238.
15 J.A. McCallum, 'The Labor Party', in W.G.K. Duncan (ed.), *Trends in Australian Politics*, Angus & Robertson, Sydney, 1935, p. 50.
16 Henry Mayer, 'Some conceptions of the Australian party system', *Historical Studies*, no. 27, 1956, pp. 15–27.
17 Davies, *Australian Democracy*, p. 1.
18 Ibid., pp. 123–33.
19 Sol Encel, *Equality and Authority*, Cheshire, Melbourne, 1970, p. 58.
20 Sol Encel, 'Metropolitan societies and dominion societies', in S.N. Eisenstadt (ed.), *Patterns of Modernity*, Frances Pinter, London, 1987, pp. 94–6.
21 Tocqueville, *Democracy in America*, pp. 202–3.
22 Encel, *Equality and Authority*, p. 76.
23 Paul Kelly, *The End of Certainty*, Allen & Unwin, Sydney, 1993, p. 45.
24 Michael Gordon, *A Question of Leadership*, University of Queensland Press, St Lucia, 1993, pp. 212–13.
25 Ibid., pp. 194–8.
26 Geoffrey Blainey, *All for Australia*, Methuen Haynes, Sydney, 1984.
27 Peter Smark, 'Time to bury Ming', *Sydney Morning Herald*, 15 March 1993.
28 Kenneth Wiltshire, 'The Australian flirtation with privatisation', in Alexander Kouzmin and Nicholas Scott (eds), *Dynamics in Australian Public Management: Selected Essays*, Macmillan, Melbourne, 1990, p. 224.
29 Ibid., p. 234
30 Peter Botsman et al., *Telefuture — Who Foots the Bill?*, H.V. Evatt Memorial Foundation, Sydney, 1991, pp. 22–39.
31 Michael Pusey, *Economic Rationalism in Australia*, Cambridge University Press, Melbourne, 1991.
32 Tocqueville, *Democracy in America*, pp. 137–8.
33 Donald Horne, *The Lucky Country*, Penguin, Ringwood, 1964, p. 73.
34 A.J. Marshall, *Australia Limited*, Angus & Robertson, Sydney, 1942, pp. 86–7.
35 Brian Fitzpatrick, *The Australian Commonwealth*, Cheshire, Melbourne, 1956, pp. 152–3.
36 Henry Mayer et al., 'Images of politics', *Australian Journal of Politics and History*, vol. 6, no. 2, 1960, pp. 23–31.
37 N.T. Feather, 'Attitudes towards high achievers in public life', *Australian Journal of Psychology*, vol. 43, no. 2, 1991, pp. 25–34.
38 Hugh Mackay, *Reinventing Australia*, Angus & Robertson, Sydney, 1993, p. 135.
39 Ann Daniel, *Power, Privilege and Prestige*, Longman Cheshire, Melbourne, 1983, pp. 183–4.

40 Henry Mayer and Ross Curnow, 'The ideal prime minister' in Henry Mayer (ed.), *Australian Politics: A Second Reader*, Cheshire, Melbourne, 1969, p. 73.
41 Quoted in Sol Encel, *Cabinet Government in Australia*, 2nd ed., Melbourne University Press, Melbourne, 1974, p. 42.
42 Sol Encel, 'The larrikin leaders', *Nation*, 25 May 1968; reprinted in K.S. Inglis, *Nation: The Life of an Independent Journal of Opinion*, Melbourne University Press, Melbourne, 1989, pp. 175–8.
43 Michael Sexton, *Illusions of Power*, Allen & Unwin, Sydney, 1979, p. 19.
44 Graham Freudenberg, *A Certain Grandeur*, Macmillan, Melbourne, 1977, p. 249.
45 Ibid., pp. 68–9.
46 Sexton, *Illusions of Power*, pp. 4, 25.
47 Paul Kelly, *The Hawke Ascendancy*, Angus & Robertson, Sydney, 1984, pp. 47–9.
48 Blanche d'Alpuget, *Robert J. Hawke*, Schwartz, Melbourne, 1982, pp. 1–32
49 Kelly, *The Hawke Ascendency*, pp. 214–15.
50 Craig McGregor, *The Australian People*, Hodder & Stoughton, Sydney, 1980, p. 80.
51 Gordon, *A Question of Leadership*, pp. 193–8.
52 Anthony King, 'Margaret Thatcher as a political leader', in Robert Skidelsky (ed.), *Thatcherism*, Chatto & Windus, London, 1989, p. 58.

9
INTELLECTUALS

James Walter

This chapter deals with an emerging pattern in the political life of our nation, the pattern that links knowledge and the control of ideas with political power and our failure to understand that pattern sufficiently. Part of the task is to better identify the people who make the pattern — the intellectuals. But this chapter also assumes that political battle for control of the state is in one sense a battle to define national consciousness. Each side appeals to some notion of, say, the 'Australian character', which, if accepted, will persuade us to adopt one set of political behaviour, serving one set of interests, rather than another. Each side, that is, offers us a different ideal of the state.

But why are things so provisional as to allow such competing definitions licence? And who is it that gives voice to competing ideals and definitions? I begin my answer to this question by making four points. First, that every community devises shared systems of meaning that help it to make sense of its collective experience. The concepts of 'nation' and 'nationalism' have been at the core of this enterprise. Second, the ideas that come to dominate in any period are never settled for long. They always best suit one set of interest groups and are therefore always challenged by others seeking their place in the sun. So we should expect conflict, trace its origins and look for winners and losers. Third, there will be particular sets of people in specifiable institutional roles whose task is to define and articulate ideas appropriate to their context. We may call them intellectuals, although, as I will show, the term *intellectual* needs broader definition than is commonly allowed. Fourth, by exploring the vicissitudes of national consciousness in many spheres, we can understand the choices that shaped our history, the choices that determined the kind of society we live in now.

The leading story in our social life, then, is the story of competition over persuasive interpretations of what Australia should be, the values such interpretations appropriate as a tactic of legitimation and the choices we are induced to make once persuaded. It is those choices that have led to our present situation, and we should be seeking a way of telling the story of those choices.

That said, where should we look for those who define the meanings of our social life? It might seem obvious that we should start looking among the ranks of mainstream politicians. For instance, Australia's longest-serving post-war prime minister, Sir Robert Menzies, was not only a leader but also a man of ideas. He had many of the qualities of the scholar–statesman: a distinguished academic record, a legal career that manifested an outstanding legal intellect, a history of learned speeches and informed debate, a respectable publication rate of books and pamphlets. The documents and publications that remain testify to a continuing concern with articulating his version of liberalism and why it was appropriate for Australian society. His intellectual influence was substantial. Judith Brett persuasively shows that one of Menzies' radio speeches, 'The forgotten people', broadcast in 1942, was the foundation for the renascence of anti-Labor politics in the 1940s and was hence decisive in the reshaping of post-war political life.[1]

'The forgotten people' was certainly a speech full of ideas about values and about what Menzies believed Australia should be like. It might well serve to describe what was to come, in the 1950s, under Menzies' rule. In 'The forgotten people' Menzies appeals to and seeks to mobilise the middle class whose stake in the country was its responsibility for homes — 'homes material, homes human, homes spiritual'. He stressed home and family as central to national life, linking the health of the home and the health of society, civilisation to the family, patriotism with defence and preservation of the home.

Menzies' intervention came at a time when people more broadly felt that there were opportunities for a new start — a new post-war order. The values that should inform the new order were very much in contention, making it an ideal moment to explore the question of where ideas were coming from and who were the bearers of these ideas. Yet, while Menzies might have made a crucial intervention with his appeal to the 'forgotten people', he was not the only player, even on his own side. He himself gives one indication of an important alternative source for understanding the success of the anti-Labor message in praising the non-parliamentary Institute for Public Affairs' (IPA) policy work in the 1940s as the 'finest statement of basic political and economic problems made in Australia for many years'.

I will return to the question of who was behind Menzies presently. We must not ignore his predecessors, the 1940s Labor Party Government, whose dominant spokesmen were John Curtin and Ben Chifley. Were they the catalysts for the ALP's ambitious post-war programs? Dr H.C. Coombs was centrally involved in the policy determinations of those years, and his fine memoir of that time, *Trial Balance*,[2] gives a clear perspective on this question.

After the outbreak of war in 1939 Coombs was released from the Commonwealth Bank to act as economist to the Treasury. When Labor assumed power in 1941, Coombs' ideas proved consonant with those of Treasurer Chifley and Prime Minister Curtin, and he become a close adviser to both. Asked by Curtin to establish a rationing commission, Coombs showed entrepreneurial flair in going beyond the bureaucracy to draw on his contacts within banks, universities and the professions. Impressed by this ability, Chifley appointed him Director-General in the new Department of Post-war Reconstruction in 1942. Under Coombs this became a 'brains trust' on a significant scale. He proved receptive to people with ideas and built up a team of talented enthusiasts whose age was below that of traditional department heads; Coombs himself was only thirty-six at the time of his appointment as head of the department. This group, moved by notions of equity and reform, was centrally involved in landmark White Papers on full employment and the economy and in hammering out the details of a rehabilitation that would, it was hoped, produce a new and better Australia.

Coombs gives illustrative samples of the originators of the reconstruction programs. On his reckoning they were mainly university economists, bankers and public servants. He names such figures as R.C. Mills, Trevor Swan, Jack (later Sir John) Crawford, Wilmot Debenham, Jock Phillips, L.F. Giblin, Douglas Copland, Gerald Firth, Dick Downing, Thor Hytten, J.M. Garland, Alfred Davidson, Leslie Melville, Leslie Bury, James Plimsoll, Arthur Tange, E.B. Richardson and himself as constituting an informal network in which the 'ideas were being formulated which were to make the conduct of the war when it came and the transition from war to peace exercises in the application of Keynesian economic theory'.[3]

There was also a wider group of publicists generating ideas about a better order; people such as Lloyd Ross, a former Communist and Trotskyist who moved to a more pragmatic position and influence in the ALP, an activist in the Workers Educational Association (WEA), New South Wales secretary of the Australian Railways Union and eventually Director of Public Relations with the Department of Post-War Reconstruction; Georgina Sweet, prominent Melbourne scientist and social reformer, active in the YWCA and the Australian Pan Pacific Women's Committee; Flora Eldershaw, a well-known writer appointed to brief the UAP Government on women's issues regarding reconstruction; Mary Ryan, who worked with Chifley in the regional ALP and was appointed by him to the Commonwealth Housing Commission; A.P. Elkin (Professor of Anthropology at Sydney) and E.H. Burgmann (an Anglican clergyman prominent in the WEA), both Christian theologians and social theorists whose books and pamphlets argued that acquisitive self-interest was a product of capitalism and was not necessarily natural to the social order; and W. MacMahon Ball, who was to become Professor of Political Science at the University of Melbourne and advocated an autonomous voice for Australia in its region.[4] The key point is that these people were all members of the liberal intelligentsia of the time. All were debating the potential for a new order and, in some cases, the theory for its implementation before the opportunities of the 1940s context presented themselves. Significant numbers of them were strategically placed in academia and the financial community and could be drawn from both of these sources to form Coombs' 'brains trusts'[5] and Chifley's 'official family'[6] when the moment for change seemed ripe.

But there were other views of the Australian future, those Menzies came to represent. And behind Menzies was another group intent on seeing an alternative program realised. It had its origins in the informal association of business people who banded together in the aftermath of the disintegration of the Menzies-led United Australia Party in 1941, with the specific purpose of tidying up the affairs and clarifying the philosophy of non-Labor interests. There were initially two strands within this association: old-order conservatives seeking a return to pre-war values and practices and progressive businessmen who saw benefits in a new status quo but were intent on ensuring private sector leadership within it.[7] The progressives were by and large the more influential, and it was they who banded behind the IPA and who were influential in formulating the IPA program.[8] Menzies seized on the IPA program for the reorganisation of anti-Labor political factions as the Liberal Party.

Business progressives were strongly committed to the debate about ideas and the future and were ceaselessly active in promoting their views through speeches, pamphlets and books. Among their number were Essington Lewis, chief executive of the Broken Hill Propriety Company Limited and appointed by the ALP as Director of Munitions during the war; W.S. Robinson, youngest son of an influential business family, one-time journalist and sharebroker, but by this period an internationally recognised figure in mining and industrial circles and in business association politics; Gerald Mussen, once industrial relations officer for Broken Hill Associated Smelters, a notorious figure on the Barrier but by now a director of Associated Pulp and Paper Mills and a proponent of industrial self-government; H.E. Brookes, a director of Australian Paper Manufacturers (APM) and a progressive in employer–employee relations; and Leslie McConnan, general manager of the National Bank and an activist who spoke for a wider group of influential businessmen including Walter Massey-Greene, A.W. Warner, W.A. Ince, Keith Murdoch and Ian Potter. All of them were concerned to mobilise opinion through the IPA to counter the threat to business autonomy that ALP reconstruction plans were seen to represent.

It is instructive to note the intellectual capital on which the contending parties drew. Among the reconstructionists, Lloyd Ross displays a persuasive and extensive familiarity with many major bodies of social theory (and varieties of business opinion) of his time, from Mises, Hayek and Robbins on one hand to Laski, Keynes, Carr and Robinson on the other.[9] Coombs, having emphasised Keynes as the centre of his intellectual universe, spoke of the influence of Lewis Mumford, Frank Lloyd Wright, Walter Burley Griffin, J.L. and Barbara Hammond, William Morris, Peter Kropotkin, the spillover of ideas from the Bauhaus, and the English initiatives for new towns on the reconstructionists' ideas of community.[10] Rowse closely plots the influence of T.H. Green, H.J. Laski and the British Liberals on the reconstructionists.[11] Since the 1930s in Australia attention had been paid to the work of William

Beveridge, director of the London School of Economics, central to Britain's 1911 Social Insurance Scheme and author of the 1942 Beveridge Report on social welfare.[12]

In contrast, the business progressives, while also familiar with and accepting the general thrust of the Beveridge Report, drew sustenance for their views on business–government relations from other sources. Hay alerts us to the influence of the reconstruction proposals of a British group led by the chairman of Imperial Chemical Industries, Lord McGowan, which eventuated in the document *A National Policy for British Industry*, as well as reports by the Federation of British Industries, individuals like Sir Ralph Wedgwood and Samuel Courtauld, and the Nuffield College, Oxford, Reconstruction Conferences.[13] 'Much of this information was known and appreciated in Australia — and it was summarised for the IPA by C.D. Kemp.'[14] Models of business–government partnership were sometimes drawn from the American experience. R.G. Casey saw in the Tennessee Valley Authority a prototype of government acting as 'development stimulator', then leaving private enterprise to do the rest.[15]

There is no questioning the influence of Hayek on the business progressives. Rowse also shows the impact of Peter Drucker and James Burnham as theorists of industrial society.[16] Both of them legitimated a balance between state power and the social power of the corporation in which the latter would dominate, and both predicted the ascendance of the managerial 'middle' class.

What the post-war reconstruction debate offered was a moment when the competing value systems implicit in the polity at that time were clearly articulated. We can see a clear set of oppositions; oppositions voiced by the bureaucratic reconstructionists on the one hand and the business progressives on the other, but taken up as the genesis of their post-war ideologies by the Labor Party and the emerging Liberal Party respectively. These oppositions might be summarised as follows.[17] For the bureaucratic reconstructionists the central value is identified as that of individual opportunity to enjoy fulfilling human relationships, but this ideal is said to be contingent on material security that can only be achieved collectively. This leads to a normative investment in cooperation and communality. Political institutions are seen as legitimate agents of social change since they are the site of the collective will; government indeed is obliged to act for the people.

The business progressives also invest primary value in the

individual but posit individual autonomy as an absolute not contingent on the community or collective action. Indeed, collective action is seen as a potential threat to individual autonomy. Opportunity consists of creating one's own chances. The central appeal is to freedom, and the symbol invoked is that of the courageous individual exercising (and free to exercise) initiative and enterprise. Political institutions are said to be unable to provide solutions to economic problems or to generate social improvement since they are subject to the dictates of public opinion. Agencies of social action, therefore, have to be individuals and private organisations. Further, to the extent that political institutions are allowed to increase their power, they will inevitably be exploitative because they are peopled by competitive individualists who will use that power to pursue their own advantage. Business leaders also have power and privilege but they are constrained by the self-regulation of market forces. Thus, government at most should play a balancing role as more would lead to totalitarianism.

Consider the context in which those ideas were played out. The war confirmed a new economic order with industrial power at its centre and with enhanced expectations about social planning and the efficacy of expertise. Who was to take control? The ALP, in government from 1941 to 1949, found in the measures associated with war the means for implementing reform and sought a message that would justify extension of those measures into post-war economic planning. A newly emergent intelligentsia, product of an interwar expansion in educational opportunities, provided just such a message. Business and finance, while happy to work with Labor in the 'total effort' demanded by war because it offered opportunities for restructuring and plant development, were concerned to preserve their freedom of movement in peace, and the IPA intellectuals were mobilised to formulate the program that would legitimate the dominance of the new management élite. On the anti-Labor side of politics, in concert, there was the demand for a rationale to act as catalyst in an effective regrouping. Robert Menzies' role is crucial. He needed a new platform to play out his ambitions, a platform that would distance him from the collapse of the United Australia Party in 1941 and deny his part in that failure. This entailed removing himself from pre-war habits of conservative thought and rhetoric through adopting a 'progressive' program yet at the same time establishing a clear differentiation from Labor. The IPA intellectuals provided him with the ammunition for this rhetorical project, and he carried it brilliantly into the public arena.

That the Liberal Party, with Menzies at its helm, eventually emerged the victor from these battles of the 1940s meant that a certain idea of political culture, which invoked individual freedoms as a restraint on the collective and on government action, was reinforced as the received wisdom. This was not to prevent a degree of government management of central sections of the economy; government, after all, was conceded a role as balancing force. Nor was it to mean that post-war governments would always satisfy business interests. It was to mean, however, that the invocation of the 'collective good' would largely remain a questionable strategy in Australian political debate. It was also to mean that the crucial decisions about the post-war direction of the Australian economy would remain in the realm of business rather than government.

The 1940s case study supports the argument that the search for meanings is a constant in social life. By extension there will always be some play of ideas, and there will always be bearers of ideas, those who emerge within social institutions whose task is to create and articulate meanings. That is to say, there is an intellectual function that depends on invocations and interpretations of 'political culture'.

But are those who perform this intellectual function — the reconstructionists or the business progressives in Australia in the 1940s, say — properly called intellectuals? It is unlikely that they would ascribe such a term to themselves; they are clearly not a part of the traditional tiny élites of high culture and academia to which we conventionally attach the term. However, if we adhere to such traditional usage and seek to explore the role of intellectuals in politics, we might risk being diverted towards a search for 'major' thinkers and 'great' traditions, and lose sight of the intellectual core of everyday politics. It is sensible to retain the term as a means of indicating those who do the thinking that — via the political process — produces the states of mind that we come to take for granted.

We can be clearer in our purpose if we keep in mind Gramsci's useful distinction between 'traditional' intellectuals — the detached 'professional' critics in our various ivory towers who define their activity in terms of a tradition of intellectual life — and 'organic' intellectuals — the thinking and organising elements of a social class who specialise in giving it homogeneity and an awareness of its function.[18] It is the work of constructing and modifying the shape of social understanding that characterises the organic intellectuals, whether or not they would describe themselves as intellectuals or fit into those niches we conventionally associate with intellectual careers. And it is that sort of work we should seek to explore if we are to understand those changes in our political culture that legitimate one course of action rather than another. Thus, the political culture is recurrently contested as the intellectuals stir the pot, giving new twists to received traditions, feeding in contemporary theories from transnational intellectual networks and adding initiatives appropriate to their context.

Institutional changes since the 1940s mean we must look more closely at where intellectuals are located in contemporary politics. In every modern state a sophisticated career bureaucracy emerges, and in each such polity there comes a moment when the political leadership feels that the bureaucracy has grown beyond its control. A popular cultural manifestation of this was evident in the British television series, *Yes Minister*. When the bureaucracy no longer seems a productive stable other measures will be taken. The flowering of the modern bureaucracy in Australia is late. It is essentially a development of the post-war years and with it, as I have demonstrated elsewhere,[19] we see in time an increase in the political executive's experience of frustration with the apparent resistance or unresponsiveness of the bureaucracy, along with the suspicion that the bureaucracy is not a neutral instrument. Whether or not this is so — and top public servants continue to argue that it is not — political executives conceive the idea that they need help in managing and coordinating administrative machinery, along with a source of fresh ideas. While conservative leaders (like McMahon and Snedden) gave voice to this attitude, Whitlam's reformist Australian Labor Party Government acted on it, bringing in both bureaucratic change and a system of personal advisers to the political executive.

Whitlam's government, elected in December 1972, was the first ALP Government since 1949. Twenty-three years had been long enough to build a tradition, a body of expectation and precedent, that any government attempting to assert a stronger managerial line, let alone to effect political intervention and reform, would find a formidable barrier. The Labor Government believed it had good reason to feel suspicious of the bureaucracy.

The Labor Party determined on change on coming to power. The initiative has been said to have come from Whitlam himself but, if this was so, almost certainly the detailed preparatory planning was carried forward by others.[20] With a general concern for strengthening the hands of ministers in their dealings with their departments, the idea of ministerial 'cabinets' along French lines was toyed with,[21] before it was decided to expand and upgrade the role of ministerial staff. Allied to the concern with enhancing ministerial power was the conviction that Labor's program of reform and change would impose quite different demands on the bureaucracy than those that had stemmed from the previous government's preoccupation with managing the status quo.

To the extent that the 'smooth' functioning of government that had prevailed under the LCP coalition was disrupted, the inner workings of the public service were opened up to ministerial scrutiny and challenge. The public service was gingered up, forced to argue for and justify its case in an unprecedented way.[22] While staffers were dependent on their ministers, many of them were left free to define their own roles and did so in ways that gave them considerable scope for action.

Since Whitlam's time, it has become clear that the distinction between advice to government (the preserve of the public service) and advice to ministers (the bailiwick of personal advisers) has become reified and that subsequent governments have continued to place high value on the latter. At first, the Fraser LCP Government (1975–83) publicly signalled a repudiation of Labor initiatives in developing the private office, but there was soon a resurgence in ministerial staff numbers, testifying to the need of ministers for such resources. More importantly, under Fraser there was a considerable augmentation of the prime minister's office such as to make it a significant policy resource. The Hawke and Keating ALP Governments (since 1983) inherited the advantages of an institutionalised ministerial staff and of the sophisticated prime ministerial office structure developed under Fraser. To these were added a mechanism for scrutinising the appointment of ministerial staff and provision for ministers to amplify their private office resources through the appointment of consultants. The theme, then, is of increasing recognition of the importance of politically and philosophically attuned minders, and the progressive subordination of the bureaucratic element, in ministerial offices.

In considering the role of ministerial staff as organic intellectuals, it is germane to note briefly who they are and what they do. Research on the personal staffs of political executives in Australia, America, Britain and Canada reveals similar characteristics.[23] In all four countries, despite different political practices, a congruent pattern attaching to political advisers can be seen: the pattern of relative youth, middle-class origins, a high levels of education, specialist credentials and the leap from academic or governmental — but rarely political — backgrounds into the inner circle of leadership.

In what ways do the characteristics of advisers serve to differentiate them from mainstream politicians and bureaucrats? As it happens, relatively high socioeconomic status and levels of education considerably higher than the norm are characteristics shared by parliamentary politicians and by bureaucrats.[24] It is true, however, that in Australia recent private office staffers have had a higher level of tertiary qualifications than either parliamentarians generally or the ministry, which itself is more highly qualified than the parliamentary norm. Advisers are in general in their thirties, a decade younger than politicians and about the age when serious bureaucratic careers are getting underway.[25] Most obviously, advisers are differentiated from politicians by their preference for the private office rather than the public podium and from bureaucrats by their admission of political commitment. The primary role of personal advisers is that of supporting a political master, and the components of that work will sometimes be personal, often technical or expert and nearly always political.

Their knowledge and, more importantly, their ability to tap sources of knowledge, have been important factors in their arrival in the inner circle. To this extent they are expected to provide a technical service. If expert, they will be expected to contribute their expertise directly to relevant policy discussion. More usually, as generalists, they will be expected to bring a critical intelligence to bear in sifting through the papers, submissions and briefings that come to their minister. They will be expected to be informed devillers with the skill to chase ideas through 'ideas networks' — research institutions, libraries, archives, other experts. To this end they will be expected to have, or to have the ability to acquire, a range of contacts in institutions relevant to their minister's policy area. Having marshalled information, they might be expected to be able to abstract themselves in order to think through debates and issues and then to provide relevant commentary. As a concomitant they will be expected to have skills of articulation and communication: the ability to summarise relevant research succinctly, to prepare coherent briefing papers and to draft speeches. In short, it is through a range of technical skills — an outcome of their education — that they will be expected to contribute to policy formulation, not through being the originators of policy ideas. The exercise of such skills will usually be mediated by attention to political imperatives.

It is unlikely that advisers generally will be able to maintain a watch on the internal politics of the bureaucracy since as a group they are disliked by the public service. On the whole advisers will probably serve their ministers more successfully by closely monitoring the bureaucracy's execution of policy decisions. A range of roles is possible, and most ministerial staff will not work across the range. Some will concentrate on administration, others on research and writing, some will specialise in personal support and some in party, bureaucratic or public liaison. Most ministerial staff are sensibly aware of the limitations of being a subordinate. Those I surveyed in the preparation of my book *The Ministers' Minders* were also circumspect in speaking of details. Yet most staffers felt there were some means of direct input into policy deliberations.

In some cases a vacuum might be created by a minister's lacking interest in part of the area for which he or she is responsible and being happy for a staffer to 'administer' that. But a more generalised need for most ministers is for expert knowledge and for that expertise to be informed by philosophies and assumptions congenial to the minister's politics. Certainly most departments have such extensive resources as to be able to claim a virtual monopoly of expert knowledge and technical capacity in policy areas — and most staffers rightly concede their inability to compete on this level. Yet knowledge and the deployment of technical capacity are not value-neutral, and the political executive will frequently experience the values of their departments as inimical to their own. Thus, for instance, an economic adviser to an Australian Labor Government remarked:

> the fault with Treasury is not to do with its competence or expertise, but that the people within it work on certain unprovable assumptions about the real world, and are very doctrinaire about them. If you operate on different assumptions, you can simply never see eye to eye.

This situation could give a handful of 'Davids' on the ministerial team the upper hand in playing the politics of expertise against the 'Goliaths' of the bureaucracy. Instances are relatively easy to identify, as I have demonstrated elsewhere.[26]

Looking at contemporary politics I would suggest that while both politicians and bureaucrats now commonly have qualifications that identify them as part of the intelligentsia, along with the advisers and, for that matter, business managers, journalists, academics and so on, the intellectual function of the power élite falls to the advisers.

The tasks of analysis and articulation are inevitably political, but the bureaucrat forgoes these to become a supposedly neutral expert in 'apolitical' information and administration while the politician can pay less attention to them because of the survival demands of combat politics. At first, the institutional disjunction caused by the failure of bureaucrats to provide what politicians want creates tension and strain at the institutional interface — and disillusion in a sector of the intelligentsia about politics and bureaucracy. But at the next stage the political stratum, in order to maintain its dominance, must demand help and thus demands the services of personal advisers, incidentally creating avenues for that sector of the intelligentsia obsessed with the importance of politics but disillusioned about the available avenues of electoral representation or public service.

> Thus there are historically formed specialised categories for the intellectual function. They are formed in connection with all social groups, but especially in connection with the more important, and they undergo more extensive and complex elaboration in connection with the dominant social group.[27]

Yet this is a subsidiary role, a service role; speaking for the powerful is not the same as being in power.

I conclude by noting one more twist in the story. Until relatively recently, the staff of the 'counter-bureaucracies' had been, like the public servants, generalists, albeit highly trained and politically committed. Recently, however, and as a further result of the preoccupation with applied knowledge, there has been an increasing resort to specialists who bring particular expertise relating to specific programs.

Such program professionals have regularly cropped up on the fringes of government. For instance, a particular group of economists in Australia in the 1930s and 1940s, led by L.F. Giblin and D.B. Copland, was at the core of the informal group traced by Coombs above and contained visible and vocal proponents of what was to become the reconstructionist line. Of late, however, such people have been drawn into the centre, with perceptible effects on the public culture.

One manifestation of this tendency was the provision in 1984 by the Hawke Government for ministers to appoint consultants on top of their established staff entitlement — still further power to the counter-bureaucracy. It had always been possible to appoint consultants for specific tasks within departments. The next development was to rationalise the staffing establishment of the public service by shedding some permanent staff and transferring discrete tasks to consultants on limited contracts. This development, however, was only one face of the resort to specialist advice. The public service more broadly was transformed in the 1980s according to an agenda of managerial and economic efficiency and in ways that accentuated a particular intellectual agenda.[28] Suddenly people with quite narrow specialties had considerable sway not just at the ministers' sides but in the public service generally. The specialties most frequently favoured were management and economics.

Managerial and economic efficiencies in government are certainly worthy ends, but the monetarist cant many of these program professionals brought with them has given a specific inflection to the political culture and had a marked influence on public life.[29] Everything has come to be judged in terms of so-called economic efficiency and market competition. This trend has had unfortunate effects on areas where it is hard to discern a market product. For instance, in the social welfare area, lacking any other measure, the tendency has been to judge productivity in terms of the relative rapidity with which 'clients' are processed, with the result that people with complex and time-consuming problems are given Band-aid solutions to get them through the system or simply pushed aside. There is no question that the provision of welfare services has deteriorated.

To take another instance, the tertiary education sector — the extent and calibre of which was perhaps the finest achievement of the Menzies era and showed the Deakinite heritage of Australian liberalism at its best — has suffered radical government intervention in the interests of achieving 'economies of scale' and processing larger numbers of students at ever more marginal costs. This is not to say that there were no problems in the tertiary education sector but that an approach based on consolidating unlike institutions, on processing 'units' rather than attending to needs and which took no account of pedagogical issues, has not been the most effective way to address those problems. In general, the problem has not been the failure of market-style solutions but the failure to differentiate between those areas of the public sector where market solutions are appropriate and those where they are not. Specialist knowledge has too readily been seen to provide a universal panacea.

Of course, the influence of economic rationalism is equally evident in other western polities, although given greater impetus where anti-labour governments (Britain's Conservatives, America's Republicans) have prevailed. That the process has taken place in Australia under Labor governments, however, indicates, I think, the importance of the intellectual fashions followed by the organic intellectuals of the day. The program professionals can, at last, override party platforms and ideology.

We have observed in this chapter an evolution of the process by which intellectuals contribute to mainstream politics. At the general level, a process that commenced with informal networks of quite public intellectuals (such as Copland, Giblin, Coombs and Ball) has ended with the dominance of institutionalised, in-house, technical specialists. Ironically, the process was given its greatest fillip by a genuinely reformist government — the Whitlam Government — revising institutions to bring organic intellectuals into the centre.

The needs for informed decision-making and for specialist skills in a modern polity are clear. But when every political problem is seen as demanding a technical solution the shortcomings become evident. Instead of listening to the community and attempting to respond to its needs, political leaders swing to telling the community what it should have or do. The swing increasingly away from persuasion — Menzies' call to the 'forgotten people', Whitlam's call to the 'men and women of Australia', Hawke's 'fellow Australians', Keating's 'true believers' — to prescription — Keating perhaps most famously on the 'recession we had to have' — in modern political rhetoric has been remarkable.

The apogee of the process is perhaps manifest in the failed aspirant prime minister of 1993, John Hewson, a man who had leapt the divide from an academic then ministerial advising career to leadership of the Liberal Party, it seemed on specialist credentials alone. The contrast between Hewson's dogmatic certainties as a type of intellectual and the wide-ranging curiosity and spirit of enquiry of such predecessors as Nugget Coombs could not be more marked. The absurdity of an organic intellectual as political leader was clear — Hewson, in effect, was not a politician. He prescribed 'answers' but seemed incapable of listening or, in the end, of knowing whom to address or how. Perhaps his defeat, in an election it was thought the Liberal Party and its coalition partner could not lose, might stimulate the realisation that information and specialist skills must be in the service of politics, rather than dictating the agenda.

In reviewing this process, I do not suggest that politicians have been at the mercy of their advisers. Rather, it has been a symbiotic process, one of collusion, where politicians who are too caught up in the exigencies of combat politics to devise solutions have been provided with ready-made answers by the dominant intellectual movement of the day. That this is a moment when everything is seen to hinge on a quite specialist form of economic knowledge, and one apparently devoid of any sense of history or of the collective interest, reveals the potential shortcoming of the organic intellectuals. They can be too specialised, too much the creatures of their context and their political masters, incapable of taking the long view. This leads me to the conclusion that it is time for the renaissance of the generalist intellectual — the 'traditional intellectual', if you like — in public life. It is time for the capacity for general overview to be reasserted, time for dissenting, detached and critical intellectuals to leave their ivory towers and insist on their place in the public culture.

Notes

1 R.G. Menzies, 'The forgotten people', radio broadcast, 22 May 1942, reprinted in G. Starr (ed.), *The Liberal Party of Australia: A Documentary History*, Drummond/Heinemann, Richmond, 1980, p. 59; Judith Brett, *Robert Menzies' Forgotten People*, Pan Macmillan, Melbourne, 1992.
2 H.C. Coombs, *Trial Balance: Issues of My Working Life*, Macmillan, Melbourne, 1981.
3 Ibid., p. 6.
4 Ross, Elkin, Burgmann and Ball are discussed by Tim Rowse in 'Political culture: A concept and its ideologues', in G. Duncan (ed.), *Critical Essays in Australian Politics*, Edward Arnold, Melbourne, 1978, pp. 5–27; details of Sweet, Eldershaw and Ryan are to be found in Carolyn

Allport, 'Women and the new order housing', in Women and Labour Publications Collective, *All Her Labours*, Hale & Iremonger, Sydney, 1984, vol. 2, pp. 129–68.
5 See James Walter, *The Ministers' Minders: Personal Advisers in National Government*, Oxford University Press, Melbourne, 1986, p. 66.
6 See L.F. Crisp, *Ben Chifley: A Biography*, Longman, London, 1955.
7 Cf. Marian Simms, *A Liberal Nation: The Liberal Party and Australian Politics*, Hale & Iremonger, Sydney, 1982, p. 20.
8 See J.R. Hay, 'The Institute of Public Affairs and social policy in World War II', *Historical Studies*, vol. 20, no. 79, 1982, pp. 198–216.
9 Lloyd Ross, 'A new social order', in D.A.S. Campbell (ed.), *Post-war Reconstruction in Australia*, Australasian Publishing Co./Australian Institute of Political Science, Sydney, 1944, pp. 183–230.
10 Coombs, *Trial Balance*, p. 60.
11 T. Rowse, *Australian Liberalism and National Character*, Kibble Books, Malmsbury, Vic, 1978, pp. 37ff. and pp. 150 ff.
12 See R. Watts, 'The origins of the Australian welfare state', *Historical Studies*, vol. 19, no. 75, 1980, pp. 175–98.
13 Hay, 'The Institute of Public Affairs and social policy in World War II', pp. 201–2.
14 Ibid., p. 202.
15 Marian Simms, ' "Private enterprise and progress": The genesis of Liberal Party ideology', in H. Mayer and N. Nelson (eds), *Australian Politics: A Fifth Reader*, Longman Cheshire, Melbourne, 1980, p. 309.
16 Rowse, *Australian Liberalism and National Character*, pp. 171–4.
17 For a more detailed discussion of the opposing sets of speeches, policy statements, pamphlets etc, see James Walter, 'Intellectuals and political culture' in B. Head and J. Walter (eds), *Intellectual Movements and Australian Society*, Oxford University Press, Melbourne, 1988, pp. 251–61.
18 Antonio Gramsci, 'The intellectuals', *Selection from the Prison Notebooks* (ed. and tr. Quintin Hoare and Geoffrey Nowell Smith), Lawrence & Wishart, London, 1971.
19 See Walter, *The Ministers' Minders*, esp. chapter 2.
20 See J.M. Anthony, 'The politics of the bureaucracy and the role of ministerial staff', in R. Wettenhall and M. Painter (eds), *The First Thousand Days of Labor*, vol. 2, Canberra College of Advanced Education, Canberra, 1975; and cf C.J. Lloyd and G.S. Reid, *Out of the Wilderness: The Return of Labor*, Cassell, North Melbourne, 1974, pp. 149–50.
21 Peter Wilenski, 'Ministers, public servants and public policy', *Australian Quarterly*, vol. 51, no. 2, 1979, p. 36.
22 For responses that illustrate the disquiet of senior public servants, see M. Roberts, 'Ministerial advisers: A background paper', Research

Paper No. 6, *Royal Commission on Australian Government Administration*, AGPS, Canberra, 1976, pp. 26–37.
23 See Walter, *The Ministers' Minders*, chapters 2 and 5.
24 Joel D. Aberbach et al., *Bureaucrats and Politicians in Western Democracies*, Harvard University Press, Cambridge, Mass., 1981, pp. 80–1.
25 Ibid., p. 69.
26 Walter, *The Ministers' Minders*, chapter 6.
27 Gramsci, 'The intellectuals', p. 10.
28 See a summary account of public service reform in the 1980s in James Walter, 'Prime ministers and their staff' in P. Weller (ed.), *Menzies to Keating: The Development of the Australian Prime Ministership*, Melbourne University Press, Melbourne, 1992, pp. 39–43.
29 The most extended account is to be found in Michael Pusey, *Economic Rationalism in Canberra: A Nation-building State Changes Its Mind*, Cambridge University Press, Melbourne, 1991.

10
CRINGERS

Elaine Thompson

Australian cultural history has suffered badly from the fact that too little attention has been given to a sensitive understanding of the insecurities of an isolated small, ex-colonial society and to the discontinuities in cultural development that inevitably occur out of such a condition. Rather than the good being appreciated along with the bad, Australian egalitarianism was blamed — that, like some cultural steamroller, egalitarianism levelled all before it, downwards. The bleakest social commentaries believed that downward egalitarianism abounded because Australia — the land itself and the society — was a wasteland that 'lacked history'. To such commentators, even God was absent from Australia.[1] The stereotype was of a society that positively encouraged only the second-rate with its supposed social norms of 'she'll be right' and 'near enough is good enough'.

Whatever else might be true of them, Australians have shown a special enthusiasm for the printed word, have been committed to self-improvement and have been supporters of the arts (including theatre, poetry, music, painting, sculpture and dance), worshipping excellence. More Australians pay to go to the theatre and the opera than to sporting events, and in 1989 they spent $250 million on admission charges to theatre, dance, concerts and opera. Polls conducted around the same time showed that 95 per cent of Australians say that the success of their artists and performers gave them a sense of pride in Australia's achievements.

Commitment to the arts is not new. In colonial times Australians strove to develop a 'civilisation of the mind'.[2] By the twentieth century they seemed to have come a long way towards achieving this objective. In 1911 Australia supported a much larger number, per capita, of authors, artists and journalists than did Britain.[3] By the late 1980s the *Directory of Australian Authors* (1989) listed a thousand published Australian writers of imaginative literature, although the editor admitted there were many more than this number.[4] Between 1900 and 1969 Australian writers produced more than 5000 novels. This figure doubled again to 1993.[5]

Patronage of the arts has not always been equal to the endeavour of the writers and artists themselves but in 1908 the Commonwealth Government established the Commonwealth Literary Fund to assist Australian authors who were in indigent circumstances, as well as make provision for their families. The fund was renovated and extended in 1939, and in 1973 it formed the basis of the Literature Board of the Australia Council.[6] In 1993 threats that the philosophies of economic rationalism might see the end of arts funding galvanised opinion within artistic communities and helped to ensure the victory of Paul Keating's Labor Government over the Liberal–Country Coalition's Fightback package. And although writers and artists have proved themselves at times to be a tribal lot, debates among them none the less have been both vigorous and positive. This is in marked contrast to the period before World War II when they clung together out of insecurity and agreed to limit criticism of one another.

In the 1930s the Carnegie Corporation's report on Australian museums and art galleries found that

> in general it may be said that where the decades of the nineteenth century witnessed the establishment of museums . . . the first fifteen years of the twentieth century saw them enriched and expanded in a most remarkable manner. Governments, scientists, men of wealth and even artists, combined in this remarkable development.[7]

In his keynote address to the Council for Australian Museums Associations annual conference in 1991, David Lowenthal, Professor of Geography at the University of London and author of the influential *The Past is a Foreign Country*, noted: 'The Australian museum world is blessed . . . '[8]

Australians do not take such achievements lightly or for granted. The traumatic interwar years focused attention on the need for greater cultural enterprise, and when Australia was cut off from its traditional European roots during World War II feelings towards national culture intensified. The 1930s depression and World War

II were watershed decades for Australian creative writing, and the influences lasted through to the 1960s[9] when a new set of conditions, what Gelder and Salzman have called the 'new diversity', began to impact.[10] The 1930s were important also for the establishment of the Australian Broadcasting Commission (1932). The ABC acted not only as a broadcaster but also as the founder, by 1937, of the orchestras, which provide music in each capital city. ABC orchestras toured throughout Australia and provided regular employment for the growing community of musicians. Australian composers were also encouraged by a regulation that required the ABC to broadcast a small percentage of Australian work. From its foundation the ABC in radio and, from 1956, in television provided music, expert talks, book reviews, history, science programs and features and drama. It was also about the only regular employer of Australian dramatists. By the 1940s almost half the plays and serials broadcast by the ABC were Australian in origin and of high standard. 'After leaving school', Ken Inglis wrote of the 1940s in his history of the ABC (1983),

> I listened with devotion to old Dr A.E. Floyd talking about music; I heard productions of plays not being done on Australian stages; I cherished the liberalism of Vance Palmer and MacMahon Ball, the one talking about books, the other on Australia and the Pacific.[11]

The ABC went on to become one of the world's quality broadcasters, and in 1993 installed a satellite service that beams Australian television into the Asia-Pacific region.

An astute visiting observer, Thomas Wood, stressed: 'Universities exist, excellent ones. Bookshops exist, excellent ones. Bush Libraries exist, excellent ones . . . the Press, generally, is good: infinitely better than stay-at-homes in England would give credit for.'[12] A 1935 report on *Australian Libraries* berated the state of free libraries but noted that wherever free library service was offered the response of readers was as eager as in England and America. As well, the report stressed the extensive use of the state reference libraries in all the capital cities.[13] It stirred into action the free library movements, which resulted ultimately in the establishment of an excellent public library system throughout Australia. In addition, as the 1946 silver anniversary issue of the book-trade journal *Ideas* noted, there had been a dramatic growth since the 1920s of rental lending libraries. Australia had the largest Left Book Club outside Britain, and it was estimated that the number of books borrowed from Melbourne's rental libraries in 1940 (when the circulating library movement was at its peak) was around 12 million per annum, which compared well with the one million (approx.) books borrowed from the public libraries in that city in the same year. Many of these libraries served as meeting places for discussions of books, and a few made serious attempts to include both quality overseas and Australian literature.[14]

The emergence of the New Theatres in Sydney, Melbourne, Newcastle and Brisbane strengthened a tradition of social realist drama that had flickered since the early experiments by Louis Esson and Vance Palmer in the 1920s. At the other end of town, in 1954 the Australian Elizabethan Theatre Trust was established, dedicated to the establishment of a theatre of Australians by Australians for Australians through an Australian drama company, an Australian opera company, assistance to playwrights and training of young artists. The same year saw 12,000 regular subscribers to the Sydney orchestral concert season. By the 1980s tens of thousands of Australians each season began attending the democratic Opera in the Park.

Confidence in Australian drama was significantly increased in the 1960s by the success of Ray Lawler's *Summer of the Seventeenth Doll* and Alan Seymour's *The One Day of the Year*. It was again strengthened in the 1960s and 1970s with the establishment of the Australian Performing Group at Melbourne's Pram Factory, which gave rise to the talents of David Williamson, Jack Hibbert, John Romeril and actors such as Graeme Blundell, Max Gillies and Bruce Spence. The National Institute of Dramatic Arts was founded in the late 1950s under the auspices of the Elizabethan Theatre Trust and the ABC. It came into prominence in the 1970s and 1980s with the rise to acclaim of actors Helen Morse, Judy Davis (who won a British Academy Award for her part in Gillian Armstrong's film of Miles Franklin's *My Brilliant Career*) and Mel Gibson.

Alongside their liking for the film medium, the introduction of television in 1956 and the continuing vast impact of magazines, Australians in 1960

> still spent more per head on books than any other English-speaking people; bought more than a quarter of British book exports and had relatively twice as many book-shops as Britain and four or five times as many as the United States — and almost half the residents in local government areas which had libraries were enrolled as borrowers.[15]

Today Australia remains the largest, per capita, English-language market in the world and is the second largest importer of books from Britain behind the US.[16] With changes in 1992 to import practices and what were previously called traditional market agreements, Australia is becoming a bigger market for books originating in the US.

Nowhere in Australia's cultural history is there clear, unambiguous evidence of an Australian tendency to chop down tall poppies. On the contrary, Australians have worshipped individual excellence: 'Nobel prizes, Olympic golds, Covent Garden triumphs, best-selling books, brilliant political cartoons, pop-music fortunes. Ordinary Australians revere . . . them all.'[17] Terry Smith has looked in some detail at Australian painters and rejected the notion that the 'general public' is philistine or 'suspicious of art'.[18] Political analyst Bill Rubinstein examined the history of Australia's wealthiest people and found that there is 'remarkably little evidence to support the contention that Australians do cut down wealthy tall poppies'.[19] In chapter 8, 'Politicians', Sol Encel points out that neither N.T. Feather's (1991) thirty-year study nor Hugh MacKay's (1993) qualitative research into Australian attitudes in the 1990s could find evidence that Australians disliked high achievers.

Similarly Susan Mitchell's title *Tall Poppies* (1984), a series of nine interviews with successful women and her opening statement — 'Australians have always liked to cut down their successful people, their "tall poppies"' — is hardly borne out in the interviews. Nor in the foreword by Mary Beasley, which instead suggests the opposite: 'We live in a nation where the talents of half our population are not utilised. Women represent vast amounts of gold in Australia which for various reasons are not being mined.'[20] *Tall Poppies* went through six reprints in its first year and was made into a television series. One might suspect that the appeal for readers and viewers related to role-modelling rather than poppy-cutting.

Given the enthusiasm of Australians for learning and culture, why have so many commentators, historians, critics and writers painted so negative a picture of Australian's egalitarian ways? In part they drew on the powerful and well-understood trait of the cultural cringe by which Australian culture was automatically assumed to be at best second-rate, if not totally worthless. Only British and European cultures and history were considered worthy of study. A dramatic expression of the cringe came in 1935 from an

Englishman, G.H. Cowling, Professor of English Literature at the University of Melbourne, who argued among other things that Australia lacked the sort of history from which literature reflecting past glories could spring.[21]

A.A. Phillips maintained in his classic essay, 'The cultural cringe', that a 'minatory Englishman' resides inside the Australian cultural critic. Phillips disdained the 'intellectual's habit of denigratory criticisms at the Australian community without any attempt to check their accuracy'.[22] George Nadel's 1957 examination of colonial culture suggested that the image of England as a cultural homeland might have developed as a contrast to Australia, which was seen as the land of economic success. England, which offered no economic opportunity to the worker, was sentimentalised as the bearer of all things cultural. A deluded belief emerged that there was an inverse relationship between economic success and cultural achievement. Critics of Australia saw the acquisition of money by workers as a 'fatal facility'. Indeed mind and mammon were antithetical.[23] Cultural dependence meant that England not Australia was seen as the grail that artists had to seek in order to fulfil their artistic destiny. Australia was the land of non-culture.[24] The result was, in Manning Clark's words, that the British past 'would continue to weigh on the brain of the living . . . the myth of the past would come between the people and their emancipation from such domination'.[25]

The colonised imagination was the logical corollary of Australia's colonised economy — in Alomes' terms, 'dominion economics supported by dominion culture'.[26] Australian history of any serious sort had not commenced at universities until the 1930s.[27] Even the most rudimentary study of American, Asian and Pacific history did not begin until the 1950s, and Australian politics and society had to wait until the 1960s before a reasonable body of intellectual work about them started to emerge.[28] Perhaps more damaging was the sort of Australian history that was created and embalmed, as Henry Reynolds has discussed more fully in chapter 1, 'History'.

The consequence of the Anglo-coloured lenses through which Australia viewed itself was psychic damage to our imagination. The damage had been wrought not by the little Aussie battler, the egalitarian, but by the people in élite positions, especially those in universities, the horsemen of the cultural apocalypse. In the mid 1960s Hugo Wolfsohn attacked this group for having created an intellectual mediocrity and called on Australian intellectuals to 'exonerate the Australian working and lower middle classes from the slur of philistinism'.[29] While Wolfsohn was overwhelmingly concerned with the impact of a conservative élite on intellectual life, his observation is equally true regarding other forms of culture. In the 1970s John Docker (1974) and David Walker (1976) turned around a number of assumptions related to Australian intellectuals by demonstrating that the 'radical legislature' of Australian cultural life actually existed outside institutions.[30] With the expansion of the university system from the 1960s onward, a startling new range of intellectual traditions (as Andrew Milner points out in chapter 12, 'Culture') have now moved from outside into the academies.[31]

But damage was done. Until 1965 Australian English departments produced only two PhD theses on Australian subjects and, despite an increase in the staff between 1947 and 1973 (from 26 to 246), the percentage of Oxbridge or London degrees barely changed.[32] Such figures beg the big question: if our universities were not teaching Australian subjects, what opinions were being formed by graduates about their own culture? How perfectly was the cringe reproduced in each graduation ceremony? The first chair in Australian literature was not created until the 1960s,[33] and further research undertaken by Feather in 1993 has demonstrated that students in the 1990s were less likely to suffer the 'cringe' of their forebears.

But if things for many years were straitened inside the academies they could be equally bad in other institutions. Although foresight had been shown in expanding the Commonwealth Literary Fund in 1939, beginning in that decade and carrying well into the Cold War, federal governments indulged in a binge of authoritarian and autocratic behaviour. Dictation tests in inappropriate languages were used to prevent visits by political radicals and people whose morals the government did not like. The Customs Act, the Telecommunications Act and the full weight of the Attorney-General's Department were used for the censorship, on both political and moral grounds, of works such by Marx, Engels, Lenin, Balzac, D.H. Lawrence and James Joyce. Among censored Australians were Norman Lindsay, Frank Walford, J.M. Harcourt,[34] Jean Devanny and Christina Stead. Robert Close was sent to prison for *Love Me Sailor* in the 1940s while Frank Hardy, in a celebrated case, only just escaped a sentence following the publication of *Power*

Without Glory. In the 1980s and 1990s Avon Lovell battled alleged police corruption in Western Australia where two of his books have been banned because of their content. Plays were banned from performance. The governors of the Adelaide Festival prohibited Alan Seymour's now classic play, *The One Day of the Year*, in the early 1960s, and there was even a bomb threat against it, while Alex Buzo's *Rooted* carried the distinction at its opening in New York of having being 'Banned in Wagga Wagga'. The antagonism between those in positions of power and intellectual communities was intensified with the philistine attack on modernism, strongly supported by Menzies and carried pubicly by the media into the 1970s with the furore over the Whitlam Government's purchase of Jackson Pollock's *Blue Poles* for what was then an unprecedented amount of money for a single work of art — $1.3 million.

Many writers and artists took as their benchmark an 'overseas' constructed out of all nations, especially Britain and Europe. There is nothing intrinsically wrong with doing this, but the contrast was habitually negative and used to downgrade cultural achievement on the pretext of nationality — to prove that, on account of its Australianness, Australian art and literature are, as a matter of course, inferior to art and literature produced elsewhere. There is surely a deep-seated perversity in this critical position, a self-hatred that defies reason. And no single nation's cultural development could withstand comparison within such a construct. The result was an analytic tradition of conservatism and sometimes of vicious derisory complacency. For example, in 1945, when giving one of the pioneering Commonwealth Literary Fund lectures, Professor T. Stewart chose to talk on D.H. Lawrence's *Kangaroo* because, he said, there was no Australian literature worthy of consideration. Again that 'minatory Englishman' — this time described in the words of R.M. Crawford (1955) — 'whose ghost sits in on the tête-à-tête between Australian reader and writer, interrupting in the wrong accent'.[35]

What this tradition of analysis did was to take certain facts and weave a destructive web: that Australian writers, frustrated by the struggle to make a living at home, went abroad, almost invariably to Britain, although some also went to other European countries and the US, expressing feelings of bitterness, and spin a web of theory about the dead hand of egalitarianism. That theory ignored other facts: that the Australian population was very small (in 1993 around seventeen million); that the cultural cringe existed in the élite institutions; that those in positions of economic power in the cultural marketplace were colonised by conservative values of Anglo origin; and that the talented might have gone overseas anyway in order to seek recognition in the metropolitan centres of intellectual and artistic development. Each of these facts had a powerful impact on Australian writers and artists. Too often negative feelings about Australia's intellectual worlds were transferred uncritically to other areas of cultural activity.

Economics, not fears of a dead-level culture, was more the engine driving expatriation. London paid at least five times the amount that Australia did for a story and had other sources of income for writers, including reviews and broadcasting.[36] An Australian book published in London and sold in Britain, which was in any case the centre of a much larger market, paid three times as much in royalties as were paid for Australian sales, which were calculated on a flat 'overseas' rate. About half of the Australian novels published between 1900 and 1970 were published in London and, in a world where returns were small enough, in which only one or two out of the thousands trying made a living from writing, the temptations to try London first were strong. Australian writers suffered because of the dominance of the local market by English publishers but were routinely told, even by Australian publishers, to send their sweated manuscripts 'Home', meaning to London.[37]

While the Australian public should not be expected to have any special commitment to the Australian product, a key problem was that Australian books and magazines were in direct competition in both price and quality with easily available English, American and European periodicals. In the years before World War II, books published in London were sold in Australia in 'colonial editions' for about a third of the cost of locally produced books and were dumped in Australia to shore up the cartel practices of British publishers. At the end of the war, the cartel moved a number of operations to Australia and further manoeuvred to shut out indigenous publishers. Add a monopoly of distributors and, as a Prices Surveillance Authority report on the book trade in the late 1980s revealed, the retail price of books increased inordinately to between a third and a half more than the price of same title in Britain and the US.[38] Australia was a captive market.

The problems for local publishers of ensuring that the local product was of the same quality as the imported, and of producing a mix of locally crafted and overseas product in magazines, were often critical. Ronald Campbell, editor of the *Australian Journal*, commented satirically that he

> wanted to publicly contradict a report which has gained currency since the increase of overland travel through central Australia to the effect that in a cave on the north side of Central Mount Stuart there lives an individual, free, white, twenty-one and Australian, who has not yet written a short story![39]

To be published was quite another matter. Campbell, like other editors, turned away thousands of stories. Syndicated fiction from Britain but increasingly from the US could be bought by publishers for about a quarter of the cost of the local product because these stories had already appeared in several publications. The same principle did not work in reverse, although there were a few Australians like Alice Grant-Rosman who 'cracked' into the international circuit.

An additional problem was that Australian writers competed with all those writing in English and 'lacked the natural protection by language which writers in countries of comparable size, like Holland and the Scandinavian countries, have had'.[40] By the 1960s British book sales in Australia were worth about four million pounds per year. By the 1990s the trade had expanded to be worth more than a hundred million dollars. But it was not until the 1970s that British publishers seriously tried to develop a local market for local products, let alone attempted to promote that product. Indeed British publishers had been so utterly uninterested in the Australian literary culture that they did not contribute any of their revenue to Australian literary magazines 'whose literary criticisms help sell the books'.[41] The production deference to the metropolitan centre was maintained. 'What happens to a country, a culture, when one of its most enduring influences, that of its native literature, is in the hands of another culture?' asked Laurie Muller, president of the Australian Book Publishers Association, as late as 1986. 'Should we be put in the ignominious position of having to import our own culture?'[42] Clearly the answer is 'No'.

When the New South Wales Bookstall Company of Sydney launched mass-market paperback publishing in 1904, authors and stories were almost exclusively Australian with an explicit company policy of avoiding British or American themes. The company was highly successful, and its authors included Steele Rudd. By the time of the founder's death in 1922, around five million copies had been published, 'a significant effort for a single publisher at that time, given the size of Australia's population — 5.4 million in 1921'.[43] Unfortunately the successors to this publishing firm fell into the conservative norm, taking little interest and fewer risks, with the result that the Bookstall series petered out around 1928. Had it continued it might have provided a continuing base for an Australian identity through the successful publishing of popular material written by Australian authors. P.R. Stephensen's attempts to establish a national publication company in the 1930s also failed. Although there were many reasons for the collapse, Stephensen blamed the cartel of distributors who refused to market his books for a reasonable price.

Angus & Robertson has been the Australian literary flagship for much of the twentieth century, although it has not always enjoyed good relations with key authors. Among those turned away include Miles Franklin, Katharine Susannah Prichard, Vance Palmer and M. Barnard Eldershaw, who were forced to seek publication overseas. Even Ion Idriess, who went on to become one of Angus & Robertson's bestsellers, had his first book in manuscript returned unread. Yet Angus & Robertson was the key player behind the remarkable Pocket Library series, which appeared during World War II. These cheap paperbacks were published in print runs of 25,000 copies and did a great deal to popularise Australian literature at a time when the country might well have felt that it really needed to know more about itself.

Other important publishers in the post-war period included F.W. Cheshire, Lloyd O'Neill and the Australasian Book Society, which published around ninety titles between 1952 and 1978.[44] Since the advent of university presses, as Geoffrey Dutton has pointed out, more and more Australian intellectual and cultural work is getting into print and achieving a wider circulation.[45] The lists of major national and international presses such as Queensland University Press and Oxford University Press, and the Australianisation via management buy-out of Allen & Unwin in the early 1990s, demonstrates that there is a stable market for this kind of material. The publications lists of the phenomenally successful McPhee Gribble in the 1970s and 1980s reads like the 'new diversity' of Australian literature. But like so many Australian publishers, it could really only operate in the gaps between the big multinational corporations, whose headquarters have traditionally been London. And as the fate of McPhee Gribble, which was taken over by Penguin in 1990, illustrates, even the most successful Australian imprint is not safe with success.

Australia's only 'special' feature was the tyranny of distance — that until the jet, it was a very long way from the great intellectual, artistic, economic and scientific centres of the world. That physical distance might have meant that Australian artists experienced a more acute sense of isolation than was the norm overseas. Moreover, if writers or artists wanted to travel to other cultural centres, even for a visit, before air travel, this almost certainly implied expatriation. There were no Australian internationalists of consequence based in Australia before the jet aircraft.[46] Now they abound, moving between London, New York, Rome and Australia: Peter Carey, Thomas Keneally, Shirley Hazzard, David Malouf and so on.

Infected by the cultural cringe, a colonised imagination and a tradition that feared egalitarianism, many conservative social critics, writers and academics remained insensitive to the positive forces of democracy. Russel Ward believes that they had always been deeply elitist, setting themselves apart from the hoi polloi.[47] Conservative critics have almost always found Australia wanting, and the 1960s and early 1970s saw the publication of a plethora of titles such as *The Australian Ugliness* and *The Great Australian Stupor*, which were countered by the likes of *Wowsers* and *Knockers*. Very few conservative writers have attempted to write positively for the masses or to raise levels of appreciation. Rather they had developed a highly negative attitude. A.A. Phillips pointed out their mistake:

> It is sometimes assumed that the indifference by Australians to the best work of their own writers is due to the alleged materialism of the average Australia. I do not believe it . . . I can find no convincing evidence that there is proportionately more Philistinism in Australia than in any other Anglo-Saxon country . . . The Australian writer's difficulty lies less in the indifference of the average man to serious writing than in the indifference of a large section of our cultivated minority to Australian writing.[48]

But Phillips' analysis went largely unheeded even among those who might have otherwise agreed with the sentiment. In 1954 in his influential work, Th*e Legend of the Nineties,* Vance Palmer argued that the Australian pioneering successes of the nineteenth century — the ability to 'make do' — led in the twentieth century to a 'tolerance of mediocre standards in life and art'.[49] In other societies that same trait, labelled human ingenuity, has been seen as the explanation for entrepreneurial successes!

At the same time as Palmer was writing, Dobell, Boyd and Drysdale, to name the most obvious, were creating masterpieces, and by the 1960s Australian artists were consciously rejoicing in painting urban Australia — most notably Donald Friend's paintings of Double Bay and Sali Herman's terraces. In 1962 the Whitechapel exhibition introduced Australian art to an overseas audience when it opened in London. Friend was among those who exhibited, as were Boyd, Dobell, Nolan and a 22-year-old Brett Whiteley, who just a year or so earlier had won his first art competition at the Bathurst show. Robert Hughes wrote the catalogue.

Critics emerged but slowly from the cultural cringe. In 1962 Robert Hughes addressed sardonic comments about conservative attitudes in art towards the trustees of the state galleries, not the little Aussie from the suburbs. Yet the cultural cringe remained so strong that Hughes, while praising the distinctiveness and genius of the great Australian artists, still had to disparage the second-rate rubbish on which 'critics and public alike spend most of their time'.[50] By 1964 *The Lucky Country* centred its attack on the mediocre nature of those in positions of power. It did not attack Australian egalitarianism. In 1965 Cecil Hadgraft, a sensitive examiner of Australian writing over the century (novels, short stories, poetry and plays), declared that in 'quality and volume combined, it seems indisputable that the Australian [writing] yields to no other of the Commonwealth literatures'.[51] In 1966 Hugo Wolfsohn challenged intellectuals to look at themselves and their assumptions.

Yet remnants of the cringe and its conservatism have remained, and it is not really surprising that as late as 1985 a member of the English department at the University of Sydney, Leonie Kramer, was still casting doubt on the quality of things Australian. To Kramer the cultural cringe was a more or less static state of mind, a kind of mental tariff barrier, which, like protectionism to manufacturing, excluded excellence and allowed in its place the conditions for second-rate products to thrive and be acclaimed. Under her pen Australian cultural products were not seen as competitive because they were not being judged by internationally known high standards:

> Australia still lacks a rigorous, constructive critical tradition . . . there is still an inclination to deal with local writers tenderly . . . a reluctance on the part of critics to subject local works to rigorous scrutiny . . . The notion of Australian creative life as a tender plant that needs special nurturing.[52]

Yet it is Kramer herself who is exhibiting classic cringe. She is an example of the tough social critic who seeks out the negative rather than looking sympathetically at what has been positively achieved. And it might well be that Australian culture has needed special nurturing. Not everything behind tariff barriers needs automatically to be second-rate. Japan's barriers enabled it to produce first-rate products that beat the world.

Despite Kramer and others like her, we have finally stopped kicking the dog and recognised the cur as a new pedigreed breed. Since the 1970s vast decolonisation of the imagination and redefinition has taken place in the arts and in Australia's intellectual and cultural life. Looking back it is clear that the critics of the early 1960s — Donald Horne in *The Lucky Country*, Hugo Wolfsohn and Henry Mayer, among others who contributed to the first Mayer reader on *Australian Politics* and the authors who wrote for Peter Coleman's *Australian Civilisation*, including Ken Inglis, James McAuley, Robert Hughes and Vincent Buckley — were the midwives of changes to the limitations and strictures of Australia's literary, intellectual and artistic life.

Vincent Buckley wrote in his 1962 essay on Australian intellectuals that he expected European immigrant intellectuals to make their voices heard 'as soon as they master the local idiom'.[53] The cultural richness, complexity and sophistication whose birth was seen by these insightful commentators took until the mid 1970s to come to maturity. As David Malouf commented: 'I think of myself as belonging to the first generation in Australia . . . in which men and women of predominantly non-Anglo-Saxon or Celtic background have felt free to speak out and make themselves visible'.[54]

In the 1980s Aboriginal and white writers and playwrights began to write about racism and the experiences of Aborigines in white Australia — a clear sign of cultural maturity. A number of Greeks have now been acclaimed as major Australian poets. Dimitris Tsaloumas, following the publication of a bilingual edition of his poems *Observatory* in 1983, was awarded the National Book Council Award. In 1985 his bilingual poetry collection *The Book of*

Epigrams received similar recognition, and the following year he was appointed writer-in-resident at the University of Melbourne.[55]

In the 1990s individual artists are still underpaid and exploited, but Australian art takes second place to none and, within it, Aboriginal art takes a pride of place. Craft has been redefined so that it no longer shuts out the long tradition of women's craft: weaving, embroidery, quilt-making and tapestry. Australians are now confident that their judgement is good enough. And the contributions to the arts by non-Anglo Australians are being recognised and cherished. Minority cultures had survived and managed to thrive — especially among the Chinese, Germans and Italians — despite policies of integration and assimilation. However, they had survived apart from the dominant culture and, because of the apartness, had been ignored.

During the very period in which Australian cultural élites were berating the suburban conservatism of our non-cosmopolitan environment, the Viennese, for example, had created in Sydney — in 1941 — the Viennese Theatre, producing not only fine plays in German with fine acting but also a 'series of bilingual satirical revues which showed Austrian refugees confronting life in Anglo-Australia society and the resulting cultural collisions'.[56] It started regular performances in English, as well as German, following World War II — performances that were reviewed in the mainstream press. That theatre and others were to continue and thrive. Just after World War II the Warrawee home of Fritz Mandl and his sister Mrs Selby because the birthplace of Musica Viva. In 1946 the Wenkarts' 'castle' was founded in Wahroonga, a house that was 'part of the postwar injection of European influence'.[57]

Some immigrants made culture their business. Rudy Komon, a Czech immigrant, opened an art gallery in Sydney in 1958 and became a celebrated patron of and expert on Australian art. Gisella Scheinberg, a Hungarian immigrant, founded the Holdsworth Art Gallery in 1969. Andrew Fabinyi, also Hungarian, became managing director of the publishing houses F.W. Cheshire and Pergamon and was noted for his advocacy of Australian textbooks and publishing — before the advent of the university presses. Fabinyi is an example of multiculturalism in action: he drew on his knowledge of the Hungarian Book Day of pre-war times and introduced the Australian Book Week.[58]

In music, dance and sculpture the embracing of non-Anglos proceeded much more quickly. The lists of names are impressive, and multiculturalism is a reality in that the 'ethnic' aspects of the immigrants and their children merged and blended with their Australian characteristics and add to mainstream culture as a whole. The following names are only examples: among the Austrians were the symphony orchestra conductors Henry Krips and Georg Tinter; in art and sculpture were Herbert Flugelman and Louis Kahan who in 1962 won the Archibald Prize; architect Karl Langer; a leading expressionist painter Leonard Hessing; Tibor Paul is a Hungarian musician, Judy Cassab a Hungarian painter. Hungarian cartoonist and writer George Molnar added joy to post-war Australia. Edouard Borovansky, a Czech who emigrated in 1939, is regarded as the father of Australian ballet. The Bodenwieser Ballet, headed by a leading figure in the world of dance, was caught in Australia by the outbreak of war. The ballet was embraced quickly by the Australian public. By 1941 they had performed in fifty-two towns and 'had become part of the cultural scene . . . contributing something vital to dance in Australia'.[59]

Asian cultures began to be embraced in the 1960s. Sydney University, for example, was teaching Indonesian and Malayan studies in the early 1960s. By the 1980s the Australian National Gallery had such an extensive collection of regional textiles that it published a definitive book on the subject, in conjunction with an exhibition. The Australian ambassador to Laos said that there no collection of Lao textiles in that country, and surprise was expressed that another country should include Laotion textiles in its collection. There is no national collection of Malaysian or regional textiles and, according to an internal Foreign Affairs document of August 1990, the 'students were amazed that Australia had seen fit to gather such a substantial collection as was evident from the book'.

Australian cultural development suffered from colonisation. It suffered for longer than it might have because the 'most enduring forms of colonisation are cultural'.[60] And Australia was colonised twice over: the first time was when the English arrived and brought their values with them; the second was when the cultural cringe developed. The emergence of Australia from its limited imagination was brought about by the shrinking of the tyranny of distance by the jet in the 1950s and later by satellite communications and microchip technologies. The second great change has been the commitment to immigration and multiculturalism and the end of the egalitarian paradox of white Australia.

Notes

1 Patrick O'Farrell, 'Spurious divorce? Religion and Australian culture', *Journal of Religious Studies*, vol. 15, no. 4, 1989, p. 522.
2 *Annual Report of the Sydney Commercial Reading Rooms and Library* (1843).
3 Richard White, *Inventing Australia: Images and Identity*, Allen & Unwin, Sydney, 1981, p. 89.
4 Mary Lord, *Directory of Australian Authors*, National Book Council, Melbourne, 1989.
5 Richard Nile, *The Fiction Industry*, University of Queensland Press, St Lucia, 1994.
6 Thomas Shapcott, *The Literature Board: A Brief History*, University of Queensland Press, St Lucia, 1988.
7 C. Hartley Grattan, *Introducing Australia*, Angus & Robertson, Sydney, 1949, p. 168.
8 David Lowenthal, 'Antipodean and other museums', *Working Papers in Australian Studies*, no. 66, 1991.
9 Ian Reid, *Fiction and the Great Depression in Australia and New Zealand*, Edward Arnold, Melbourne, 1979.
10 Ken Gelder and Paul Salzman, *The New Diversity*, McPhee Gribble/Penguin, Melbourne, 1989.
11 K.S. Inglis, *This is the ABC*, Melbourne University Press, Melbourne, 1983, p. 2
12 Thomas Wood, *Cobbers*, Oxford University Press, Melbourne, 1943, pp. 156–7.
13 Documented in F.K. Crowley (ed.), *Modern Australia in Documents*, Wren, Melbourne, 1973, p. 551.
14 John Arnold, 'Cultivating the armchair reader: The circulating library movement in Melbourne, 1930–1960' in David Walker et al. (ed.), *Books, Readers, Reading*, special issue of, *Australian Cultural History*, vol. 11 1992, pp. 73–5.
15 Geoffrey Serle, *From Deserts the Prophets Come: The Creative Spirit in Australia*, Heinemann, Melbourne, 1973, p. 335.
16 Jan Paterson, *The Future of Australia as an Export Market*, Sir Stanley Unwin Foundation, London, 1989.
17 Hugh Stretton, 'The quality of leading Australians', in *Australia: Terra Incognita*, special issue of *Daedalus*, vol. 113, no. 1, 1985, p. 198.
18 Terry Smith, 'Australian painting', in S.L. Goldberg and F.B. Smith (eds), *Australian Cultural History*, Cambridge University Press, Melbourne, 1988, p. 195.
19 W.D. Rubinstein, 'Men of wealth', in ibid., p. 115.
20 Susan Mitchell, *Tall Poppies*, Penguin, Ringwood, 1984.
21 For a discussion of the argument and response by P.R. Stephensen see Craig Munro, *Wild Man of Letters*, Melbourne University Press, 1984.

22 A.A. Phillips, *The Australian Tradition: Studies in Colonial Culture*, F.W. Cheshire, Melbourne, 1958, pp. 92, 94.
23 George Nadel, *Australia's Colonial Culture: Ideas, Men and Institutions in Mid-Nineteenth Century Eastern Australia*, Harvard University Press, Cambridge, Massachusetts, 1957, pp. 65–6.
24 Richard White, 'Bluebells and fogtown: Australians' first impressions of England, 1860–1950', *Australian Cultural History*, no. 5, 1986, pp. 45–8.
25 C.M.H. Clark, *The People Make the Laws*, Volume 5, *A History of Australia*, Melbourne University Press, Melbourne, 1981, p. 138.
26 Stephen Alomes, *A Nation at Last? The Changing Character of Australian Nationalism*, Angus & Robertson, Sydney, 1988, p. 93.
27 Stuart MacIntyre, 'History, the university and the nation', Trevor Reece Memorial Lecture, London, 1992.
28 P.H. Partridge, 'The Australian universities' in W.V. Aughterson (ed.), *Taking Stock*, F.W. Cheshire, Melbourne, 1953, p. 57.
29 Hugo Wolfsohn, 'The ideology makers' in Henry Mayer (ed.), *Australian Politics: A Reader*, Cheshire, Melbourne, 1966.
30 John Docker, *Australian Cultural Elites*, Angus & Robertson, Sydney, 1974; David Walker, *Dream and Disillusion: A Search for Australian Cultural Identity*, Australian National University Press, Canberra, 1976.
31 See Brian Head and James Walter (ed.), *Intellectual Movements and Australian Society*, Oxford University Press, Melbourne, 1988.
32 Alomes, *A Nation at Last?* p. 255.
33 Richard Nile and Robert Darby, 'Introduction' to Lesbia Harford, *The Invaluable Mystery*, McPhee Gribble/Penguin, Melbourne, 1987.
34 See J.M. Harcourt, *Upsurge* [1934], facsimile edition, University of Western Australia Press, Nedlands, 1986, with Introduction by Richard Nile.
35 R.M. Crawford, 'The Australian national character: Myth and reality', *Journal of World History*, no. 2, 1955, p. 723.
36 Serle, *From Deserts the Prophets Come*, p. 126.
37 See Richard Nile and David Walker, 'Marketing the literary imagination' in Laurie Hergenhan (ed.), *New Literary History of Australia*, Penguin, Ringwood, 1988; also Richard Nile, 'Cartels, capitalism and the Australian book trade' in Albert Moran (ed.), *The Media of Publishing*, special issue, *Continuum*, vol. 4, no. 1, 1990.
38 Prices Surveillance Authority, *Inquiry into the Book Trade* reports 1989 and 1990.
39 Reported in *All About Books*, July 1934, p. 147.
40 Serle, *From Deserts the Prophets Come*, p. 57.
41 Jeanne MacKenzie, *Australian Paradox*, Cheshire, Melbourne, 1961, p. 145.
42 *Sydney Morning Herald*, 16 March 1986.
43 C. Mills, 'The Bookstall novel: An Australian paperback revolution,

1904–1946', in D. Walker et al. (eds), *Books, Readers, Reading*, special issue of *Australian Cultural History*, vol. 11, 1992, pp. 87–8, 96.
44 Jack Beasely, *Red Letter Days: Notes from Inside an Era*, Australasian Book Society, Sydney, 1979, pp. 161–4.
45 Geoffrey Dutton, *Snow on the Saltbush: The Australian Literary Experience*, Penguin, Ringwood, 1984, pp. 231–2.
46 Andrew Taylor, 'From sea to air: The impact of jet travel on Australia's "Australia" ' in Werner Senn and Giovanna Capone (eds), *The Making of a Pluralist Australia*, Peter Lang, Bern, 1993.
47 Russel Ward, *A Nation for a Continent: The History of Australia 1901–1975*, Heinemann, Richmond, 1977, p. 213.
48 A.A. Phillips, 'Australian literature' in W.V. Aughterson (ed.), *Taking Stock: Aspects of Mid-Life in Australia*, Cheshire, Melbourne, 1961.
49 Vance Palmer, *The Legend of the Nineties*, Melbourne University Press, 1954, p. 172.
50 Robert Hughes, 'Painting' in Peter Coleman, *Australian Civilization*, F.W. Chesire, Melbourne, p. 134.
51 Cecil Hadgraft, 'Literature' in A.L. McLeod (ed.), *The Patterns of Australian Culture*, Oxford University Press, Melbourne, 1963, p. 99.
52 Leonie Kramer, 'The media, society and culture', *Australia Terra Incognita*, pp. 304–6.
53 Vincent Buckley, 'Intellectuals' in Coleman, *Australian Civilization*, p. 102.
54 M. Jurgensen, 'Literature and ethnicity' in James Jupp (ed.), *The Australian People: an Encyclopaedia of the Nation, its People and their Origins*, Angus & Robertson, Sydney, 1988, pp. 907–8.
55 C.A. Price, 'Greeks' in ibid., p. 529.
56 M.J. Norst, 'The Austrians', ibid., p. 279.
57 Karl Bittman (ed.), *From Strauss to Matilda: Viennese in Australia 1938–1988*, Wenkart Foundation, Sydney, 1988, p. 298.
58 E.F. Kunz, 'Hungarians', ibid., p. 540.
59 Ibid., pp. 38–40.
60 Graeme Davison cited in Arthur Martin, 'The emigrant public servant', *Australian Journal of Public Administration*, vol. 48, no. 4, 1989, p. 398.

11
STRUTTERS

Chris Wallace-Crabbe

It was the pioneering cultural critic, A.A. Phillips, who coined the phrase *the cultural cringe*, hardly guessing at the time that it would catch on like mad, so that it is by now one of the standard Australian clichés, among cringers and strutters alike. Phillips came from a distinguished family of lawyers and painters; he was educated at one of the most Anglophile of Melbourne's privileged private schools; he taught at another, having majored at university in that assertively named discipline, English. Throughout his life, then, Arthur Phillips was even more aware than most of us of the double moulding pull of the old world and the new — of the culture that came from imported books and that which came from life. He knew something of the decisions Uncle Manny — the painter E. Phillips Fox — had made negotiating the themes, motifs, gestures and colorations of European and British painting to arrive at his lively images of the bourgeoisie, leisured, parasolled, at play beside blue water in wonderfully striped and spotted dresses. No doubt, too, Phillips' Jewish background made him all the more acutely aware of problems of cultural definition, problems to be encountered in relating older, sacred texts to the factual and political present.

The cultural cringe caught on, then, as an explanatory term, as a critical tool and, later, as a cliché. It could be applied to any circumstance in which the new world deferred to the old. It entered the common pot. It could be applied to assumptions in the old Anglophile families or in Germanic music teaching, to the notorious G.H. Cowling who thought that there were no conditions appropriate to the development of an Australian literature, to the Cambridge-oriented arts faculties of the 1950s and 1960s (when few Australian scholars went to America), and to the writers of 1968 who recognised no writing that failed to ape American styles.

It is a blunt tool that can be used for almost anything, anywhere. Is the recent proliferation of literary theory in Australia (described by Andrew Milner in chapter 12, 'Culture') a fresh outgrowth of the cringe, for example? Some would think so. For others the curious mélange or bricolage of French and American ideas is typically post-colonial, even distinctively Australian in juxtaposition — an interesting argument suggested to me by Paul Carter, but which I shall not pursue here.

There is an emphasis that I would share with Carter, however: an obvious one but one that needs frequent repetition as a charm against laziness. It is that Australian culture can never be neatly separated from the myriad threads that have webbed into it from other states and times. There are many complexities of such filiation, which begin to spring to mind if I merely list such categories as Australian democracy, Christianity in Australia, Australian publishing, Australian cricket, Australian Marxists, immigration, spelling, forestry, biochemistry, ethics and history. These things do not have an ocean around them, I am afraid.

Still, our emergence from some perceived model of inferiority to the old countries does not depend on naively merging with them. The irritating proponents of post-modernism are simply wrong if they go so far as to assert that all countries are going to blend in one weakly ironic megaculture, imitative, parodic, rootless, multinational and commodified. Nation states have a need — megapsychic, if you like — to assert their separateness, their perceived individuality.

It is commonly believed now that we have grown beyond the cringe. Perhaps we have passed over it again and again. In a National Arts Week supplement to the Melbourne *Age*, theatre critic Peter Weiniger has expounded on the theme, 'Melbourne theatre passes stage [pun?] of cultural cringe'. His article takes the form of a vigorous response to some nameless lady who has just returned from London, breathless about the quality of West End theatre. Weiniger proceeds to discuss the twenty professional theatre companies working in Melbourne, the quality and range of their productions. His piece is marked by some of that same anxiety that we Australians often evince when talking about the country's 'coming of age' in this or that field and, in the favoured current banality, about Australian being 'flavour of the month' in this or that centre overseas.[1]

The epidemic of this figure of speech over the last few years has been remarkable. The trope itself is an odd one, apparently coming from ice-cream parlour parlance. It does, however, combine perfectly two kinds of Australian usage: exaggeration and irony, surely two of the hallmarks of our popular speech. It is both a boast and a shrug, like the Warholian prospect of being famous for fifteen minutes. In his tauntingly titled article, 'Bad Australian art', Eric Michaels has linked this quaint usage with a thesis about postcolonial anxiety. He begins:

> During 1987 the Australian press reported frequently that Aboriginal Art, especially Western Desert acrylic 'dot paintings', had become flavour of the month in New York, Paris and Munich. Flavour of the month is an odd description Australians over-use to resolve the incompatibility of such reports of Australian success overseas with a cherished and characteristic myth of the second rate, sometimes labelled cultural cringe. Indeed Australia now has a suspiciously elaborate terminology for identifying the contradictions of colonialism and creativity. The notion of radical unoriginality is claimed to privilege this discourse, so that Sydney for example now asserts itself as the most dislocated, imitative, unoriginal, and therefore, *postmodern* city (which only goes to show that Sydneysiders never make it north to Brisbane).[2]

Whatever the full implications of the 'flavour of the month', its use does typify an ever-louder insistence on the part of Australian commentators that, yes, our arts *are* being noticed overseas. Of course this is in part justified. The success of our previously minimal film industry has kick-started an awareness of Australian themes and images in many overseas countries, many places that used to perceive Australians as sportsmen and sportswomen, first of all.

Regional anxiety can respond to the liveliness of, say, our film industry, that shining light in the gloom of the 1980s and 1990s, by worrying once again whether our other products are distinctive enough. Thus, another *Age* article was headed 'Australian style: Does it exist? If not, why not? And does anybody care?', thus having its cake, chucking it away and eating it all at the same time.[3]

Generalisations about our country, its values and attitudes, are based on communal self-consciousness. And this is not a bad thing.

Without self-consciousness, how would any of us ever know anything of significance? For Australians, the problem is often this: just how should a country of our size, our population and our history behave? The cultural templates of our upbringing — which might have been Greece and Rome, Britain, France, perhaps the United States — will seldom have been a good fit. There are some countries — Canada and Argentina — that resemble us spatially; in population we are comparable with, say, Holland, Chile, Malaysia, we are somewhat less than Canada, vastly more than New Zealand, and we seldom compare ourselves with either, for all the cultural similarities of our condition.

Alan Davies categorised our problems and — as he saw it — our lack of confidence under the head of 'small country blues'.[4] In his oft-quoted and frequently recontextualised poem, 'Australia', A.D. Hope wickedly depicted our big cities as seedbeds of 'second-hand Europeans'.[5] A land that is also a continent teases the imagination. So does the fact that our Aboriginal predecessors and fellow citizens appear to have inhabited this enormous space for about three hundred times the two hundred years that white culture has. The European word *Australia* cannot usefully refer to that 60,000 years. We must save it for the new nation state. The problem, then, is that so many of the fascinatingly distinctive features of Our Place spring from the older times. It is easy to feel that we have added very little.

A sense that we have indeed added very much in the last decades of the twentieth century emerges strongly if one turns to Peter Coleman's imaginative 1962 anthology, *Australian Civilisation*. His book seems to have sprung from a small, anxious Australia, whether in such enthusiastic essays as those by Robert Hughes and James McAuley — both of them mapping a cultural production that now seems unrecognisable — or Vincent Buckley's rather superior put-down of bourgeois intellectuals. A few of the best chapters — Ken Inglis on the press and Sol Encel on power — have not dated, and we can all still brood over A.A. Phillips' conclusion that the 'Australian teacher is never quite sure whether he wants to sting his pupils into the dissatisfaction which is most readily receptive of a European culture, or whether he wants to accept and encourage the achievements of happiness', in which the only quaint note is the assumption that a school teacher will be male.

Coleman's volume is of great historical interest. It is a belated product of the 1950s, that great decade of reborn Australian nationalism. Its anxieties record shadows that were already falling across the prosperous post-war nation. Thus, Max Harris concluded his chapter with questions about the arrival of the 'admass age', fearing that 'Within this large arena national culture may have only a fragile and unremarkable existence'.[6] He might be surprised at how confidently, in many areas, Australia has survived transnational bullying and how noisily it has moved into the next post-colonial stage — that of guilty nationalism.

In *Ideas for a Nation*, Donald Horne has written:

> Of the modern-industrial societies, Australia belongs to the subset of the post-colonial. It was not only born modern. It was born colonial. It is crazy to feel any peculiar inferiority or shame about this, and equally crazy not to recognise it.[7]

His book is properly complicated and argumentative, unlike some of the simple generalisations offered by expatriates who no longer know what is going on in Australia — often at the request of Australians who *want* to hear stirring simplifications about their country from star-encrusted expatriates. Let me add that some expatriates, Clive James being a sparkling example, do take care to observe, think, note and carefully analyse the phenomena of home on which they are passing comment. But comments as off the top of the head as Shirley Hazzard's lazy remarks about Australian philistinism in her Boyer lectures (1988) have the kind of broad newsworthiness that will always get a response somewhere.[8] And, in defence even of Hazzard's excesses, one may turn to the psychologically intriguing remark in Katharine Gallagher's 'London Letter' of the Bicentennial year: 'It is quite diverting to "imagine" your own Australia. School children and teachers do it all the time. Expatriates do it of necessity.'[9] Sweet are the uses of necessity.

Of course, there is another good reason why our *émigrés* come up from time to time with utterances that we find at once harsh and cringing. Often they have lived for years in a country with a larger population and a more brutal clout, with the result that they feel obliged to remind their homeland that it is only a Belgium or a Norway in their eyes. Population as essential power is a knot that political sociologists and psychopoliticos would do well to explicate further. Also the question: in what ways can nations manifest cultural power without the employment of gunboat diplomacy?

And, as soon as I use the phrase *cultural power*, we are brought back to a phenomenon that is inescapable in the modern ecumene. Such power is gained by the association of the produce with the name of a particular nation state. Certain nations — France and Canada — put a great deal of energy into this business of giving their products national identification — every French thinker wears a little tricolour. And writers who are deracinated will commonly have trouble in building for themselves a Fame-coloured Career, a Name. Think of the trouble Christina Stead experienced in establishing who and what she was.

Most of our models for what is happening in a country's modern history are constructed on a surf-like sinusoidal curve, a manic-depressive undulation. The troughs are periods of depression, recession, colonialism or cringe; the peaks, high times of independence, boom, strut or 'coming of age'. Recurrent accounts of our economy have become the tail that wags the dog that wags the country. Repeated warnings about our adverse balance of payments, our gross deficit, our lack of technological inventiveness, our *retardataire* dependence on the export of raw materials, these have progressively shaken our self-confidence. In a rapid turn-around of assumptions, our Labor governments have striven to be drier than Mrs Thatcher, or to take a leaf from Japan's book, or from Singapore's: in each case plucking the desired effects from *part* of an alien economy while ignoring those aspects of the other society which are unlike their own, even thoroughly undesirable.

Australians have been trying to cope with this economic angst for some years now, introjecting the warnings of crisis, having nowhere to turn politically, since socialists and conservatives are offering virtually the same policies and since there is no longer any communist threat to help the latter lot back into government. Before he became prime minister our federal treasurer described the country as in danger of becoming a 'banana republic'. A typical newspaper comment, full of economic cringe, was the *Weekend Australian* for 12–13 August 1989, headed, 'What the world really thinks of our economy'.

Sometimes the shock tactics in our business pages flaunt their own brand of boastful strut. Thus Terry McCrann, passing judgement on the collapse of the Alan Bond financial empire, wrote:

> This will be by far the biggest collapse in Australia's corporate history, and quite possibly the biggest collapse anywhere in the world. Losses will run into hundreds of millions, and quite possibly billions of dollars.[10]

But McCrann is hardly an optimist. Nor is he a nationalist. The zest of his utterance is that of someone giving a schoolboy six of the best or at least a large spoonful of cod liver oil. Such doses of punishment are by now a regular part of economic life. And very few indeed are those who are willing to look at our problems laterally, independently, from an entirely new angle. A rare example is that very distinguished thinker, Hugh Stretton, who recommended a complete about-turn of policy and the re-regulation of the Australian economy. I do not know if there was any response from the admired and much-hated Paul Keating — although at his 1993 victory speech he spoke of the 'true believers' and something of a return to Australian values while reminding his personal staff about that powerful mix of 'econocrats and bleeding hearts'.

The checks and balances of a national psyche are like those of an individual. We purchase our freedoms by way of our repressions. We build our confidence on a foundation provided out of our traumata. As Freud assumed, there are many ways in which the psyche has laws paralleling the operation of the physical laws in a closed system. This, no doubt, is one of the reasons why Australians cry up the quality of their creative arts so loudly. If our economy is crook, our sporting teams patchy — except, thank God, for swimming and rugby — and our manufacturers in staggering disarray, if there is drought in the heartland, it is still possible to point proudly to the arts — a field in which quality cannot be measured.

In his *Little Organon for Theatre*, the irrepressible Bertold Brecht complained of German culture that 'with us even materialism is abstract'. In Australia, as is right and proper for the Antipodes, the opposite impulse prevails; solid practice being preferable to ivory steeples of theory, number-crunching to pure mathematics, engineering to physics and the carrot of administration leading the donkey of research. Art is also valued far above theory, but I shall come back to that. And it is no accident that the philosophical movement for which Australia is internationally known is brain physicalism, a movement at least as sceptical as Gilbert Ryle was, and one that presses to reduce psychic or intellectual phenomena to their material bases. I should add that Australian philosophy is also famous for its contribution to animal liberation, a deeply moral concern for the complex fate of wordless creatures. I prefer to draw no conclusions from this.

In reviewing a book on intellectual life in Australia, Judith Brett drew attention to the broad streak of pragmatism and materialism in our thoughts. She observed that one of the chapters

> highlights the dominance of positivist forms of knowledge in the social sciences in Australia over more critical and humanist traditions in sociology and psychology. The sociology that flourished here was the sociology useful to governments in their solutions of practical problems . . . The pragmatic social scientist advising the government is a more typical Australian intellectual than wide-ranging, European-style critic.[11]

From intellectual life — how *could* intellectual life be general? asked the caterpillar — let us turn back to art culture, to those kinds of imaginative creation commonly dignified as 'creative'. These include many of the phenomena modern Australia tends to be particularly proud of: films, painting, some novels, more poetry, immigrants' writing, recent short stories and an expanding proliferation of writing by Kooris. Even taken together these constitute a narrow version of the word *culture*, but I will continue to concentrate on these things of 'high' culture because their status in Australia is distinctive.

Some years ago I quoted in an article Clive James' description of Australia as a 'land gone mad about art', and I want to use it once again as a peg to pitch my tent. It is a cheeky comment but contains a hard nut of truth. Australian life is marked with, or divided by, a modern version of court culture. It is a diffused Antipodean Urbino, an Esterhazy kangaroo court, the pomp and glitter of Versailles without *le Roi Solei* — we have the sunshine but the king's gone bush.

Of course there is some exaggeration in this little string of tropes but they are all gesturing at the same phenomenon: the peculiar post-religious prestige that many Australians allow the arts. Painting, especially, is a focus of fashionable and influential society in a way that would be unimaginable in Britain. There is a fine novel by Melbourne writer Janine Burke, entitled *Company of Images*, which deals with this peculiar social power of the visual arts and its ramifications in various lives. To be a successful painter, film-maker or actor is to be at the visible centre of Australian cultural life. Like athletes or footballers, they deal in visible achievement — in Australia the eye is far more important than the ear.

Let me look back to the question: why do Australians invest so much pride in their élite art productions, in the arts generally? One reason has been suggested: the economy of hope required a bullish area to balance our bearish economy. The Bicentenary was another trigger; on such a pompous occasion one finds things to boast and swagger about — quantity, quality and comings of age.

There is another, more objective, ground for this kind of pride. All of us who are in our middle years can remember a time when the Australian books in a good bookshop would be presented on one small table, all the others being filtered through English methods of cultural control. Now the bookshops, and even the better suburban newsagents, stock a wide array of Australian titles, all the way from literary solids to ephemeral chuckles. Parallels can be felt between this and the rise, *ex nihilo*, of an Australian film industry. In the late 1960s I wrote that local audiences would titter nervously if local suburbs were actually recognised in a film. A little later I had a walk-on, actually a dance-on, part in the first local feature film to have been made for years. Now they can be seen everywhere, in the cinemas, on TV or by way of the local video shop. As a result, the very nature of *film* in our consciousness has altered, and it can be used to understand ourselves.

Again, overemphasis and skiting are ways of striking out if staking our a bold claim for our belated culture in the teeth of great powers — both living powers and the heavy legions of the dead. Australians might 'overdo it' as a way of slouching lairily through the nightmare of history. To barrack loudly is to forget the millstones round your neck. Hence the visible and audible excess that Barry Humphries has sketched in his one-liner: 'In Australia we've got culture up to our freckles.' To prove that you have high culture is to stand up courageously to Europe and to vanquish America, a nation we are in danger of resembling if we do not stand up for ourselves. And since modern works of art are by definition New they are precisely what we call for to represent a new country against the threatening parental authority of the old world. Paintings and poems are our rollerblades and Heavy Metal. Often, too, we underwrite this sense of being young and new by boasting of something we call vitality in our own productions — a human body is commonly the template for the leviathan culture.

Alan Davies sees how far this show of overconfidence can be the product of two kinds of division. The first is the

> imbalance and tension between imported and local ideas. Cultural rifts of portentous depth and sharpness open up between a corps of

importers of ideas which live like merchants exacting their percentage from the knowledge products they bring in and render fit for local distribution, and a corps of loyal protectionists, who buy the locally-made for preference and mock their adversaries' abject 'Cultural Cringe'.

This is a social division, in short: a demarcation between the universalists and the parochials, the deconstructors and the barbecue set. Often the former group includes academics, avid for an imaginary Paris or New Haven, for a platonic, papery, squeaky-clean Oxford or Berkeley. And the protectionists can easily be dismissed as blinkered and reactionary. Nationalism is often a dirty word.

Davies goes on and upward to say:

However, a genuine pathos lies behind the ritual jousting, a chronic and painful doubt about the achievable quality of life in a small country. In part this is just the modern burden that Simmel detected in the 'over-growth of objective culture', the oppressive weight of the sheer mass of cultural objects and artifacts already in existence set against our limited capacity to learn about, master, or meaningfully assimilate them. So each new generation everywhere — and not merely the small country's — finds itself torn between an 'empty too much' (a wild dash to crop; hurried, skewed choice; an inability to say 'no' to any new fad) and a 'pure too little' (hanging back; staying loose; resignation to one's restrictive niche and its harsh filters).[12]

So, in the post-colonial consciousness, there is also a psychic division. Not only do we recognise our peers as belonging to one or other of opposing parties, but also we recognise those parties — or their psychic analogues — warring within ourselves. And such an anxiety in the psyche has the effect that we can find in other kinds of neurosis: compulsion to overstate the case, to make too large a claim, to swagger, to strut.

Other grounds come to mind. For example, the Australia Council, modelled in some ways on the Canada Council, has played a brightly visible part in funding and foregrounding the arts, in pressing for the recognition of their necessity, in 'protectionism'. Its achievement is striking. In an interview Sandra Forbes, newly appointed director of the council's literature unit, discussed the council's contribution to a scene in which 'We've achieved enormous recognition in the past twenty years, in all the Australian arts'. After pointing out that there were about twenty novels published in Australia in 1973 as against 300 in 1988 (annus mirabilis!), she goes on: 'We live in a country where all the statistics seem to show that people want the arts. But it's government-provided.'[13] Looking from another, ironic, angle the avant-garde writer Chris Mann sportively observed:

> The Australia Council's aggressive pursuit of mediocrity is not in and of itself a bad thing. It does maintain our links to a subscriber magazine culture . . . It does maintain a surrogate free expression/ free enterprise model. It does guarantee a market. It does mean that we can compete.[14]

Either way, the government-subsidy model is intrinsic.

Another slant: anyone who — like myself — has taken children overseas from Australia and enrolled them for a time in British or American schools might well have been struck by how little emphasis is placed on the creative arts in those school systems, as against the Australian norm.

I can particularly vouch for this in the case of Victorians travelling OS. The Victorian education system places a good deal of stress from the earliest years on such activities as drama, music, 'creative' writing, art and even a primitive kind of publishing. The Victorian Department of Education is still powerfully driven by seventiesish principles of education for leisure. Indeed, many of us are inclined to believe that recycled hippies run the department. In the 1970s, we should remember, Australia began to have significant unemployment for the first time in forty years. Educational policies were progressively developed on this basis to ensure that burgeoning generations would have the leisure skills, the self-motivating depths, to cope with the changed circumstances in which unemployment, part-time employment or early retirement would cast people back on themselves. These policies are still in place. There is a wide gap between the populist idealism of education in Victoria and the mean-hearted reality principle of federal authorities. (Neither of them, let me add, has managed to stem the decay of science teaching in Australia.)

It will be noted that many of the factors I am discussing turn on government policies, government initiatives. A small population in a gigantic land must always look yearningly towards the generous hand of government. Most Australians have grown up with a belief, which I still firmly hold, that — food and clothing aside — essentials are provided for us by the public sector, luxuries by the private sector. Given such a belief, I can extract no joy from privatisation and look on in horror when Labor governments take Thatcherite aridity as one of their models.

None of us can write a definitive history of the future, of course. But now, the pragmatic Federal Government has insisted more and more on bureaucratically draconian categories of relevance — the big dry skills — so that we keep seeing the gap I mentioned between federal Dawksquark and existing patterns of education around the country. No doubt Canberra has the final capacity to crack the whip, a whip made of purse-strings, and the art–leisure imperatives of the state systems will be, in Henry Lawson's words, 'educated down'. There you go, then; and here we go too. But it does seem a grave pity to see a volatile education pattern shifting from the arts and sciences over to accounting and computer technology. We live in a guided democracy of discourse systems. Auden wrote, long ago, that 'Time will say nothing but I told you so', but only time will tell us what it was that worked and to what end.

I have failed to mention one additional factor causing the overvaluation of cultural products. This is the emergence since the late 1970s of promotional hype. New books, however mediocre, tend on the American model to arrive with interviews, broadcasts, published extracts, fancy blurbs and all the trimmings. The flummery deluge can be persuasive and/or intimidating, with the result that reviewers slide into believing much of it. Clearly, Australian reviewers are timid about passing judgement. The review pages of the Saturday and Sunday papers can be as uniformly approbatory as the *New York Times Book Review*. Too often one reads them and groans, muttering, 'Not *another* great novel, this week, as well!'

All this blandness and optimism has been criticised, especially from the right. P.P. McGuinness, for instance, claims: 'The basic problem is that there's been an enormous increase in the output of writing in Australia, but most of it is of pretty low quality; the fiction and the non-fiction both.'[15] And Greg Sheridan links inflated literary reputations to Australia's insecure cultural élite.[16] Sheridan also links this insecurity to the development of restrictive ghettos of Australian studies in universities. I agree with this as a potential danger but would reply, as the director of an Australian studies outfit myself, that there is no need at all for Australian studies to be thin and weedy. It should be free to deal with the reception of Bartok or Shakespeare in Australia, with sociology or cosmology, with international law, with intellectual transmissions of Wittgenstein or of Derrida, with feminist discourse theory.

Both the debates over education and discussion of the creative arts in Australia — painting especially — raise questions about standards, quality, judgement. Stroppy conservatives are fond of quoting Allan Bloom's *The Closing of the American Mind*, that wilful curate's egg of a book. They have their eyes narrowed not only against sloppy, rawhide-and-stringybark Australian artiness but also against the feminist–Marxist–semiotic hegemony in the arts faculties of Australian universities. Their objection to these academic theorists is partly based on a presumption of radicalism but also on the fact that the academic theorists hold that there can be no such thing as quality, only the ever-restless interactions of power-seeking discourse systems.

This is one point on our journey at which the cultural importers meet up with the enthusiastic protectionists. Both theorists and the barbecue set undermine canons (by some crude pun, canons are held to be masculine), critical preferences, moral interpretations, all manifestations of value-based judgement. Any book, however stupid or incompetent, is evidence of something or other, and bad books, because of their flat crudity, are far easier to write about. From a small, flat materialist base, you can erect a theoretical superstructure as grandiose as Xanadu, as vertiginous as the Hanging Gardens of Babylon, as discursive as the Tower of Babel.

It is not only from the right that doubts about our high-flying self-valuations have been expressed. In his Barry Andrews Memorial Lecture for 1989, the historian Geoffrey Serle offered his considered 'Ruminations on Australia and the arts over fifty years'. After describing the recent proliferation of artistic production, Serle goes on to sound a warning note. His critical tone is the more striking because it occurs in an account of Australian life and culture which is marked by Serle's old Fabian optimism and which perceives the society as tolerant, kindly and peaceful, a view I broadly share. Serle writes:

> In no country ever, possibly, has it been easier to be published; we readers are flooded, and the mediocre tend to drive out the good: nevertheless, one able reviewer in a broad survey of fiction in 1988 joyfully praised all 35 books. Only a very few more writers make a decent living. Leaving aside recent vicious attacks on Australian writing by ignorant journalists, among writers and critics there is a growing concern . . . that some writers are grossly over-praised and

have bubble reputations . . . in general I fear that many of our novelists lack not intelligence but breadth, as well as the narrative gift. I particularly regret that not many have much to say on the great universal issues and especially the state of Australia. If so, *why* is a big question: one possibly demoralising answer is that most of the novelists have had too narrow an education, have not read enough, have not knocked around enough in the world.[17]

There we are, then, unquestionably Australians, held firmly in our place by history and by geography. Our sociological character might change — take, for example, the way our population was significantly Europeanised after World War II, then significantly Asianised after the Vietnam War. Our policies might change, in immigration and education, and our power relations might change in ways that include economic subservience to Japan and bemused astonishment at the economic success of western Europe. But we are locked into our Australian identities incorporating male and female, Aboriginal, immigrant and Anglo, young and old. As Kay Schaffer writes in her sharply critical study, *Women and the Bush* (1989):

> The impulse to find a national identity arises out of man's desire, a desire to know origins, beginnings and endings. It proceeds through an assertion of national character which has a history, a presence, a voice, a landscape of values, and evolving tradition. This construction functions as a principle of national unity which protects the national character and a complete identification with England, on the one hand, and a complete fragmentation into culture without distinction, on the other.[18]

For Schaffer the danger inherent in this impulse is a tendency to masculinist reading, its often tacit urge to see both the land and women as the 'Other'.

However, women as well as men share this desire to find something distinctly Australia that helps to name *them* and will protect their personal and communal identities from compete fragmentation. Judith Wright, in an early poem, apostrophises 'your delicate dry breasts, country that built my heart', in a line that could otherwise be read as masculinist and feels her identity as constructed out of Australian places, Australian discourse: 'South of my days' circle/I know it dark against the stars, the lean high country/full of old stories that still go walking in our sleep'.[19]

Like most countries in the world, Australia is vulnerable to the cultural imperialism of the United States; like other English-speaking countries, acutely vulnerable. The vulnerability of our publishing companies to multinationals or to hard pruning in a time of recession has painfully underlined this. One often feels that it is suicidal not to be nationalistic; it is passively to will one's own annihilation.

A good deal of post-colonial theory merely advocates passivity. Such definitions of post-colonial discourse see it as inevitably subject to the economic and material coercion of the great powers and its modes, therefore, as merely ludic: parody, imitation, collage, bricolage or lampoon. It is no accident that such theorists are often hostile to nationalism. They are Davies' 'importers', ideologically employed by the Great Powers whose causal force they in fact admire. The 'protectionists' might look naive by international standards, whatever *that* means, but they are correct in knowing they have something substantial to protect. They know that overstatement, even a show of overconfidence, is the only way out.

In the long run nobody can show us what is the proper degree of confidence for a recently developed nation of not quite seventeen million people to display. Countries that we resemble in population, like Sri Lanka, are historically too different; while the civilisations on which we have been educated — Rome, Great Britain, fifth-century Athens and the children of Israel — all exercised kinds of power, coercive authority and discursive priority that Australia can never emulate. There is no book of etiquette to which we can turn. And our becoming a minimalist republic will solve very few problems, if any.

I hope that Australians could believe passionately in the products of their own civilisation, in the best products, that is. In short, I am all for an intense confidence in what sustained discrimination has suggested as the most vivid, acute, fresh, complex and memorable works of the Australian imagination. They rejustify the nation's existence. And above all, they feed back into it.

Notes

1 Peter Weiniger, 'Melbourne theatre passes stage of cultural cringe', *Age*, 7 October 1989.
2 Eric Michaels, 'Bad Australian art', *Art and Text*, no. 28, 1988, p. 59.
3 'Australian style: Does it exist?' *Age*, 26 September 1989.
4 Alan Davies, 'Small country blues', *Meanjin*, no. 2, 1985, pp. 244–5.
5 A.D. Hope, 'Australia', 1939.
6 Robert Hughes, 'Painting'; James McAuley, 'Literature and the arts'; K.S. Inglis, 'The daily papers'; Sol Encel, 'Power'; A.A. Phillips, 'The

schools'; Max Harris, 'Morals and manners', all in Peter Coleman (ed.), *Australian Civilisation*, F.W. Cheshire, Melbourne, paperback edition, 1963.
7 Donald Horne, *Ideas for a Nation*, Pan, Sydney, 1989, p. 151.
8 Shirley Hazzard, *Postscripts*, Boyer Lectures, ABC, 1988.
9 Katharine Gallagher, 'London letter', *Overland*, no. 3, 1988, p. 78.
10 Terry McCrann, *Sunday Herald*, 31 December 1989.
11 Judith Brett, review of *Intellectual Movements and Australian Society* (B. Head and J. Walter, eds, OUP, Melbourne, 1988), *Island*, no. 70, 1988, p. 71.
12 Davies, 'Small country blues', pp. 244–5.
13 *Age Extra*, 1989.
14 Chris Mann, *The Rationalist*, self-published, Melbourne, 1986.
15 P.P. McGuinness, *Airways* (Qantas in-flight magazine), November/December 1989.
16 Greg Sheridan, *Weekend Australian*, 13–14 January 1990.
17 Geoffrey Serle, 'Ruminations on Australia and the arts over fifty years', *Notes and Furphies*, 1989.
18 Kay Schaffer, *Women and the Bush*, Cambridge University Press, Melbourne, 1989, p. 24.
19 Judith Wright, 'South of my days', 1946.

12
CULTURE

Andrew Milner

The classic account of the historical evolution of the term *culture* and of the culturalist tradition is Raymond Williams' *Culture and Society*. Williams argued that in the nineteenth century the concept of 'culture' increasingly emerged as an 'abstraction and an absolute', merging two distinct responses:

> first, the recognition of the practical separation of certain moral and intellectual activities from the driven impetus of the new kind of society; second, the emphasis of these activities, as a court of human appeal, to be set over the process of practical social judgement and yet to offer itself as a mitigating and rallying alternative.[1]

Culture was originally a noun of process referring to the tending of crops and animals, and it was only in the late eighteenth and early nineteenth centuries that it developed into an independent noun referring to a distinctly human world of values, which would become increasingly counterposed to that equally human, but less humane, realm of 'civilisation', defined as encompassing essentially the worlds of economics and politics.[2]

Culture thus understood, that is, as separate from and yet superior to both economics and politics, was initially the creation of European Romanticism. At one level the term clearly denotes the arts and perhaps especially literature: 'Poets are the unacknowledged legislators of the world', wrote Shelley.[3] But the importance of art, and the ultimate legislative power of poetry, reside in their status as expressions of the distinctive 'spirit' of a people, very often especially the people understood as 'folk'. Which is why art as culture becomes counterposed to the mechanism of industrial civilisation. This social sense of the term continues to inform twentieth-century literary humanisms.

From Arnold on, English culturalism decisively opted for the nation-state-sponsored system of education as the mechanism by which culture could be preserved and extended and as the centre of resistance to the driving imperatives of an increasingly mechanical and materialist civilisation.[4] In the late nineteenth century and even more so in the twentieth, this culturalist discourse became institutionalised in Australia within the academic discipline we now know as 'English'. English literature justified itself as a discipline essentially in terms of its contribution to the maintenance of a unitary English national culture. It was thus inextricably connected both to the development of modern English nationalism and to that of its wider imperial extension, Greater British imperial nationalism.

Nationality, it is now widely agreed, is not so much a matter of natural 'fact' as a form of collective imagining. A nation, in Benedict Anderson's phrase, is an 'imagined political community . . . imagined as both inherently limited and sovereign'.[5] And professional intelligentsias have, of course, been central to the design of such imaginings. Whatever its ultimate fate, the imagined community of the Greater British imperial nation came to exercise considerable sway over late nineteenth-century Australian society. It was this notion of the imperial nation and its language and literature that inspired much of the initial development of English studies in Australia. The key figure here is almost certainly Sir Mungo MacCallum, who held the chair of modern literature at the University of Sydney from 1887 until 1921 and succeeded in transforming it into what became, in effect, Australia's first chair of English literature. MacCallum pioneered the development of extension classes. He founded and became first and only life president of the Sydney branch of Sir Henry Newbolt's English Association. His career, a successor would recall, came to represent 'his main and conscious offering to the labours of empire'.[6]

The central intellectual influence over the subsequent professionalisation of English studies was undoubtedly Leavisism. Contemporary debate tends to treat the Leavises unkindly, not only as irascibly mistaken but also as of merely 'historical' interest, essentially figures from the 1930s.[7] But F.R. Leavis didn't actually die until 1978, Q.D. Leavis until three years later, and both continued to write and publish during the 1970s. Their notion of culture is quintessentially 'culturalist'. It is the 'knowledge of basic human need that is transmitted by . . . "cultural tradition" '.[8] Culture is a 'third realm', neither private nor public, but the collaborative creation of a whole community. Thus understood, culture is also necessarily singular: 'We have no other; there is only one, and there can be no substitute.'

The inspirational effect of the Leavises' work should not be underestimated. Leavisism provided a powerful sense of purpose for English teachers in schools and universities alike, in Australia as in England, for much of the 1950s and 1960s. The key figure here was S.L. Goldberg, Professor of English by turn at the Universities of Sydney and Melbourne, and longstanding editor of the *Critical Review*, itself an often enthusiastically Leavisite journal. Kathy MacDermott's analysis of first-year university examiners' comments has shown that, even as late as the early 1970s, English studies at Melbourne was still clearly dominated by a distinctively Leavisite 'ideologeme'.[9] Uldiz Ozolins has argued persuasively that Victorian Higher School Certificate examiners' reports betray evidence of a similarly Leavisite ethos.[10]

For the Leavises, as for their predecessors, English studies had remained a fundamentally nationalist enterprise. Such nationalism informed the discipline's central organising device, that of the national literary 'canon' or 'tradition', as also F.R. Leavis' own improbable affirmation of the non-arbitrary nature of the English linguistic sign.[11] In England itself this nationalism continued powerfully to underwrite the emotional and intellectual appeal of English studies. Such appeal was very obviously much less generally effective in Australia. And, as is well known, at the University of Sydney in particular an older dilettantish liberal humanism combined with a local variant of American New Criticism so as powerfully to obstruct Goldberg's Leavisite intentions.[12] But MacCallum's heirs continued in their imperial labours none the less. As *Windows onto Worlds*, a 1987 Australian Government report on higher education, was to discover, English was then still a very much less 'Australianised' discipline than geography, sociology, political science or anthropology.[13] The discipline's initial construction, as 'English' rather than as 'literature' or 'modern literature' or 'comparative literature', had left it mortgaged to its earlier imperial ideological underpinnings. Little wonder, then, that Australian university English departments have remained one of the last important British garrisons east of Suez.

The culturalist tradition had clearly embraced in one important register a deeply conservative reaction against capitalist modernity but in another a profoundly radical aspiration to go beyond that modernity. If English studies has represented the characteristically conservative form of Australian culturalism, then its radical obverse has been nationalist cultural criticism. Such radical nationalisms relocated both the national community itself and the national literary canon to which it would bear witness, away from an imperial past and toward a liberal–democratic or even socialistic future, away from England and towards Australia.

From the 1890s until the 1970s Australian cultural studies remained organised around an apparently enduring structural opposition between an Anglophile 'imperial' literary criticism located in the university English departments and a radical nationalist cultural criticism located initially in local journalism, later within the subdiscipline of Australian history. The ultimate fate of Greater British imperial nationalism is now no longer a matter for reasonable doubt. That of Australian radical nationalist cultural criticism remains to be seen. In the 1990s it appears to enjoy official patronage and sponsorship by Labor governments, in particular, but also in the wider debates over republicanism. Moreover, it shares with the older Leavisite criticism a whole set of underlying culturalist theoretical assumptions, which could facilitate its importation into the literary–critical academy.

Resistance to radical nationalism remains formidable. Furthermore, the radical nationalist challenge to literary studies has been consistently overshadowed in recent years and, as it were, out-radicalised by a set of often self-consciously cosmopolitan, intellectual alternatives: those represented theoretically by western Marxism, structuralism, post-structuralism and post-colonial theory; politically by second-wave feminism and 'ethnic' multiculturalism.

'Cultural studies' as currently constructed in Australia is itself theoretically indebted to another British prototype, especially to the work of the Birmingham Centre for Contemporary Cultural Studies. As Graeme Turner, a founding editor of the *Australian Journal of Cultural Studies* and key figure in the development of cultural studies at the University of Queensland, puts it: 'the Birmingham Centre . . . can justifiably claim to be the key institution in the history of the field'.[14] British cultural studies provided the occasion for a sustained encounter between an earlier tradition of

English 'literary' criticism on the one hand and a variety of French structuralist and more generally 'continental' western Marxist and sociological traditions on the other. It has often been alleged that the fundamental difference between such English 'culturalisms' and French structuralisms was essentially that between, respectively, an atheoretical empiricism and an aprioristic theoreticism.[15] This seems to misconstrue the situation. For, no matter how apparently 'empirical' its particular reference points, British culturalism, as much as French structuralism, remains irretrievably 'theoretical' in nature.

The cultural politics of the early Australian New Left had borne more than a passing resemblance to the 'left culturalism' of Raymond Williams and historian E.P. Thompson, albeit with a distinctly radical nationalist inflection. The central Australian figure here is Ian Turner. A slightly younger generation of New Left scholars, shaped by the student movement and by the politics of the Vietnam War, found its own theoretical inspiration elsewhere, in the successive translations into English during the late 1960s and the early 1970s of the key works of the major western Marxist thinkers, Gramsci and Lukacs in particular. Despite Knight and Wilding's *Radical Reader* (1977), the disciplinary focus for these newer Marxisms was provided, initially at least, not so much by English studies as by history and politics; witness the work of Humphrey McQueen (1970) and Alastair Davidson (1977).[16]

As the 1970s proceeded, however, New Left Marxism found a second home in the newer disciplines of sociology, women's studies, Australian studies and cultural studies. Perhaps the most significant figure here was Bob Connell, Professor of Sociology at Macquarie University from 1976 to 1992, whose work combined a political commitment to Australian nationalism and the Australian Labor Party with an intellectual commitment to the more explicitly humanist themes in both radical sociology and western Marxism. Connell's interest in 'sex, class and culture', as the subtitle of an influential collection of essays defined itself, clearly fed into the work of each of these 'new' disciplines.[17] More cosmopolitan appropriations of culturalist Marxism informed the work of the social theory journal, *Thesis Eleven*, especially as it became more obviously indebted to Agnes Heller and Ferenc Feher, both former students of Lukacs and both resident in Melbourne during the early 1980s. Significant and scholarly contributions to contemporary debates in neo-Marxist cultural and social theory have been made by Australian associates of this émigré 'Budapest school': Pauline Johnson's *Marxist Aesthetics* (1984), for example, John Rundell's *Origins of Modernity* (1987) and David Roberts' *Art and Enlightenment* (1991). As for *Thesis Eleven* itself, it has reproduced the characteristic themes and preoccupations of western European 'critical theory' much more accurately than has any other journal in Australia.

The term *ideology*, as distinct from quasi-culturalist conceptions such as hegemony, was effectively reintroduced into western cultural theory only through Althusserian structural Marxism and especially through Althusser's influential essay 'Ideology and ideological state apparatuses' (1971). Contemporary debate has dealt with Althusser almost as unkindly as with the Leavises, although perhaps with better reason. As Elizabeth Grosz recalls, 'he murdered his wife — a well-known feminist. He never came to trial but was hospitalised. His name is consequently rarely mentioned today, and always in hushed tones'.[18]

Althusserianism entered Australian radical intellectual life initially by way of the Marxist journal *Intervention*. It exercised a considerable fascination not only for Marxists but also for very many feminists and perhaps especially for those working in sociology. Althusser's exclusion from intellectual respectability after 1980 resulted in a kind of ritualised 'significant absence' of his name from subsequent Marxian and feminist texts. These none the less very often still bear the clear impress of the theory of ideology in its more or less Althusserian form. That there is some substance to the position seems more than probable. Our society and our culture are irreparably marked by divisions of class and gender, and these are repressed by unitary conceptions of culture.

The notion of ideology remains flawed, none the less, by its insistent reduction of problems of value to matters of class or gender interest or, in the more strictly Althusserian formulation, to those of the social reproduction of social inequalities of class and gender. It is not that such interests are irrelevant; it is only that culture entails a great deal more than this. As Raymond Williams observes:

> cultural tradition and practice are ... much more than superstructural expressions ... of a formed social and economic structure. On the contrary, they are among the basic processes of the social formation itself and, further, related to much wider areas of reality than the abstractions of 'social' and 'economic' experience.[19]

Structuralist and semiotic theoretical motifs became current in Australia only in the early to mid 1970s, and they did so, initially at least, by way of Althusserianism. It was in journals such as the Sydney-based *Working Papers* during the mid 1970s that more properly semiotic themes first gained currency. A much less radical and much more respectable version of semiotics had meanwhile been introduced into the erstwhile heartland of Australian Leavisism, with the appointment of Howard Felperin to the chair of English literature at the University of Melbourne in 1977.

In February 1981 the first ever national conference devoted to semiotics was organised in Sydney. As the conference title, 'The foreign bodies conference: Semiotics in/and Australia' clearly attested, much of the appeal of semiotics consisted in its transparent exoticism and novelty, in the fact that 'the ideas dealt with are not widely recognised in Australia'.[20]

But structuralist and post-structuralist thematics rapidly acquired both theoretical and institutional recognition. M.A.K. Halliday in linguistics at Sydney, John Frow at Murdoch's School of Human Communications, Ian Reid in humanities at Deakin, all lent powerful encouragement to the development of semiotics in Australia. The *Australian Journal of Cultural Studies*, centred on Frow and John Fiske at Curtin University, proved successful enough to be taken over by Methuen and internationalised as the new journal *Cultural Studies* in 1987. Structuralist and post-structuralist preoccupations also became central to journals such as *Art and Text*, *Scripsi* and *Southern Review* and to academic associations such as the Sydney Association for Studies in Society and Culture (SASSC) and the Australian and South Pacific Association for Comparative Literary Studies (ASPACLS). By July 1984, when the SASSC convened a second national semiotics conference, Australian semiotics had indeed 'come of age'.[21]

Australian semiotics had begun from the conviction that intellectual work, as theoretical demystification, could contribute to a radical reorganisation of Australian society and culture. Its theoreticism and cosmopolitanism had evolved by way of an entirely legitimate reaction against the insidious anti-intellectualism, on the one hand, and the quasi-corporatism of the appeal to a national unity that represses difference, on the other, that so often characterised radical nationalist discourse. As Meaghan Morris, one of the more convincingly radical of radical semioticians, had complained at the Foreign Bodies Conference, cultural nationalisms 'seem to impose a discourse on identity — not just national or cultural identity . . . but also the call for a program in which speakers identify themselves, take a position in a struggle'.[22]

Morris' remarks seem pertinent not only to cultural nationalism but also to all culturalisms. It is possible, however, to construe this peculiar 'solidarity effect' much more positively than did Morris, at least insofar as the solidarity thus invoked is genuinely emancipatory in its practical, political and cultural implications. And this has very often been the case for those solidarities by which subordinated communities of class, gender or race have sought to organise their collective lives. Solidarity, community and culture need not always prove bogus. They might even render social life meaningful, creative and, indeed, genuinely cooperative. Yet this has not been so and could not have been so for the imagined community of the nation state, if only because it remains unimaginable except as superordinate to and sovereign over other imaginable communities. It was, then, one of the central achievements of Australian radical semiotics to have established the theoretical grounds from which one might proceed to defamiliarise, demythologise and thereby deconstruct the cultural politics of Australian nationalisms, radical or otherwise.

During the 1980s Australian semiotics achieved institutional recognition, but only at the price of a sharp diminution in its analytical and critical purchase. And as the decade proceeded even its previously intransigent cosmopolitanism became progressively compromised. Hence the production of a collection of essays in semiotics, commissioned by the Bicentennial Authority no less, which would celebrate at least as much as demystify 'myths of place in Australian culture'.[23] The editors of the 1984 semiotics conference proceedings had already promised the end of a 'semiotics derived largely from French theory. In its place is a semiotics which is peculiarly Australian'.[24] The eventual outcome would be at its very worst a celebration of the banalities of Australian suburban life,[25] as enthusiastic as any ever contemplated in radical nationalist historiography.

The shift from structuralism to post-structuralism further belied the promise of a new structuralist science of demystification. Thus both Howard Felperin's comfortably apolitical 'deconstruction' and John Frow's self-consciously 'Marxist' Foucauldianism shared a common rejection of the possibilities for a structuralist science of the text.[26] More recent encounters with deconstruction have proved more properly Derridean than Felperin, those with post-Marxism more properly Foucauldian than Frow. By far the most significant instance of the former has been Kevin Hart's quite remarkable attempt to read deconstruction as in effect a negative theology, a reading intended not so much to bury deconstruction as to praise theology;[27] of the latter, Tony Bennett's determinedly Foucauldian critique of Marxist literary theory and Simon During's ambitious attempt at a 'genealogy of writing'.[28]

In a different context During has insisted that in 'writing in a First World colony like Australia, one ought to be nationalistic' and that 'nationalism in post-colonial nations has virtues that perhaps it lacks elsewhere'.[29] The central 'post-colonialist' argument, as advanced in Ashcroft, Griffiths and Tiffin's *The Empire Writes Back* (1989), is that settler literatures such as that of Australia can meaningfully be assimilated to the literatures of the formerly colonised societies of Africa and Asia as analogously 'post-colonial'. Here the category of the post-colonial is expanded to include not simply the post-independence period but also all writing 'affected by the imperial process from the moment of colonisation to the present day'. It is defined, in truly post-structuralist fashion, as entailing a revolt of the periphery against the centre, the margin against the metropolis, through which all experience comes to be 'viewed as uncentred, pluralistic and nefarious'. The paradoxical effect of the argument, however, is not so much to celebrate as to obliterate difference — that between pre-independence and post-independence periods and, more importantly, that between the colonisers and the colonised. For, of course, these colonies of white settlement are not post-colonial in any sense other than that posited by a strict periodisation between pre-independence and post-independence. In every other respect they are instances of a continuing colonisation, in which the descendants of the original colonists remain dominant over the colonised indigeneous peoples.

There is, no doubt, much to be gained from the kind of analysis that seeks to show how European colonial discourse constructed the non-European as 'Other'. But such analysis can be applied neither to Australia nor to Canada. To the contrary, these colonies of European settlement were imagined precisely as overseas extensions of Europe itself, as 'Self' rather than 'Other', as New Britannias all. At this level, then, 'post-colonial literature', defined both as exclusive of non-English-language writing and inclusive of settler writing, represents little more than a fashionable refurbishment of what used to be called 'Commonwealth literature'. At a second level, however, the post-colonial rubric serves as a device by which to reinstate many of the culturalist preoccupations of an apparently discredited erstwhile radical nationalism. An insistent valorisation of the supposedly 'inevitable tendency towards subversion' on the 'post-colonial' margin, if divorced from the comparativist perspective that sustains it in *The Empire Writes Back*, would easily lend itself to a celebration of the peculiar virtues of a putatively Australian national literary canon.[30]

To be fair, During concedes a distinction between the post-colonialism of the post-colonised and that of the post-coloniser. But the latter, it seems to me, is much better characterised as 'post-imperialism'. In any case, no such distinction registers in Ashcroft, Griffiths and Tiffin, for whom the logic of their own argument compels even the inclusion of the United States within the category post-colonial. The implication that American culture is somehow subversively peripheral to a European centre seems almost wilfully perverse, given that many of the dominant cultural forms of our time — science fiction, jazz, rock, the Hollywood movie, some important television subgenres — are characteristically American in origin. Wilfully or not, the perversity is sustained only at the price of a systematic indifference to such 'popular' cultural forms and a corollary insistence on the special value of 'Literature'. For it is only in the very peculiar and, in truth, increasingly socially marginal instance of high literary studies that such notions of American marginality retain an even residual credibility. Elsewhere American centrality is surely almost self-evidently obvious.

Like the New Left, second-wave feminism aspired to a level of theoretical articulacy and sophistication unimagined by previous Australian radical movements. Like the New Left, second-wave feminism came increasingly to define cultural theory itself as a matter of both particular concern and peculiar political relevance. Contemporary feminist thought has been much influenced by Marxism, structuralism and post-structuralism. And indeed one can even discover properly culturalist themes at work. Dale Spender's *Writing a New World* (1988), for example, while exhibiting a healthy scepticism towards the possibility or desirability of a female literary canon, none the less detects in Australia a 'distinct and distinguished women's literary tradition'.[31] While Marxist feminist theoretical motifs have certainly been present in Australian literary studies — the obvious instance is the work of Carole Ferrier and some of her colleagues associated with the feminist journal *Hecate* — they have none the less proven much more influential in sociology and in history.[32]

These various socialist feminisms and the labour-movement-oriented politics that provided their practical corollary became near-hegemonic in the Australian women's movement during the period of conservative government, which lasted from the mid 1970s to the early 1980s. But as the 1980s progressed socialist feminism became progressively marginalised. Hence the deeply troubled and troubling mood of the first-person narrative that runs through *For and Against Feminism*, a retrospectively reconstructed and recontextualised collection of essays by Ann Curthoys, Professor of History in the School of Humanities and Social Sciences at the University of Technology, Sydney, and perhaps the best known of all Australia's socialist feminist historians. If Curthoys resolutely persists in her socialist convictions, then she also seems uncomfortably aware of her own political and theoretical isolation. Her work now seems 'too far away from where most people were at to spark off much real debate'.[33]

The contrary position against which Curthoys polemicises at this point is not simply radical feminism in general, it is clear, but post-structuralist feminism in particular. As the 1980s proceeded structuralist and post-structuralist claims had become increasingly pressing on Australian feminism. The resultant theoretical outcome, a combination of feminist rhetoric, Lacanian psychoanalysis and Barthesian semiotics, is celebrated by Michele Barrett as 'what might rapidly become known as "New Australian Feminism" '.[34] It is not in fact at all clear what exactly is Australian, as distinct from French, in Barrett's New Australian feminism; neither Lacan nor Barthes nor even feminist rhetoric are in any obvious sense peculiarly Australian. That said, there can be little doubt that the Australian feminist academy has indeed provided an important conduit through which French feminist theory has been introduced into the Anglophone world. The London-based publisher Verso's 'Questions for Feminism' series, which Barrett herself co-edited, provided this new Australo-French feminism with a peculiarly visible international platform.

Psychosemiotic feminisms have proved especially persuasive to scholars working in philosophy or in the more cosmopolitan areas of literary and cultural studies. A recent, representative collection ranges from French philosophy to Zola, Marguerite Duras to Strindberg, scientific narratives to soap operas.[35] At the level of high literary theory, one might well cite Marie Maclean's *Narrative as Performance*,[36] a deeply scholarly study in narratology, which takes as its 'demonstration pieces' the experimental narratives of Baudelaire and makes both extensive and elegant use of much recent French semiotic theory. A more publicly influential and politically paradigmatic instance, however, is that provided by the work of Elizabeth Grosz.

Grosz's initial theoretical formation appears to have been conditioned by the encounter with and reaction against Althusserianism. Thereafter, more properly post-structuralist influences, both 'malestream' (Lacan, Barthes and Derrida) and feminist, come to the fore.[37] Indeed, Grosz goes so far as to define contemporary feminist theory, as distinct from the feminism of the 1960s, in terms of a set of quite specifically 'French' and post-structuralist thematics: as aspiring to autonomy (difference) rather than equality; as theoretically engaged not with 'Marx, Reich, Marcuse . . . ' but with 'Freud, Lacan, Nietzsche, Derrida, Deleuze, Althusser, Foucault . . . '; as contesting singular or universal concepts of truth so as to 'encourage a proliferation of voices . . . a plurality of perspectives and interests'. Grosz's feminism is also insistently corporeal. And although she often writes with a distinctly un-French lucidity, Grosz's feminism is also ferociously and uncompromisingly 'intellectual' in character. Thus she acknowledges the not uncommon Anglophone feminist doubt that an intellectual practice centred on the deconstruction of male-dominated academic knowledge, rather than on the empirical reality of women's life in patriarchy, might prove both elitist and unfeminist, but only so as to assert to the contrary that: 'This struggle for the right to write, read and know differently is not merely a minor or secondary task within feminist politics.'[38]

Much more popular in its intellectual concerns, much more properly eclectic (and thereby perhaps more sympathetic to feminism of a very different kind), but none the less equally post-structuralist in general import, is the work of Meaghan Morris, the Sydney-based journalist, film critic and essayist. For Morris, as for Grosz, a post-structuralist semiotics enables not the discovery of the truth of some deep structure inherent in the text, but rather the production of new readings, that is, of new strategic rewritings. For Morris, as for Grosz, such rewritings can be of value only by virtue of their relationship to the political discourses of feminism. For Morris, as for Grosz, there can be no appeal beyond signification to the supposed reality of a referent.

Morris retains a residual commitment to the notion of a left that is socialist as well as feminist and a genuine and not entirely appropriative enthusiasm for malestream thinkers such as Barthes, both of which suggest a much less theoretically separatist feminism than that enjoined by Grosz. This apparent catholicism derives in part from her obvious discomfort at the more sectarian intellectual habits not only of the left but also of the academy. Hence the declared antipathy to Felperin's proposed post-structuralist rationale for the literary canon, as also the parallel enthusiasm for 'the kind of "mixed" public to be encountered at events organised on thematic or political, rather than purely professional, principles'. Hence too the characteristically defiant insistence that 'it doesn't follow for one moment that I consider the activity of "transforming discursive material" as sufficient to, or coextensive with, the tasks of feminist political struggle'. Interestingly, Morris' usage of the Foucauldian notion of the 'specific intellectual' is quite deliberately broadened in scope so as to preclude the 'myth of institutional and discursive *closure* which may emerge from the . . . academic attempt to "know your limitations"'.[39]

Intellectually generous, politically engaged and engagingly writerly, Morris' work apparently belies the general drift towards academicism within post-structuralist feminism. Much more typical of the new post-structuralist academy is Rosemary Pringle's response to Ann Curthoys' socialist feminism. Pringle's own intellectual career has run almost exactly parallel to that of the ideal-typical post-Althusserian academic, which Curthoys describes elsewhere:

> This kind of marxism . . . was . . . generally distanced from political activity, including feminist political activity, and resided principally in the universities and colleges. It was . . . a theoreticist, impenetrable, and narrow doctrine . . . Those who now identify marxism as rigid and mechanistic are often ex-Althusserians who know no other way of thinking about marxist theory.[40]

Thus Pringle chooses to berate Curthoys for an adherence to a set of supposedly 'fundamental socialist assumptions',[41] most of which are very much more typical of Althusserian structuralism than of any kind of Australian socialist feminist labour history. Curthoys has herself pointed to the manifest unfairness of this misreading.[42] What even she fails to note is the political significance of Pringle's own ultimate rationale for a Foucauldian, post-structuralist, post-modern feminism, as preferable to Curthoys' ' "superior" socialist morality'.

> One of the strengths of the women's movement [writes Pringle] has been precisely that it *is* self-interested, that its activists are acting on their own behalf and not sacrificing themselves to the interests of some larger group which they claim to represent. Many women have battled against discrimination and harassment to achieve positions of responsibility within the system and it may be that in straight occupational terms women are now more divided than they ever have been. But it is not helpful to evoke guilty self-interest amongst those who have 'made it'.[43]

'Not helpful to whom?' one is tempted to ask. For what is truly striking about Pringle's position here is its frank admission that the self-interest for which she speaks is not that of the vast majority of women who have, of course, not 'made it' to responsible positions. This is indicative of a real shift and one best understood not in terms of the move from socialism to feminism (although this is how Curthoys tends to read it) but rather that from a general to a restricted feminism. In this respect at least Pringle's views powerfully attest to the presence of a distinctly neo-utilitarian element in recent post-structuralism.

If the post-modern era is essentially coextensive with the period since World War II, then one of its constitutive features has very obviously been international mass migration. And if self-consciously intellectual 'post-modernism' is a delayed reflection on this changed politico-economic configuration, then the Australian debates over multiculturalism from the 1970s on are themselves importantly 'post-modernist'. Certainly, Australian multiculturalism as discourse remains strikingly coincidental in time with the more general debates over post-modernism. It dates from the early 1970s, specifically from Grassby's period as immigration minister in the Whitlam Government. Conservative opponents of multiculturalism have typically spoken in the name of a recognisably 'culturalist' monoculture.[44] Radical critics by contrast have sought to indict both monoculturalism and multiculturalism as similarly implicated in similarly 'ideological' conceptions of culture. They stress differences of class and gender not only within the general culture but also within each of the different ethnic subcultures. They also stress, in quasi-Althusserian fashion, the social control function performed, again both within the general social formation and within the different ethnic communities, by multiculturalism as ideology.[45] Joel Kahn, Professor of Anthropology at La Trobe University, and himself very much influenced by such radicalisms, has argued that Australian multiculturalism remains indebted to the relatively closed and unitary conceptions of culture developed within his own discipline, recommending in effect that the concept itself be abandoned. Culture, he insists in a characteristically postmodernist gesture, is only a 'construct'.[46]

By contrast Sneja Gunew's work remains much more sympathetic to a post-structuralist rewriting of multiculturalism. She deliberately invokes ethnic 'difference' as in itself a discursively and politically subversive category. In an earlier formulation she defined multiculturalism as a 'rhizome', which functions simultaneously both to signal immigrant opposition and to reinforce the dominant trajectories of Anglo-Celtic power. Despite the often overwhelming presence of the latter, Gunew concludes that multiculturalism can none the less be utilised so as to deconstruct the dominant Anglo-Celtic unified narrative. It should be retained, she argues, as a 'strategy which interrogates hegemonic unities' and perhaps even as the 'basis for constructing "signifying breakthroughs", the preconditions for a revolutionary, non-repetitive, history'.[47]

A later formulation borrows from Habermas the notion of the 'public sphere' so as to argue that a multicultural counter-public sphere can be discovered in immigrant writing conventionally excluded from Australian literary and cultural histories. There is, surely, a certain incongruity in this resort on Gunew's part to a thinker as universalist as Habermas and a notion as rationalist as that of the public sphere. But her intentions are none the less determinedly post-structuralist — by counter-public sphere she means only whatever it is that qualifies and interrogates the public sphere of 'legitimising and institutionally endorsed public statements'. The category is thus essentially discursive rather than institutional in range and disruptive rather than normatively regulative in intent.[48]

Assuming, as I'm afraid I do, that multiculturalism as sign must bear some relation to some referent, then, whatever might be true of what frightens people, what *attracts* them to multiculturalism is surely the reality of multicultural consumption, that is, the transnational commodification of cultural texts and artefacts. In this sense opponents of multiculturalism and immigration such as Robert and Tanya Birrell or Katherine Betts [49] are right to point to ethnic restaurants and foreign films as paradigmatic instances of Yuppie consumption patterns. But such patterns require neither immigration per se nor legitimation by ethnic group politics. They are rather a general phenomenon of late capitalist society, irrespective of actual immigrant flows. It is sufficient that the messages flow; quite irrelevant whether the bodies do likewise. All postmodern culture, whether north American, western European, Japanese or Australian, is in effect 'multicultural', if only because the circuits of cultural capital, although not necessarily the corollary labour flows, are everywhere already effectively transnational.

Theoretical post-structuralisms of the kind that have become widely current in contemporary Australian cultural theory clearly endorse the cultural pluralism of this contemporary post-modern condition and with it the collapse of older, institutionalised claims to authoritative cultural judgement. As Elizabeth Grosz explains: anti-humanism implies the 'dismantling of a constricting commonness and the open celebration of specificity'.[50] Analogously pluralist understandings clearly underpin much multicultural theory. This pluralism, this new play of differences, is indeed distinctively post-modern, and it does indeed allow some at least of the hitherto culturally marginalised an opportunity to assert their own specificity.

But how has this decentring of cultural authority actually arisen? It is certainly not the 'new social movements' that have displaced the cultural authority of what Gramsci termed the 'traditional intelligentsia',[51] the clergy, the academy and so on. The achievement belongs solely to the market and to the commodity aesthetics it enjoins. In short, the cultures of difference are sustained not so much by the existence of effectively organised political countercultures as by an effective monetary demand for commodifiable countercultural texts. Those of us who formed part of a once highly profitable market for Che Guevara posters will recall just how vulnerable to fluctuations in demand such 'cultures' can be.

Romantic and post-Romantic culturalisms envisaged culture not simply as separate from economy and polity but also as in itself the central source of social cohesion; society as such was inconceivable without culture. Each also, in one way or another, counterposed the claims of culture, understood as a repository of superior values, to those of utilitarian capitalist civilisation, understood as driven by the dynamics of profitable exchange. But if post-modernism is the full commodification of art, as Fredric Jameson has argued,[52] then clearly it represents a triumph of civilisation over culture. Let us be clear what is at stake here. Any society will possess some institutional arrangement or other for the regulation of symbolic artefacts and practices. In that sense, society is indeed inconceivable without culture. But these institutions might themselves be either 'political', that is, based on the ultimate threat of coercion wielded by the state, or 'economic', that is, organised through commodity exchange in a more or less (normally less) competitive market, or 'cultural', in the 'culturalist' sense, that is, based on theoretically (although often not actually) consensual arrangements for the generation of authoritative, but not in fact politically coercive, judgements of value. Soviet socialist realism provides us with an extreme instance of the first, contemporary post-modernism the second. But most cultures, we might agree, have been much more properly 'cultural'. No doubt, the old literary humanist 'common culture' was neither common nor consensual; most people were very effectively excluded from its deliberations on grounds of lack of taste.

Yet its rhetoric none the less captures an important part of what many of us still experience as the most basic of truths about our 'culture' — that our art, our religion, our morals, our knowledge, our science, are not simply matters of private revealed preference, but rather possess a validity that is ultimately social. In short, we belong to our culture very much more than it belongs to us. What post-modernism provides, then, is an index of the western intelligentsia's collective crisis of faith in its own redemptive functions. This is in itself to be welcomed. But it is still only an absence, or perhaps an opening, a space in which new options might be explored, others foreclosed. One option is indeed that of radical commodification and the effective absorption of the cultural into the economic — this is where the smart money is. A second alternative, however, would be to recognise that the old high culture was indeed elitist, to acknowledge none the less that the new post-modern commodity culture, like the older 'mass' culture before it, is both manipulative and exploitative, yet to insist on the possibility and desirability, within this new post-modern space, of an as-yet-to-be-made democratic common culture.

This was the central politico-cultural trajectory that actually informed Williams' work, and it is one that still seems to me both theoretically available and politically preferable. The ideal of a common culture is, in my view, neither inherently reactionary nor inherently utopian. At one level, it registers the truth of an already existing commonality, evident in language and in the most fundamental of moral proscriptions. At another and more important level, moreover, it registers the 'ideals' of community and solidarity, as standards against which to measure the actual deficiencies of our culture and our society. By this second level, I refer not to some reactionary medievalism, such as those entertained by Leavis, but to the real possibility in a real future of a culture truly made in common. As Williams wrote in *Culture and Society*:

> The distinction of a culture in common is that the selection is freely and commonly made and remade. The tending is a common process, based on common decision, which then, within itself, comprehends the actual variations of life and growth.[53]

For Williams, this would serve both as an indictment of traditional literary humanisms and as the prospectus for a continuation of 'the long revolution'. For us, it need only be the latter.

Notes

1. Raymond Williams, *Culture and Society: 1780–1950*, Penguin, Harmondsworth, 1963, p. 17.
2. Raymond Williams, *Keywords: A Vocabulary of Culture and Society*, Fontana, Glasgow, 1976, p. 77, 79.
3. P.B. Shelley, *A Defence of Poetry* with P. Sidney, *An Apology for Poetry* (ed. H.A. Needham), Ginn & Co., London, 1931, p. 109.
4. Matthew Arnold, *Culture and Anarchy* (J. Dover Wilson, ed.), Cambridge University Press, Cambridge, 1966.
5. Benedict Anderson, *Imagined Communities: Reflections on the Origins and Spread of Nationalism*, London, Verso, 1983, p. 15.
6. W. Milgate, 'The language and literature tradition' in University of Sydney, *One Hundred Years of the Faculty of Arts*, Sydney, Angus & Robertson, 1952, p. 47.
7. See Francis Mulhern, *The Moment of 'Scrutiny'*, Verso, London, 1979.
8. F.R. Leavis, *Nor Shall My Sword: Discourses on Pluralism, Compassion and Social Hope*, London, Chatto & Windus, 1972, pp. 92–3.
9. K. MacDermott, 'The discourse of assessment: English studies at Melbourne University', *Melbourne Working Papers*, 1982–83, p. 104.
10. U. Ozolins, 'Victorian HSC examiners' reports: A study of cultural capital', *Melbourne Working Papers*, 1981.
11. F.R. Leavis, *Revaluation*, Penguin, Harmondsworth, 1972, p. 58.

12 See John Docker, *In a Critical Condition: Struggles for Control of Australian Literature — Then and Now*, Penguin, Ringwood, 1984.
13 Committee to Review Australian Studies in Tertiary Education, *Windows on to Worlds*, AGPS, Canberra, 1987, p. 81.
14 Graeme Turner, *British Cultural Studies: An Introduction*, Unwin Hyman, London, 1990, p. 76.
15 Susan Dermody et al., 'Introduction: Australian cultural studies: Problems and dilemmas', in Susan Dermody et al. (eds), *Nellie Melba, Ginger Meggs and Friends: Essays in Australian Cultural History*, Kibble Books, Malmsbury, Vic, 1982, p. 3.
16 Ian Turner (ed.), *The Australian Dream*, Sun Books, Melbourne, 1968; S. Knight & M. Wilding (ed.), *The Radical Reader*, Wild & Woolley, Sydney, 1977; Humphrey McQueen, *A New Britannia: An Argument Concerning the Social Origins of Australian Radicalism and Nationalism*, Penguin, Ringwood, 1970; Alistair Davidson, *Antonio Gramsci: Towards an Intellectual Biography*, Merlin Press, London, 1977.
17 R.W. Connell, *Which Way is Up? Essays on Sex, Class and Culture*, Allen & Unwin, Sydney, 1983.
18 Elizabeth Grosz, *Sexual Subversions: Three French Feminists*, Allen & Unwin, Sydney, 1989, p. 235.
19 Raymond Williams, *Marxism and Literature*, Oxford University Press, Oxford, 1977, p. 111.
20 P. Botsman & R. Phillips, 'Preface' to Botsman et al. (eds), *The Foreign Bodies Papers*, Local Consumption Publications, Sydney, 1981, p. 11.
21 T. Threadgold et al., 'Preface' to Threadgold et al. (ed.), *Semiotics — Ideology — Language*, Sydney Association for Studies in Society and Culture, Sydney, 1986, p. 11.
22 M. Morris & A. Freadman, 'Import rhetoric: Semioticians in/and Australia' in Botsman et al. (eds), *The Foreign Bodies Papers*, pp. 126–7.
23 P. Foss (ed.), *Island in the Stream: Myths and Place in Australian Culture*, Pluto Press, Sydney, 1988.
24 Threadgold et al., *Semiotics — Ideology — Language*, p. 11.
25 John Fiske, Bob Hodge, Graeme Turner, *Myths of Oz: Readings in Australian Popular Culture*, Allen & Unwin, Sydney, 1987.
26 Howard Felperin, *Beyond Deconstruction: The Uses and Abuses of Literary Theory*, Oxford University Press, Oxford, 1985; John Frow, *Marxism and Literary History*, Basil Blackwell, Oxford, 1986.
27 Kevin Hart, *The Trespass of the Sign: Deconstruction, Theology, Philosophy*, Cambridge University Press, Cambridge, 1989.
28 Tony Bennett, *Outside Literature*, Routledge, London, 1990; Simon During, *Foucault and Literature: Towards a Genealogy of Writing*, Routledge, London, 1992.
29 Simon During, 'Literature — nationalism's other? The case for revision' in H.K. Bhaba (ed.), *Nation and Narration*, Routledge, London, 1990, pp. 139, 151.

30 Bill Ashcroft, Helen Tiffin, Gareth Griffiths, *The Empire Writes Back: Theory and Practice in Post-colonial Literatures*, Routledge, London, 1989, pp. 2, 12, 33.
31 Dale Spender, *Writing a New World: Two Centuries of Australian Women Writers*, Pandora Press, London, 1988, p. xv.
32 Carole Ferrier (ed.), *Gender, Politics and Fiction*, University of Queensland Press, St Lucia, 1984; Ann Game & Rosemary Pringle, *Gender at Work*, Allen & Unwin, Sydney, 1983; Ann Curthoys, *For and Against Feminism: A Personal Journey into Feminist Theory and History*, Allen & Unwin, Sydney, 1988.
33 Ibid., p. 146.
34 Michele Barrett, *Women's Oppression Today: The Marxist/Feminist Encounter*, Verso, London, 1988, p. xxix.
35 T. Threadgold & A. Cranny Francis (ed.), *Feminine/Masculine and Representation*, Allen & Unwin, Sydney, 1990.
36 Marie Maclean, *Narrative as Performance: The Baudelairean Experiment*, Routledge, London, 1988.
37 C. Pateman & E. Grosz (Gross) (ed.), *Feminist Challenges: Social and Political Theory*, Allen & Unwin, Sydney, 1986; E. Grosz, 'Notes towards a corporeal feminism', *Australian Feminist Studies*, no. 5, 1989; E. Grosz, *Jacques Lacan: A Feminist Introduction*, Routledge, London, 1990; E. Grosz, 'Feminism and anti-humanism' in Andrew Milner and C. Worth (ed.), *Discourse and Difference: Post-structuralism, Feminism and the Moment of History*, Centre for General and Comparative Literature, Monash University, 1990.
38 Pateman and Grosz, *Feminist Challenges*, pp. 190–93, 204; Grosz, *Sexual Subversions*, p. 234.
39 Meaghan Morris, *The Pirate's Fiancée: Feminism, Reading, Postmodernism*, Verso, London, 1988, pp. 5, 7, 8, 10, 123–36, 173–86.
40 Curthoys, *For and Against Feminism*, p. 55.
41 Rosemary Pringle, ' "Socialist-feminism" in the eighties: Reply to Curthoys', *Australian Feminist Studies*, no. 6, 1988, p. 26.
42 Ann Curthoys, 'What is the socialism in the socialist feminism', *Australian Feminist Studies*, no. 6, 1988, p. 173.
43 Game and Pringle, *Gender at Work*, pp. 28–9.
44 F. Knopfelmacher, 'The case against multi-culturalism' in Robert Manne (ed.), *The New Conservatism in Australia*, Oxford University Press, Melbourne, 1982; Geoffrey Blainey, *All for Australia*, Methuen Haynes, Sydney, 1984.
45 Andrew Jakubowicz, 'State and ethnicity: Multi-culturalism as ideology' in James Jupp (ed.), *Ethnic Politics in Australia*, Allen & Unwin, Sydney, 1984; J. Martin, 'Multiculturalism and women', *Social Alternatives*, vol. 4, no. 3, 1984.
46 J.S. Kahn, 'The "culture" in multiculturalism: A view from anthropology', *Meanjin*, vol. 50, no. 1, 1991, p. 52.

47 S. Gunew, 'Migrant women writers', in Ferrier, *Gender, Politics and Fiction*; S. Gunew, 'Australia 1984: A moment in the archaeology of multiculturalism', in F. Barker et al. (ed.), *Europe and Its Others*, vol. 1, University of Essex, Colchester, 1985, pp. 179, 188.
48 S. Gunew, 'Denaturalising cultural nationalisms: Multicultural readings of "Australia"', in Homi K. Bhabha (ed.), *Nation and Narration*, Routledge, London, 1990, p. 100.
49 R. Birrell & T. Birrell, *An Issue of People: Population and Australian Society*, Longman Cheshire, Melbourne, 1981, p. 225; K. Betts, *Ideology and Immigration: Australia 1976–1987*, Melbourne University Press, Melbourne, 1988, p. 101.
50 Grosz, 'Feminism and anti-humanism', p. 74.
51 Antonio Gramsci, *Selections from Prison Notebooks* (trans. Q. Hoare and G. Nowell Smith), Lawrence & Wishart, London, 1971.
52 F. Jameson (1991), *Postmodernism, or, The Cultural Logic of Late Capitalism*, Verso, London, 1991, pp. 4–5.
53 Williams, *Culture and Society*, p. 322.

BIBLIOGRAPHY

Aberbach, Joel D., et al., *Bureaucrats and Politicians in Western Democracies*, Harvard University Press, Cambridge, Mass., 1981.

Allport, Carolyn, 'Women and the new order housing', in Women and Labour Publications Collective, *All Her Labours*, Vol. 2, Hale & Iremonger, Sydney, 1984.

Almond, Gabriel, 'Political theory and political science', *American Political Science Review*, vol. 60, no. 4, 1966.

Alomes, Stephen, *A Nation at Last? The Changing Character of Australian Nationalism*, Angus & Robertson, Sydney, 1988.

Altman, Dennis, *The Homosexualization of America*, Beacon Press, Boston, 1983.

Altman, Dennis, *AIDS and the New Puritanism*, Pluto Press, Sydney, 1986.

Altman, Dennis, 'The creation of sexual politics in Australia', *Journal of Australian Studies*, no. 20, May, 1987.

Altman, Dennis, *A Politics of Poetry*, Pluto Press, Sydney, 1988.

Altman, Dennis, 'A closet of one's own', *Island*, no. 48, Spring, 1991.

Altman, Dennis, *The Comfort of Men*, Heinemann, Melbourne, 1993.

Anderson, Benedict, *Imagined Communities: Reflections on the Origins and Spread of Nationalism*, Verso, London, 1983.

Arnold, Matthew, *Culture and Anarchy* (J. Dover Wilson, ed.), Cambridge University Press, Cambridge, 1966.

Ashcroft, Bill, Helen Tiffin and Gareth Griffiths, *The Empire Writes Back: Theory and Practice in Post-colonial Literature*, Routledge, London, 1989.

Aughterson, W.V. (ed.), *Taking Stock*, F.W. Cheshire, Melbourne, 1953.

Ballard, J., 'The politics of AIDS' in H. Gardner, *The Politics of Health*, Churchill Livingstone, Melbourne, 1989.

Barbalet, J.M., *Citizenship*, Open University Press, Milton Keynes, 1988.

Barker, F. et al. (ed.), *Europe and its Others*, Vol. 1, University of Essex, Colchester, 1985.

Barrett, Michele, *Women's Oppression Today: The Marxist/Feminist Encounter*, Verso, London, 1988.

Bean, C.E.W., *The Story of Anzac*, Vol. 1 of *Official History of Australia in the War of 1914–18*, Sydney, Angus & Robertson, 1933.

BIBLIOGRAPHY

Beasely, Jack, *Red Letter Days: Notes from Inside an Era*, Australasian Book Society, Sydney, 1979.

Beilharz, P., 'Social democracy and social justice', *Australia and New Zealand Journal of Sociology*, vol. 25, no. 1, 1989.

Bennett, Bruce, *An Australian Compass: Essays on Place and Direction in Australian Literature*, Fremantle Arts Centre Press, Fremantle, 1991.

Bennett, Bruce, 'An interview with András Domahidy', *Westerly*, vol. 37, no. 2, 1992.

Bennett, Bruce and Susan Miller (eds), *A Sense of Exile: Essays in the Literature of the Asia–Pacific Region*, Centre for Studies in Australian Literature, University of Western Australia, Nedlands, 1988.

Bennett, Bruce and Dennis Haskell (eds), *Myths, Heroes and Anti-heroes: Essays on the Literature of the Asia–Pacific Region*, Centre for Studies in Australian Literature, University of Western Australia, Nedlands, 1992.

Bennett, Tony, *Outside Literature*, Routledge, London, 1990.

Betts, K., *Ideology and Immigration: Australia 1976–1987*, Melbourne University Press, Melbourne, 1988.

Bhahba, Homi K., *Nation and Narration*, Routledge, London, 1991.

Birch, A.H., 'The rights of man and the rights of ethnic minorities', unpublished paper, Research School of Social Sciences, Australian National University, Canberra, 1987.

Birrell, R. and T. Birrell, *An Issue of People: Population and Australian Society*, Longman Cheshire, Melbourne, 1981.

Bittman, Karl (ed.), *From Strauss to Matilda: Viennese in Australia 1938–1988*, Wenkart Foundation, Sydney, 1988.

Blainey, Geoffrey, *Triumph of the Nomads: A History of Ancient Australia*, Macmillan, Melbourne, 1975.

Blainey, Geoffrey, *All for Australia*, Methuen-Haynes, Sydney, 1984.

Botsman, Peter et al. (ed.), *The Foreign Bodies Papers*, Local Consumption Publications, Sydney, 1981.

Botsman, Peter et al., *Telefuture — Who Foots the Bill?* H.V. Evatt Memorial Foundation, Sydney, 1991.

Brain, R., *Rites Black and White*, Penguin, Ringwood, 1979.

Brett, Judith, *Robert Menzies' Forgotten People*, Pan Macmillan, Melbourne, 1992.

Bridge, Ernie, *The Great Australian Dream*, cassette tape recording arranged and directed by Ernie Bridge, DR 9001, Perth, 1990.

Broinowski, Alison, *The Yellow Lady: Australian Impressions of Asia*, Oxford University Press, Melbourne, 1992.

Bryce, James, *The American Commonwealth*, abridged edn, Macmillan, New York, 1896.

Bryce, James, *Modern Democracies*, Vol. 2, Macmillan, London, 1921.

Burgmann, Verity, *Power and Protest*, Allen & Unwin, Sydney, 1993.

Calwell, A.A., *Be Just and Fear Not*, Lloyd O'Neill, Melbourne, 1972.

Camm, J.C.R. and John McQuilton, *Australians: A Historical Atlas*, Fairfax Syme & Weldon, Sydney, 1988.
Clark, C.H.M., *A History of Australia*, Vols 1–6, Melbourne University Press, Melbourne, 1979–84.
Clark, C.H.M., *Manning Clark: Occasional Writings and Speeches*, Fontana, Melbourne, 1980.
Clark, C.M.H., *The People Make the Laws*, Vol. 5, *A History of Australia*, Melbourne University Press, Melbourne, 1981.
Clark, Kenneth, *Civilisation*, BBC Books and John Murray, London, 1992.
Coleman, Peter, *Australian Civilization*, F.W. Cheshire, Melbourne, 1963.
Committee to Review Australian Studies in Tertiary Education, *Windows on to Worlds*, AGPS, Canberra, 1987.
Commonwealth of Australia Parliamentary Debates Session 1901–2 (House of Representatives, 23 April 1902).
Connell, R.W., *Which Way is Up? Essays on Sex, Class and Culture*, Allen & Unwin, Melbourne, 1983.
Conway, Ronald, *The Great Australian Stupor*, Sun Books, Melbourne, 1971.
Coombs, H.C., *Trial Balance: Issues of My Working Life*, Macmillan, Melbourne, 1981.
Copp, D., 'The right to an adequate standard of living: Justice anatomy and the basic needs', *Social Philosophy and Research*, vol. 9, no. 1, 1992.
Crawford, R.M., 'The Australian national character: Myth and reality', *Journal of World History*, no. 2, 1955.
Crisp, L.F., *Ben Chifley: A Biography*, Longman, London, 1955.
Crowley, F.K. (ed.), *Modern Australia in Documents*, Wren, Melbourne, 1973.
Curr, E., *The Australian Race, Its Origins, Languages, Customs*, Victorian Government Printer, Melbourne, 1886–87.
Curthoys, Ann, *For and Against Feminism: A Personal Journey into Feminist Theory and History*, Allen & Unwin, Sydney, 1988.
Curthoys, Ann, 'What is the socialism in the socialist feminism?', *Australian Feminist Studies*, No. 6, 1988.
Dahrendorf, R., *The New Liberty*, Routledge & Kegan Paul, London, 1975.
d'Alpuget, Blanche, *Robert J. Hawke*, Schwartz Publishing, Melbourne, 1982.
Daniel, Ann, *Power, Privilege and Prestige*, Longman Cheshire, Melbourne, 1983.
Davidson, Alistair, *Antonio Gramsci: Towards an Intellectual Biography*, Merlin Press, London, 1977.
Davies, A.F., *Australian Democracy*, Melbourne, Longman, 1964.
Davies, Alan, 'Small country blues', *Meanjin*, no. 2, 1985.
Davis, Jack, *Kullark (Home) and The Dreamers*, Currency Press, Sydney, 1982.
Davis, Jack, *The First-born and Other Poems*, J.M. Dent, Melbourne, 1983.

BIBLIOGRAPHY

Department of Immigration, Local Government and Ethnic Affairs, *Australian Population Trends and Prospects*, Australian Government Publishing Service, Canberra, 1988.
Dermody, Susan et al. (eds), *Nellie Melba, Ginger Meggs and Friends: Essays in Australian Cultural History*, Kibble Books, Malmsbury, Vic., 1982.
Dessaix, Robert (ed.), *Australian Lesbian and Gay Writing*, Oxford University Press, Melbourne, 1993.
de Tocqueville, Alexis, *Democracy in America*, World's Classics, London, 1946.
Dixon, Miriam, *The Real Matilda*, Penguin, Ringwood, 1974.
Docker, John, *Australian Cultural Elites*, Angus & Robertson, Sydney, 1974.
Docker, John, *In a Critical Condition: Struggles for Control of Australian Literature — Then and Now*, Penguin, Ringwood, 1984.
Domahidy, András, *Shadows and Women* (trans. Elizabeth Windsor), Aeolian Press, Claremont, WA, 1989.
Duncan, Graeme (ed.), *Critical Essays in Australian Politics*, Edward Arnold, Melbourne, 1978.
Dutton, Geoffrey, *Snow on the Saltbush: The Australian Literary Experience*, Penguin, Ringwood, 1984.
Dworkin, R., *Taking Rights Seriously*, Duckworth, London, 1978.
Edwards, J., 'Justice and the bounds of welfare', *Journal of Social Policy*, no. 18, 1988.
Ellinghaus, M.P. et al. (eds), *The Emergence of Australian Law*, Butterworth, Sydney, 1989.
Emy, H.V., *The Politics of Australian Democracy*, Macmillan, Melbourne, 1974.
Encel, Sol, 'The concept of the state in Australian politics', *Australian Journal of Politics and History*, vol. 5, no. 1, 1960, republished in C.A. Hughes (ed.), *Readings in Australian Government*, University of Queensland Press, Brisbane, 1968.
Encel, Sol, *Equality and Authority*, Cheshire, Melbourne, 1970.
Encel, Sol, 'Metropolitan societies and dominion societies', in S.N. Eisenstadt (ed.), *Patterns of Modernity*, Frances Pinter, London, 1987.
Encel, Sol, 'The larrikin leaders', *Nation*, 25 May 1968; reprinted in K.S. Inglis, *Nation: The Life of an Independent Journal of Opinion*, Melbourne University Press, Melbourne, 1989.
Eyre, E.J., *Journals of Expeditions of Discovery*, T. &W. Boone, London, 1845.
Feather, N.T., 'Attitudes towards high achievers in public life', *Australian Journal of Psychology*, vol. 43, no. 2, 1991.
Felperin, Howard, *Beyond Deconstruction: The Uses and Abuses of Literary Theory*, Oxford University Press, Oxford, 1985.
Ferrier, Carole (ed.), *Gender, Politics and Fiction*, University of Queensland Press, St Lucia, 1984.
Firth, R., 'Anthropology in Australia', *Oceania*, vol. 3, no. 1, 1932.

Fiske, John, Bob Hodge and Graeme Turner, *Myths of Oz: Readings in Australian Popular Culture*, Allen & Unwin, Sydney, 1987.
Fitzpatrick, Brian, *The Australian Commonwealth*, Cheshire, Melbourne, 1956.
Flood, J., *Archaeology of the Dreamtime*, Collins, Sydney, 1983.
Foss, P. (ed.), *Island in the Stream: Myths and Place in Australian Culture*, Pluto Press, Sydney, 1988.
Freudenberg, Graham, *A Certain Grandeur*, Macmillan, South Melbourne, 1977.
Frow, John, *Marxism and Literary History*, Basil Blackwell, Oxford, 1986.
Gallagher, Katharine, 'London letter', *Overland*, no. 3, 1988.
Game, Ann and Rosemary Pringle, *Gender at Work*, Allen & Unwin, Sydney, 1983.
Gelder, Ken and Paul Salzman, *The New Diversity*, McPhee Gribble/Penguin, Melbourne, 1989.
Gerster, Robin, *Big-noting: The Heroic Theme in Australian War Writing*, Melbourne University Press, Melbourne, 1987.
Goldberg, S.L. and F.B. Smith (eds), *Australian Cultural History*, Cambridge University Press, Cambridge, 1988.
Gordon, Michael, *A Question of Leadership*, University of Queensland Press, St Lucia, 1993.
Gramsci, Antonio, 'The intellectuals' in *Selections from the Prison Notebooks* (ed. and tr. Quintin Hoare & Geoffrey Nowell Smith), Lawrence & Wishart, London, 1971.
Grattan, C. Hartley, *Introducing Australia*, Angus & Roberston, Sydney, 1949.
Grey, G., *Journal of Two Expeditions of Discovery*, T. & W. Boone, London, 1841.
Griffiths, Gareth, 'The dark side of the Dreaming: Aboriginality and Australian culture', *Australian Literary Studies*, vol. 15, no. 4, 1992.
Grosz, E., 'Notes towards a corporeal feminism', *Australian Feminist Studies*, no. 5, 1989.
Grosz, E., *Sexual Subversions: Three French Feminists*, Allen & Unwin, Sydney, 1989.
Grosz, E., 'Feminism and anti-humanism' in Andrew Milner and C. Worth (ed.), *Discourse and Difference: Post-Structuralism, Feminism and the Moment of History*, Centre for General and Comparative Literature, Monash University, Melbourne, 1990.
Grosz, E., *Jacques Lacan: A Feminist Introduction*, Routledge, London, 1990.
Gunew, Sneja and Kateryna O. Longley (eds), *Striking Chords: Multicultural Literary Interpretations*, Allen & Unwin, Sydney, 1992.
Gunn, Jeannie, *The Little Black Princess: A True Tale of Life in the Never-Never Land* [London, 1905], Melville & Mullen, Melbourne, 1906.
Gunn, Jeannie, 'A real story completed: Australia's little "Bett-Bett" is now a grandmother', *Age*, 15 January 1955.

Gunn, Jeannie, *We of the Never-Never* [London 1908], Hutchinson, Melbourne, 1982.
Hallam, Sylvia, *Fire and Hearth*, AIATSIS, Canberra, 1975.
Hamilton, Annette, 'Fear and desire: Aborigines, Asians and the national imagery', in *Australian Cultural History*, 9, 1990 (special issue: *Australian Perceptions of Asia*, ed. David Walker et al.).
Hancock, W.K., *Australia*, Benn, London, 1930.
Harcourt, J.M., *Upsurge* (facsimile edition with introduction by Richard Nile), University of Western Australia Press, Nedlands, 1986.
Harford, Lesbia, *The Invaluable Mystery* (introduction by Richard Nile and Robert Darby), McPhee Gribble/Penguin, Melbourne, 1987.
Hart, Kevin, *The Trespass of the Sign: Deconstruction, Theology, Philosophy*, Cambridge University Press, Cambridge, 1989.
Hay, J.R., 'The Institute of Public Affairs and social policy in World War II', *Historical Studies*, vol. 20, no. 79, 1982.
Hazzard, Shirley, *Postscripts*, Boyer Lectures, ABC, 1988.
Head, Brian and James Walter (eds), *Intellectual Movements and Australian Society*, Oxford University Press, Melbourne, 1988.
Healy, J.J., *Literature and the Aborigine in Australia*, University of Queensland Press, St Lucia, 1978.
Held, D., *Political Theory and the Modern State*, Cambridge University Press, Cambridge, 1989.
Hergenhan, Laurie (ed.), *New Literary History of Australia*, Penguin, Ringwood, 1988.
Hill, R., 'Still in the closet', *Bulletin*, 13 October 1992.
Hirst, John, 'The pioneer legend', *Historical Studies*, vol. 18, no. 71, 1978.
Hodge, Bob and Vijay Mishra, *The Dark Side of the Dream: Australian Literature and the Postcolonial Mind*, Allen & Unwin, Sydney, 1991.
Hong, Ee Tiang, *Tranquerah*, Department of English Language and Literature, National University of Singapore, Singapore, 1985.
Hong, Ee Tiang, 'Coming to', *Westerly*, no. 3, 1986.
Horne, Donald, *The Lucky Country*, Penguin, Ringwood, 1964.
Horne, Donald, *Time of Hope*, Angus & Robertson, Sydney, 1980.
Horne, Donald, *Ideas for a Nation*, Pan, Sydney, 1989.
House of Representatives Standing Committee on Legal and Constitutional Affairs, *Half Way to Equal*, Report of the Inquiry into Equal Opportunity and Equal Status for Women in Australia, AGPS, Canberra, 1992.
Hungerford, T.A.G., *Australian Signpost*, Cheshire, Melbourne, 1956.
Inglis, K.S., *This is the ABC*, Melbourne University Press, Melbourne, 1983.
Jameson, F., *Postmodernism, or, The Cultural Logic of Late Capitalism*, Verso, London, 1991.
Jayasuriya, Laksiri, 'Citizenship and welfare: Rediscovering Marshall', in Peter Saunders and Sara Graham (eds), *Beyond Economic Rationalism: Alternative Futures for Social Justice*, SPRC Reports and Proceedings, No. 105, 1993.

Jenkins, R. and J. Solomos, *Racialism and Equal Opportunity Policies in the 1980s*, Cambridge University Press, Cambridge, 1987.
Johnston, C., 'From gay "movement" to gay "community"', *Gay Information*, no. 5, 1985.
Johnson, Colin, *The Song Circle of Jacky and Selected Poems*, Hyland House, Melbourne, 1986.
Johnson, Colin (Mudrooroo Narogin), *Dalwurra: The Black Bittern*, Centre for Studies in Australian Literature, University of Western Australia, Nedlands, 1988.
Jupp, James, *Arrivals and Departures*, Cheshire-Lansdowne, Melbourne, 1966.
Jupp, James (ed.), *Ethnic Politics in Australia*, Allen & Unwin, Sydney, 1984.
Jupp, James (ed.), *The Australian People: An Encyclopaedia of the Nation, its People, and their Origins*, Angus & Robertson, Sydney, 1988.
Jupp, James, *The Challenge of Diversity: Policy Options for a Multicultural Australia*, AGPS, Canberra, 1989.
Kahn, J.S., 'The "culture" in multiculturalism: A view from anthropology', *Meanjin*, vol. 50, no. 1, 1991.
Kelly, Paul, *The Hawke Ascendancy*, Angus & Robertson, Sydney, 1984.
Kelly, Paul, *The End of Certainty*, Allen & Unwin, Sydney, 1993.
King, Anthony, 'Margaret Thatcher as a political leader', in Robert Skidelsky (ed.), *Thatcherism*, Chatto & Windus, London, 1989.
Knight, S. and M. Wilding (ed.), *The Radical Reader*, Wild & Woolley, Sydney, 1977.
Kovesi, Julius, 'The alienated big animal', *Westerly*, no. 2, 1962.
Kovesi, Julius, 'Nature and convention'. Proceedings of the First New Norcia Humanities Symposium, Perth, 1985.
Kramer, Leonie, 'The media, society and culture', in *Australia: Terra Incognita*, special issue of *Daedalus*, vol. 13, no. 1, 1985.
La Nauze, J.A., 'The study of Australian history, 1929–1959', *Historical Studies*, vol. 9, no. 33, 1959.
Labumore (Elsie Roughsey), *An Aboriginal Mother Tells of the Old and the New*, McPhee Gribble-Penguin, Ringwood, 1984.
Langford, Ruby, *Don't Take Your Love to Town*, Penguin, Ringwood, 1988.
Lawnham, Patrick, 'Scultors carve outback tribute to Hollows', *Weekend Australian*, 22–23 May 1993.
Lawson, Henry, *Collected Verse* (ed. Colin Roderick), Sydney, Angus & Robertson, 1968.
Leavis, F.R., *Nor Shall My Sword: Discourses on Pluralism, Compassion and Social Hope*, London, Chatto & Windus, 1972.
Leavis, F.R., *Revaluation*, Harmondsworth, Penguin, 1972.
Levi-Strauss, Claude, *The Savage Mind*, Weidenfeld & Nicolson, London, 1962.
Liberal Party of Australia, *Australia 2000*, Canberra 1991.

BIBLIOGRAPHY

Lloyd, C.J. & G.S. Ried, *Out of the Wilderness: The Return of Labor*, Cassell, North Melbourne, 1974.

Lord, Mary, *Directory of Australian Authors*, National Book Council, Carlton, 1989.

Lowenthal, David, 'Antipodean and other museums', *Working Papers in Australian Studies*, no. 66, 1991.

MacDermott, K., 'The discourse of assessment: English studies at Melbourne University', *Melbourne Working Papers*, 1982–83.

MacIntyre, Stuart, *History, the University and the Nation*, Trevor Reece Memorial Lecture, Sir Robert Menzies Centre for Australian Studies, University of London, 1992.

Mackay, Hugh, *Reinventing Australia*, Angus & Robertson, Sydney, 1993.

MacKenzie, Jeanne, *Australian Paradox*, Cheshire, Melbourne, 1961.

Mann, Chris, *The Rationalist*, privately published, Melbourne, 1986.

Manne, Robert (ed.), *The New Conservatism in Australia*, Oxford University Press, Melbourne, 1982.

Marshall, A.J., *Australia Limited*, Angus & Robertson, Sydney, 1942.

Marshall, T.H., *Citizenship and Social Class*, Cambridge, Cambridge University Press, 1950.

Marshall, T.H. (ed.), *Citizenship and Social Development*, Greenwood Press, Connecticut, 1973.

Marshall, T.H., *Social Policy*, Heinemann, London, 1975.

Marshall, T.H., *Rights to Welfare and Other Essays*, Heinemann, London, 1981.

Martin, Arthur, 'The emigrant public servant', *Australian Journal of Public Administration*, vol. 48, no. 4, 1989.

Martin, J., 'Multiculturalism and women', *Social Alternatives*, no. 3, 1984.

Mayer, Henry, 'Some conceptions of the Australian party system', *Historical Studies*, no. 27, 1956.

Mayer, Henry, et al., 'Images of politics', *Australian Journal of Politics and History*, vol. 6, no. 2, 1960.

Mayer, Henry (ed.), *Australian Politics: A Reader*, Cheshire, Melbourne, 1966.

Mayer, Henry and Ross Curnow, 'The ideal prime minister' in Henry Mayer (ed.), *Australian Politics — A Second Reader*, Cheshire, Melbourne, 1969.

McAuley, James, *A Map of Australian Verse*, Oxford University Press, Melbourne, 1975.

McCallum, J.A., 'The Labor Party', in W.G.K. Duncan (ed.), *Trends in Australian Politics*, Angus & Robertson, Sydney, 1935.

McGregor, Craig, *The Australian People*, Hodder & Stoughton, Sydney, 1980.

McLeod, A.L. (ed.), *The Patterns of Australian Culture*, Oxford University Press, Melbourne, 1963.

McQueen, Humphrey, *A New Britannia: An Argument Concerning the Social Origins of Australian Radicalism and Nationalism*, Penguin, Ringwood, 1970.

Menzies, R.G., 'The forgotten people', radio broadcast, 22 May 1942 reprinted in G. Starr (ed.), *The Liberal Party in Australia: A Documentary History*, Drummond/Heinemann, Melbourne, 1980.

Métin, Albert, *Le Socialisme sans Doctrines*, Alcan, Paris, 1901.

Michaels, Eric, 'Para-ethnology' [review of Bruce Chatwin, *The Songlines*, and Sally Morgan, *My Place*], *Art & Text*, 30, September–October, 1988.

Milgate, W., 'The language and literature tradition' in University of Sydney, *One Hundred Years of the Faculty of Arts*, Angus & Robertson, Sydney, 1952.

Miller, N., *Out in the World*, Random House, New York, 1992.

Minichiello, V., D. Plummer & E. Tinewell (eds), *AIDS in Context*, Prentice Hall, Sydney, 1992.

Mitchell, Susan, *Tall Poppies*, Penguin, Ringwood, 1984.

Moore, George Fletcher, *A Descriptive Bibliography of the Language in Common Usage Among the Aborigines of Western Australia*, W.S. Orr, London, 1842.

Moran, Albert (ed.), *The Media of Publishing* (special issue), *Continuum*, vol. 4, no. 1, 1990.

Morgan, Sally, *My Place*, Fremantle Arts Centre Press, Fremantle, WA, 1987.

Morgan, Sally, 'A fundamental question of identity', interview with Mary Wright, in *Aboriginal Culture Today*, ed. Anna Rutherford (special issue of *Kunapipi*, vol. 10, nos 1 & 2), 1988.

Morris, Meaghan, *Feminist Challenges: Social and Political Theory*, Verso, London, 1988.

Mouffe, C., 'The civics lesson', *New Statesman*, 7 October 1988.

Mulhern, Francis, *The Moment of 'Scrutiny'*, Verso, London, 1979.

Mulvaney, D.J., *The Pre-history of Australia*, Thames & Hudson, London, 1969.

Munro, Craig, *Wild Man of Letters*, Melbourne University Press, Melbourne, 1984.

Murray, J. & J.P. White, 'Cambridge or the bush? Archaeology in Australia and New Guinea', *World Archaeology*, vol. 13, no. 2, 1981.

Murray, Les (ed.), *The New Oxford Book of Australian Verse*, Oxford University Press, Melbourne, 1987.

Nadel, George, *Australia's Colonial Culture: Ideas, Men and Institutions in Mid Nineteenth Century Eastern Australia*, Harvard University Press, Cambridge, Mass., 1957.

Narogin, Mudrooroo, *Writing from the Fringe: A Study of Modern Aboriginal Literature*, Hyland House, Melbourne, 1990.

National Agenda for Women, AGPS, Canberra, 1988.

Nile, Richard (ed.), *Immigration and the Politics of Ethnicity and Race in*

Australia and Britain, SRMCAS, University of London, and Bureau of Immigration Research, Melbourne, 1991.

Nile, Richard, *The Fiction Industry*, University of Queensland Press, St Lucia, 1994.

NSW Advisory Council to the Premier, *A Decade of Women in New South Wales 1976–1986*, Sydney, 1987.

O'Farrell, Patrick, 'Spurious divorce? Religion and Australian culture', *Journal of Religious Studies*, vol. 15, no. 4, 1989.

Office of Multicultural Affairs, *National Agenda for a Multicultural Australia*, AGPS, Canberra, 1989.

Oldfield, Audrey, *Woman Suffrage in Australia: A Gift or a Struggle?*, Cambridge University Press, Melbourne, 1992.

Oswald, P., 'Living on the land', *Campaign*, October, 1992.

Ozolins, U., 'Victorian HSC examiners' reports: A study of cultural capital', *Melbourne Working Papers*, 1981.

Ozolins, Uldis, *The Politics of Language in Australia*, Cambridge University Press, Melbourne, 1993.

Palmer, Nettie, *Talking It Over*, Angus & Robertson, Sydney, 1932.

Palmer, Vance, *Legend of the Nineties*, Melbourne University Press, 1954.

Partridge, P.H., 'The Australian universities' in W.V. Aughterson (ed.), *Taking Stock*, F.W. Cheshire, Melbourne, 1953.

Pateman, C. and E. Grosz (Gross) (ed.), *Feminist Challenges and Political Theory*, Allen & Unwin, Sydney, 1986.

Paterson, Jan, *The Future of Australia as an Export Market*, Sir Stanley Unwin Foundation, London, 1989.

Penton, Brian, *Think or be Damned*, Angus & Robertson, Sydney, 1941.

Phillips, A.A., *The Australian Tradition: Studies in Colonial Culture*, F.W. Cheshire, Melbourne, 1958.

Phillips, A.A., 'Australian literature' in W.V. Aughterson (ed.), *Taking Stock: Aspects of Mid-life in Australia*, Cheshire, Melbourne, 1961.

Pierce, Peter (ed.), *The Oxford Literary Guide to Australia*, Oxford University Press, Melbourne, 1987.

Plant, R., *Citizenship, Rights and Socialism*, Fabian Society Tract No. 531, London, 1988.

Plomley, N.J.B. (ed.), *The Baudin Expedition and the Tasmanian Aborigines 1802*, Blubber Head Press, Hobart, 1983.

Pointer, G. and S. Wills, *The Gift Horse: A Critical Look at Equal Employment Opportunity in Australia*, Allen & Unwin, Sydney, 1991.

Preddey, Elsbeth, *Women's Electoral Lobby*, WEL Australia and WEL New Zealand, 1985.

Pringle, J.D., *The Australian Accent*, Chatto & Windus, London, 1961.

Pringle, Rosemary, '"Socialist-feminism" in the eighties: Reply to Curthoys', *Australian Feminist Studies*, no. 6, 1988.

Pusey, Michael, *Economic Rationalism in Australia*, Cambridge University Press, Melbourne, 1991.

BIBLIOGRAPHY

Pybus, Cassandra, *Community of Thieves*, Heinemann, Port Melbourne, 1991.
Ramson, W.S. (ed.), *The Australian National Dictionary*, Oxford University Press, Melbourne, 1988.
Rawls, J., *A Theory of Justice*, Oxford University Press, Oxford, 1972.
Recognition for Women in Australia: A Discussion Paper: Prepared for the House of Representatives Standing Committee on Legal and Constitutional Affairs for the Inquiry into Equal Opportunity and Equal Status for Australian Women, December 1991.
Reid, Ian, *Fiction and the Great Depression in Australia and New Zealand*, Edward Arnold, Melbourne, 1979.
Reynolds, Henry, *The Other Side of the Frontier*, Penguin, Ringwood, 1982.
Roberts, M., 'Ministerial advisers: A background paper', Research Paper, No. 6, Royal Commission on Australian Government Administration, AGPS, Canberra, 1976.
Robinson, Portia, *The Women of Botany Bay*, Penguin, Ringwood, 1993.
Roe, Jill, 'Chivalry and social policy in the Antipodes', *Historical Studies*, April, 1987.
Ross, Lloyd, 'A new social order', in D.A.S. Campbell (ed.), *Post-war Reconstruction in Australia*, Australasian Publishing Co./Australian Institute of Political Science, Sydney, 1944.
Roughsey, D., *Moon and Rainbow*, Rigby, Sydney, 1971.
Rowse, T., *Australian Liberalism and National Character*, Kibble Books, Malmsbury, Vic, 1978.
Santamaria, B.A., 'Gays must admit that AIDS discriminates', *Weekend Australian*, 23–24 January 1993.
Sawer, Marian, *Sisters in Suits: Women and Public Policy in Australia*, Allen & Unwin, Sydney, 1990.
Sawer, Marian and Marian Simms, *A Woman's Place: Women and Politics in Australia*, Allen & Unwin, Sydney, 1984.
Schaffter, Kay, *Women and the Bush*, Cambridge University Press, Melbourne, 1989.
Senn, Werner and Giovanna Capone (eds), *The Making of a Pluralist Australia*, Peter Lang, Bern, 1993.
Serle, Geoffrey, *From Deserts the Prophets Come: The Creative Spirit in Australia*, Heinemann, Melbourne, 1973.
Serle, Geoffrey, 'Ruminations on Australia and the arts over fifty years', *Notes and Furphies*, 1989.
Sexton, Michael, *Illusions of Power*, Allen & Unwin, Sydney, 1979.
Seymour, Alan and Richard Nile (ed.), *Anzac: Meaning, Memory and Myth*, SRMCAS, University of London, 1991.
Shapcott, Thomas, *The Literature Board: A Brief History*, University of Queensland Press, St Lucia, 1988.
Shelley, P.B., *A Defence of Poetry* with P. Sidney, *An Apology for Poetry* (ed. H.A. Needham), Ginn & Co., London, 1931.

Shoemaker, Adam, *Black Words, White Page: Aboriginal Literature 1929–1988*, University of Queensland Press, St Lucia, 1989.
Siegfried, André, *Democracy in New Zealand*, Bell, London, 1919.
Simms, Marian, '"Private enterprise and progress": The genesis of Liberal Party ideology', in H. Mayer and N. Nelson (eds), *Australian Politics: A Fifth Reader*, Longman Cheshire, Melbourne, 1980.
Simms, Marian, *A Liberal Nation: The Liberal Party and Australian Politics*, Hale & Iremonger, Sydney, 1982.
Smark, Peter, 'Time to bury Ming', *Sydney Morning Herald*, 15 March 1993.
Spender, Dale, *Writing a New World: Two Centuries of Australian Women Writers*, Pandora Press, London, 1988.
Stanner, W.E.H., *After the Dreaming*, ABC, Sydney, 1969.
Stanner, W.E.H., *White Man got no Dreaming: Essays 1938–1973*, ANU Press, Canberra, 1979.
Stow, Randolph, *The Merry-Go-Round in the Sea*, MacDonald, London, 1965.
Stretton, Hugh, 'The quality of leading Australians', in *Australia: Terra Incognita*, special issue of *Daedalus*, vol. 113, no. 1, 1985.
Summers, Anne, 'Sisters out of step', *Independent Monthly*, July 1990.
Teilman, R., *Homoseksualiteit in Nederland*, Bonn Meppe, Amsterdam, 1982.
Thompson, Denise, *Flaws in the Social Fabric*, Allen & Unwin, Sydney, 1985.
Thonemann, H.E., *Tell the White Man: The Life of an Aboriginal Lubra*, Collins, Sydney, 1949.
Threadgold, T. and A. Cranny Francis (ed.), *Feminine/Masculine and Representation*, Allen & Unwin, Sydney, 1990.
Threadgold, T. et al. (ed.) *Semiotics — Ideology — Language*, Sydney Association for Studies in Society and Culture, 1986.
Trioli, V., 'Hyundai makes a pitch for the gays', *Age*, Melbourne, 17 December 1992.
Turner, B.S., *Citizenship and Capitalism*, Allen & Unwin, London, 1986.
Turner, Graeme, *British Cultural Studies: An Introduction*, Unwin Hyman, London, 1990.
Turner, Ian (ed.), *The Australian Dream*, Sun Books, Melbourne, 1968.
Walker, David, *Dream and Disillusion*, Australian National University Press, Canberra, 1976.
Walker, David et al. (eds), *Books, Readers, Reading*, special issue of *Australian Cultural History*, Vol. 11, 1992.
Walker, Kath, *My People: A Kath Walker Collection*, Jacaranda Press, Brisbane, 1970.
Walter, James, *The Ministers' Minders: Personal Advisers in National Government*, Oxford University Press, Melbourne, 1986.
Ward, Russel, *The Australian Legend*, Oxford University Press, Melbourne, 1958.
Ward, Russel, *A Nation for a Continent: The History of Australia 1901–1975*, Heinemann, Melbourne, 1977.

Watts, R., 'The origins of the Australian welfare state', *Historical Studies*, vol. 19, no. 75, 1980.

Weller, P. (ed.), *Menzies to Keating: The Development of the Australian Prime Ministership*, Melbourne University Press, Melbourne, 1992.

Wettenhall, R. and M. Painter (eds), *The First Thousand Days of Labor*, vol. 2, Canberra College of Advanced Education, Canberra, 1975.

White, Patrick, *Voss*, Penguin, Ringwood, 1974.

White, Richard, *Inventing Australia: Images and Identity 1688–1980*, Allen & Unwin, Sydney, 1981.

White, Richard, 'Bluebells and Fogtown: Australians' first impressions of England, 1860–1950', *Australian Cultural History*, no. 5, 1986.

Whitlam, Gough, *The Whitlam Years: 1972–1975*, Viking, Ringwood, 1985.

Wilenski, Peter, 'Ministers, public servants and public policy', *Australian Quarterly*, vol. 51, no. 2, 1979.

Williams, Raymond, *Culture and Society: 1780–1950*, Penguin Books, Harmondsworth, 1963.

Williams, Raymond, *Marxism and Literature*, Oxford University Press, Oxford, 1977.

Williams, Raymond, *Keywords: A Vocabulary of Culture and Society*, Collins, Glasgow, 1981.

Wiltshire, Kenneth, 'The Australian flirtation with privatisation', in Alexander Kouzmin and Nicholas Scott (eds), *Dynamics in Australian Public Management: Selected Essays*, Macmillan, Melbourne, 1990.

Wolfsohn, Hugo, 'The ideology makers' in Henry Mayer (ed.), *Australian Politics: A Reader*, Cheshire, Melbourne, 1966.

Wood, Thomas, *Cobbers*, Oxford University Press, Melbourne, 1943.

Wotherspoon, Garry, *City of the Plain*, Hale & Iremonger, Sydney, 1991.

Wright, Ronald, *Stolen Continents: The 'New World' seen through Indian Eyes since 1492*, Viking, Toronto, 1992.

CONTRIBUTORS

Dennis Altman is Reader and Associate Professor of Politics at La Trobe University. He is the author of eight books, including *Homosexual: Oppression and Liberation*, *Rehearsals of Change* and the novel *The Comfort of Men*. His latest book, *Power and Community: Organisational and Cultural Responses to AIDS*, will be published by Falmer Press in 1994. He is a member of a number of international and national AIDS bodies, including the Global AIDS Policy Coalition, based at Harvard University.

John Barnes is Professor of English at La Trobe University where he has taught for many years. He is the author of *The Order of Things: A Life of Joseph Furphy* (OUP, 1990) and is editing a selection of Furphy's letters. His other interests include *Meridian: The La Trobe University English Review*, of which he is the foundation editor.

Bruce Bennett is Professor of English and head of department at University College, University of New South Wales, at the Australian Defence Force Academy, Canberra. He is the author of *Spirit in Exile: Peter Porter and His Poetry* (Oxford University Press, 1991) and *An Australian Compass: Essays on Place and Direction in Australian Literature* (Fremantle Arts Centre Press, 1991). Formerly Director of the Centre for Studies in Australian Literature at the University of Western Australia and editor of *Westerly*, he has published widely on Australian literary history and on the literature and culture of the Asia–Pacific region. He has held visiting appointments at a number of Asian, European and North American universities and was a member of the Australian National Commission for UNESCO from 1985 to 1990.

Sol Encel, Emeritus Professor of Sociology at the University of New South Wales, was a contributor to the original *Australian Civilization* (ed. Peter Coleman) in 1962. His other publications include *Australian Society* (various editions between 1965 and 1987), *Cabinet Government in Australia* (1962 and 1974), *Equality and Authority* (1970) and *Out of the Doll's House: Women in the Public Sphere* (1991). He is an honorary research associate at the Social Policy Research Centre, University of New South Wales.

CONTRIBUTORS

Laksiri Jaysuriya is Emeritus Professor of Social Work at the University of Western Australia and has held appointments in Sri Lanka, Australia and the USA. He has recently taken early retirement from the UWA where he was foundation chair of social work and social administration. He was also director of the Centre for Asian Studies at the UWA. He has published widely on multiculturalism and citizenship in Australia, and in 1985 he was awarded the Order of Australia for services to community relations.

James Jupp is Director of the Centre for Immigration and Multicultural Studies at the Australian National university and Executive Director of the Academy of the Social Sciences in Australia. He was editor of the bicentennial encyclopedia, *The Australian People* (Angus & Robertson, 1988) and has recently published *Immigration* (Sydney University Press, 1991), *National of Immigrants* (Oxford University Press, 1992) and *The Politics of Australian Immigration* (AGPS, 1993). He was born in London and has lived in Melbourne for ten years and in Canberra for fifteen.

Andrew Milner is the Director of the Centre for General and Comparative Literature at Monash University. He is the author of *John Milton and the English Revolution* (1981), *The Road to St Kilda Pier (1984)*, *Contemporary Cultural Theory* (1991) and *Cultural Materialism* (1993), and co-editor of *Postmodern Conditions* (1988), *Discourse and Difference* (1990) and *Cultural Materialism* (1993).

Richard Nile is Executive Director of the Australian Studies Centre at the University of Queensland. Formerly the deputy head of the Australian Studies Centre at the University of London and foundation director and professor of Australian Studies in Hungary, his books include *The Fiction Industry* (1995), *The Practice and Problems of Australian Studies in Australia and Europe* (1993) with Zoltan Abadi-Nagy, *Australian Aborigines* (1992), *Indigenous Rights in the Pacific and North America* (1992) with Henry Reynolds, *Workers and Intellectuals* (1992) with Barry York, *Anzac: Meaning, Memory and Myth* (1991) with Alan Seymour, *Immigration and the Politics of Ethnicity and Race* (1991), *The Gate of Dreams* (1990) with Ffion Murphy. He lives in Brisbane with Ffion and their two children, Booka and Jerra.

Henry Reynolds was born and educated in Tasmania. He taught in secondary schools there and later in London. In 1966 he began teaching at what was then the Townsville University College. Over the years he became an associate professor and the college became the James Cook University. His major work has been in the history of European–Aboriginal relations, and his publications include *The Other Side of the Frontier, Frontier, The Law of the Land, Dispossession* and *Indigenous Rights in the Pacific and North America* (with Richard Nile). He writes extensively on a range of social and political questions, and is married to Senator Margaret Reynolds.

Contributors

Margaret Reynolds is Labor Senator for Queensland. Formerly a member of the Women's Electoral Lobby, she is an active political voice and has held a number of positions in government including Minister Assisting the Prime Minister on Women's Affairs.

Elaine Thompson is Associate Professor and head of the School of Political Science, University of New South Wales. She has also been a visiting professor at Pennsylvania State University and American University, Washington DC. Dr Thompson has received a number of awards, including Fulbright and Senior Fulbright Fellowships. She has specialist research interests in public administration (bureaucracy) and American domestic politics, which she also teaches. A regular public commentator and a foundation member of the Australian republican movement, she is interested in Australian political culture and is writing a book on Australian egalitarianism.

Chris Wallace-Crabbe is the Director of the Australian Centre at The University of Melbourne, where he also holds a Personal Chair in English. Educated at Melbourne and Yale Universities, Chris Wallace-Crabbe held the Visiting Chair of Australian Studies at Harvard in 1987–88. He has published a dozen collections of poems, the most recent being *Rungs of Time* (1993). In 1995 Oxford University Press will publish his *Selected Poems*. In addition, Chris Wallace-Crabbe is the General Editor of Oxford's *Australian Writers Series*, and has edited four poetry anthologies. His collections of critical essays include *Falling into Language* (Oxford, 1990).

James Walter is Professor of Australian Studies at Griffith University and formerly the head of the Australian Studies Centre at the University of London. His books include *The Leader: A Political Biography of Gough Whitlam* (1980); *The Minister's Minders: Personal Advisers in National Government* (1986); *Intellectual Movements and Australian Society* (with Brian Head) (1988); *Australian Studies: A Survey (1989)* and *Shaping Lives: Reflections on Biography* (with Ian Donaldson and Peter Read) (1992).

INDEX

Aborigines 74, 78, 80, 81, 88
 and art 8–9, 13–14, 194, 202
 assimilation of 6, 76
 and bicentenary 37
 Buludja 45–6, 52
 comparisons with Maori 32–3
 historiographical neglect 24–7, 35–6, 44
 and inter-racial sex 34, 43, 47, 50–1, 52
 land rights 10, 27, 38, 48–9, 55
 and land use 28, 29
 and legal system 9, 10, 37
 literary representations 42–3, 45–52, 61–2
 literature 61–3, 193, 206
 and national mythologies 41–5, 60, 90
 and political activism 27, 38, 48–9, 63, 64, 85, 87
 prehistory 18, 27–8, 202
 and settlers 25, 26, 30–6
 sex and sexuality 50, 52, 111
 society 28, 30, 32
 spirituality 10–11, 50, 51, 52–4, 69
 Tasmanian 4, 25, 30, 31, 34–5
 and work 46, 47, 48, 50, 51, 134
 see also Australia; citizenship; civilisation; culture; employment; Langford, Ruby; Mabo Ruling; Morgan, Sally; race relations
academics *see* intellectuals
Adelaide 17, 78, 79, 80
Age (Melbourne) 129, 200, 201
AIDS 114, 115–17
 see also homosexuality
Allen & Unwin 190
Alomes, Stephen 185
Althusser, L. 220, 221
Anderson, Benedict 216

Andrews, Barry 211
Angus & Robertson 190
Antipodes 3–4, 5, 6, 8, 12, 15, 16, 19, 205, 206
Anzac Day 12, 36, 43, 58–9, 60, 63
Archibald Prize 195
Argentina 148, 202
Armstrong, Gillian 183
Art and Text 221
arts/artists 180–2, 183, 187, 188, 192, 193–5, 201, 205, 206–7, 208, 211–12, 215
AUSSAT 152
Australasian Book Society 190
Australia:
 and Asia 18–19, 20, 42, 68, 69, 78–9, 80–1, 89, 91
 bicentenary 9, 37, 39, 55
 and Britain 6, 20, 74–5, 77–8, 150, 151, 185, 186, 187, 189
 environment 8, 54, 82, 91, 103–4
 exploration of 12, 30–1, 36
 federation 42, 147, 148, 152
 historiography 6–7, 11, 24–7, 30
 perceptions of 3–4, 11, 12, 16
 population 81–2, 88, 91
 regionalism 17
 settlement 26, 36, 41
 terra nullius 9, 27, 38, 88
 and war 20, 74, 128
 see also Aborigines; Australian Government; citizenship; civilisation; politics; society
Australia Council 87, 181, 208, 209
Australian civilisation, *see* civilisation; Coleman, Peter
Australian Civilization 24, 94, 193, 202–3
Australian Broadcasting Commission/Corporation 16, 25, 182, 183

INDEX

Australian Legend, The 24, 41
Australian Government 181, 186, 210
   Attorney General's Department 107, 186
   British institutions/practice 88, 93, 94, 97, 98, 99
   and business 167, 168
   Community Services, Department of 99
   electoral practice 87–8, 90, 126
   federal elections 19, 121, 125, 126–7, 128, 132, 151
   Franchise Act (1902) 126
   Immigration, Department of 86
   Post Master General 152
   Office of Multicultural Affairs 86
   Office of Women's Affairs 125, 130, 131, 133, 135–6, 137
   public service 107, 134, 170, 171, 172, 173, 174
   and state 143, 144
   Telecom 152
   Trade and Customs Act 186
   see also monarchy; political culture; politics
Australian Journal 189
Australian Labor Party 9–10, 63, 76, 82, 84, 86, 87, 112, 119, 121, 130, 131, 132, 138, 142, 145, 146, 151, 152, 153, 155, 156, 157, 164, 165, 166, 167, 168, 170, 171, 173, 176, 210, 219
   and labour movement 144, 145, 146, 148, 150
Australian National Gallery 195
Australian Performing Group 183
Australian Workers' Union 76
Australians: A Historical Atlas 8

Ball, W. MacMahon 165, 176
barbarism *see* civilisation
Barnard, Majorie *see* M. Barnard Eldershaw
Barrett, Michele 225
Bean, C.E.W. 43–4
Bennett, Bruce 68, 69
Bennett, Tony 223
Bentham, Jeremy 145
Bentley, Mary Ann Moore 127
Berndt, Ronald 61–2
Betts, Katherine 230
Beveridge, William 166–7
Birrell, Robert 230
Birrell, Tanya 230
Bishop, Bronwyn 159

Bjelke-Petersen, Joh 131
Blainey, Geoffrey 4–5, 29, 151
Blewett, Neal 116
Bloom, Alan 211
Blundell, Graeme 183
Bodenweiser Ballet 195
Bond, Alan 204
Bonwick, James 25
books, bookselling 182–4, 188, 194, 207, 210, 211–12
Borovansky, Edouard 195
Boyd, Arthur 192
Boyd, Martin 77
Boyer Lectures 26–7
Bradman, Donald 68
Brecht, Bertold 205
Brett, Judith 163, 205–6
Bridge, Ernie 63
Brisbane 17, 80, 183
Britain *see* United Kingdom
Broinowski, Alison 68
Brookes, H.E. 166
Bryce, James 142, 143, 145
Buckley, Vincent 193, 202
Bulletin 20, 47–8, 75, 76
Burgmann, E.H. 165
Burke, Janine 206
Burke and Wills 12
Burnham, James 167
Buzo, Alex 187

Calwell, Arthur 76, 156
Camm, J.C.R. 8
Campaign Against Moral Persecution 113
Campbell, Robert 189
Canada 172, 202, 204, 223
   citizenship rights in 98
   as multicultural society 80, 81, 85, 86
Canberra 27, 157, 210
Capital Q 114
Carey, Peter 191
Carter, Paul 200
Cassab, Judy 195
Casey, R.G. 167
Cawley, Evonne *see* Goolagong, Evonne
censorship 186–7
Chadwick, Virginia 131
Chamberlain, Lindy 12, 13
Chartism 90, 94
Cheshire, F.W. 190, 194
Chifley, Ben 15, 82, 164
China; Chinese 42, 69, 70, 79
Chisholm, Caroline 126
Churchill, Winston 14, 158

INDEX

cinema *see* film
citizenship
  and Aborigines 93
  attitudes to 76, 78
  definitions 94–5, 102
  and immigrants 93, 97–8, 99, 100
  legislation 93, 97–8, 107
  and minorities 94, 98–107
  oath of allegiance 90, 93, 107
  principle of equality 94, 95–6, 99, 101, 102
  rights 96–7, 98, 99–102, 103, 104, 105, 106, 145
  as societal basis 94
civilisation 18, 38, 41, 58, 105–6, 107, 163, 180, 213, 215, 216, 231
  Aboriginal 4–5, 7, 9, 10–11, 28–9, 53, 54–5, 56
  Australia 1, 3–6, 12, 14, 16, 17–19, 20–21, 33, 37, 39, 56, 64, 91, 93, 94
  and barbarism 5, 6, 8
  definitions of 4–6, 16–17
  European 6, 8, 15, 17, 18, 25, 53, 62, 65, 96
  and savagery 8, 10
  see also Clark, C.M.H.; Clark, Kenneth; Coleman, Peter
Clark, C.M.H. (Manning), 5, 6–7, 13, 18, 24–5, 185
Clark, Kenneth 5
class 21, 142, 148, 222
  conflict 82, 87, 95, 103, 104, 105
  consciousness 106
  middle 49, 89, 163, 167, 172, 186
  relations 75, 95, 99, 105, 106, 107, 146
  ruling 29, 65, 74, 83, 102–3
  workers 33, 76, 89, 98, 139, 142, 156, 185
  working 12–13, 76, 83, 89, 99–100, 186
Cleary, Phil 87
Close, Robert 186
Coleman, Peter 24, 94, 193, 202–3
Colonial Times (Hobart) 34
Commonwealth Graves Commission 12
Commonwealth Literary Fund 181, 186, 187
  see also Australia Council
communism 65, 75, 82
  see also Communist Party of Australia; marxism
Communist Party of Australia 77, 82, 165

see also communism; marxism
Community of Thieves 55
Connell, Bob 219
conservatives, conservatism 66, 82, 83, 87, 88, 122, 145, 149–50, 168, 187, 191, 194, 204, 211, 218
  and land rights 10
  in legal system 98–9
  social theory 141
  and women's movement 131
  and women's suffrage 126
  see also liberalism; Liberal Party; Menzies, R.G.; multiculturalism
Coombs, H.C. 164–5, 166, 175, 176, 177
Copland, Douglas 164, 175, 176
Corruna, Daisy 50–3
Court, Charles 9
Court, Richard 9–10
Courtauld, Samuel 167
Cowan, Peter 68
Cowling, G.H. 185, 199
Crawford, R.M. 187
cultural cringe 184, 185, 186–93, 195, 199–200, 208, 210–12
  see also culture; Phillips, A.A.
Cultural Studies 218, 221
culture 106, 107, 206–8, 210, 215, 216–22, 228–32
  Aboriginal 25, 26, 28, 49, 54, 60
  Asian 68, 70, 81, 195
  Australian 181, 184–6, 188, 193–5, 202, 206, 209, 211–12, 215–16
  European 14, 65, 68, 69, 71, 189, 202, 205
  literary 60–3, 70, 189
  and nationalism 187, 190, 203–4, 216, 221–2
  popular 60, 142, 145
  public 175, 177
  see also arts; civilisation; cultural cringe; multiculturalism; political culture
Curr, Edward 33
Curthoys, Ann 225, 227–8
Curtin, John 150, 164

d'Alpuget, Blanche 158
Daniel, Ann 155–6
Dark Side of the Dream 45, 60–1
Darwin 19–20, 80
Davidson, Alastair 219
Davies, Alan 144, 146, 202, 207–8, 213
Davis, Jack 52, 63

Davis, Judy 183
Devanny, Jean 186
Dexter, Nancy 129
Dobel, William 192
Docker, John 186
Domahidy, Andrew 66–7
Drake-Brockman, Alice 50–1
Drake-Brockman, Howden 50–1
Drewe, Robert 13
'Drovers' Wife, The' 42
Drucker, Peter 167
Drysdale, Russell 192
During, Simon 223
Dutton, Geoffrey 190

economics 215
economy 95, 100, 164, 169, 185, 204–5, 207, 230
education 91, 96, 172, 173, 175–6, 209–10, 211, 212, 216, 217
egalitarianism 44, 55, 69, 75–7, 89, 90, 141, 143, 155, 156, 180, 185, 187, 191, 192
Eldershaw, Flora 165
see also M. Barnard Eldershaw
Eldershaw, M. Barnard 190
Elizabethan Theatre Trust 183
Elkin, A.P. 45, 61, 165
Ellinghaus, M.P. 37
Elton, Ben 16
employment and work 46, 48, 91, 100, 125, 126, 127, 128, 134–5, 145, 148, 209
unemployment 82, 86, 150, 209
Emy, Hugh 142, 143–4
Encel, Sol 147, 148, 149, 156, 202
environmentalism see Australia
Esson, Louis 14–15, 183
ethnic communities 79, 80, 83, 88
ethnicity 21, 70, 90, 134, 199
and political participation 80, 86, 87–8, 102–3, 104–5
see also ethnic communities; Federation of Ethnic Communities Councils of Australia
Eureka Stockade 75, 90
Europe 15, 65, 68, 83–4, 143, 207, 212, 223
Europeans 11, 12, 29, 30–6, 38, 39, 53, 54, 61, 65–7, 80–1, 83, 202
Eyre, Edward 35

Fabinyi, Andrew 194
family 59, 76, 83, 91, 121, 122, 163
see also Aborigines
fascism 148

Fatin, Wendy 131
Faust, Beatrice 129
Feather, Norman 155, 184, 186
Federation of Ethnic Communities' Councils of Australia 80
Felperin, Howard 221, 222, 223, 227
feminism 83, 101, 103–4, 112, 121, 211, 212, 224–8
international influence 125, 128
lesbians and 113–14
see also women
Ferenc, Feher 219
Ferrier, Carole 225
Fiji 68, 69, 97
film 4, 16, 38, 59, 183, 201, 206, 207
Firth, Raymond 32–3
Fischer, Tim 4–5, 9
Fiske, John 221
Fitzgerald Report see immigration
Fitzpatrick, Brian 154
Floating World, The 59
Flood, Josephine 28
Flugelman, Herbert 195
Forbes, Sandra 209
For the Term of His Natural Life 111
Forward, Ann 132
France 202, 204
Franklin, Miles 183, 190
Fraser, Malcolm 20, 84, 151, 156, 157, 171
and social reform 130–1
Freudenberg, Graham 157
Friedan, Betty 128
Friend, Donald 192
Frow, John 221, 222, 223
Furphy, Joseph 42

Gallagher, Katherine 203
Gallipoli 12, 14, 58
Gardner, Ava 16
Gelder, Ken 182
Giblin, L.F. 164, 175, 176
Gibson, Mel 16, 183
Gillies, Max 183
Goldberg, S.L. 217
Goldstein, Vida 126–7
Goolagong, Evonne 9
Gordon, Michael 158
Gorton, John 156
Gove Land Rights Case 38
government see Australian Government
Grant-Rosman, Alice 189
Greenwood, Gordon 26
Greer, Germaine 128
Greiner, Nick 84

Index

Grey, George 32
Grosz, Elizabeth 220, 226, 227
Gulipilil, David 9
Gunew, Sneja 64–5, 229
Gunn, Mrs Aeneas 47, 48, 51

Hallahan, Kay 131
Hallam, Sylvia 29
Halliday, M.A.K. 221
Hamilton, Annette 68
Hancock, W.K. 5–6, 7, 8, 32, 144, 145, 146, 147, 151, 155
Harcourt, J.M. 186
Hardy, Frank 186–7
Harris, Rolf 15–16
Hart, Kevin 223
Hawke, Bob 20, 84, 87, 132, 137, 150, 152, 158, 171, 175, 176
Hazzard, Shirley 191, 203
Healy, J.J. 61
Heller, Agnes 219
Henderson, Yvonne 131
Herbert, Xavier 68
Hergenhan, L.T. 60
Herman, Sali 192
Hessing, Leonard 195
Hewson, John 149–50, 159, 176–7
Hibbert, Jack 183
High Court of Australia 148–9
Hirst, John 41
Hodge, Bob 45, 48, 60–1
Hogan, Paul 16
Holding, Clyde 38–9
Holdsworth Art Gallery 194
Hollows, Fred 13–14
Holman, W.A. 144–5, 151
homosexuality 111, 112, 114, 115, 116, 119, 120
 attitudes to 75–6, 111–12, 115, 116, 119–20, 121
 and church 111, 121–2
 culture 113–14, 118, 119
 Gay and Lesbian Mardi Gras 110, 115, 117
 identity 111–12
 in interwar years 111–12
 as political movement 112–13, 118–19, 121
 and religion 111, 113, 120, 121, 122
 separatism 113–14, 117
 in Tasmania 113, 120, 121
 and US 112–13, 114, 117, 118–19, 121
 see also AIDS
Hong, Ee, Tiang 70
Hope, A.D. 202

Horne, Donald 76, 112, 154, 193, 203
Howard, John 85, 99
Hughes, Robert 192, 193, 202
Hughes, W.M. 20
Humphries, Barry 4, 207

Ideas 182
identity, national 42, 59, 64, 74–8, 81, 82–3, 85, 88, 90, 212, 213, 222
ideology 220
Idriess, Ion 190
immigration 14, 15, 64, 70, 151, 200, 206, 212
 Asian 78–9, 83, 84, 89
 assimilation 78, 83–4, 194
 British 74, 77–8, 80, 88, 89
 cultural contribution 194–5
 Europeans 83–4, 194–5
 Fitzgerald Report 87, 97–8
 Hungarians 65–7
 Irish 12
 Jewish 83
 opposition to 86
 and racism 24
 white Australia policy 78–9, 84
 and work 12
 see also conservatives; multiculturalism; race relations; White Australia Policy
India 69–70
Indonesia 18
industrial relations 147–8
Inglis, K.S. 3–4, 182, 193, 202
Institute of Public Affairs 164, 165, 168
intellectuals 9, 66, 75, 76, 77, 82, 83, 85, 87, 142, 168–70, 174, 202, 211, 231
 and cultural cringe 185–8, 191–3
 definitions 162, 169–70
 in government/politics 164–8, 170–7, 206
 organic 169–70, 176, 177
 specific 227
 traditional 169–70, 177, 230
intelligentsia *see* intellectuals
Island 37

Jackson, Sir Robert 15
James, Clive 203, 206
Japan 79, 81, 89, 204
Jenkins, R. 99
Jindyworobaks 54
Johnno 1
Johnson, Pauline 220
José, F. Sionil 69

INDEX

Kahan, Louis 195
Kahn, Joel 229
Kardamitsis, Bill 87
Keating, Paul 20, 39, 84, 99, 137–9, 151, 158, 171, 176, 181, 204, 205
Kelly, Ned 63
  see also Nolan, Sidney
Kelly, Paul 149, 157, 158
Kelly, Ros 137
Kemp, C.D. 167
Keneally, Thomas 37, 191
Kennedy Miller 16
Kennett, Jeffrey 99
Keynes, J.M. 165, 166
Kingsley, Henry 48
Kirner, Joan 136–7
Knight, Stephen 219
Komon, Rudy 194
Kovesi, Julia 65–6
Kovesi, Julius 65, 67
Kovesi, Paul 65–6
Kramer, Leonie 192–3
Kripps, Henry 195

La Nauze, J.A. 25
Lake Mungo 37–8
Lane, William 75
Lang, Jack 75, 155
Langer, Karl 195
Langford, Ruby 51, 52, 55
Lawler, Ray 183
Lawrence, Carmen 131, 136–7
Lawrence, D.H. 11, 186
Lawson, Henry 16, 42–3, 44, 63, 75, 210
lawyers 148–9
Leavis, F.R. 216–17, 220
Leavis, Q.D. 216–17, 220
Left Book Club 182
legend of the nineties 42, 75, 85, 86
Legend of the Nineties, The 191–2
Leichhardt, Ludwig 12
Leroy-Beaulieu, Pierre 142
Levy, Anne 131
Levy-Strauss, Claude 10, 28
Lewis, Essington 166
Liberal Party 66, 84, 85, 87, 121, 129, 130, 138, 151, 152, 167, 169, 177
  National Party coalition 133, 138, 151, 156, 171, 177, 181
  see also Menzies, R.G.; United Australia Party
liberalism 96, 115, 144, 163, 167–8, 175
libraries 182–3
Lincoln, Abraham 154

literature 69–70, 157–8, 181, 215, 216–17
  Aboriginal writers 61–3, 193
  Australian 42, 70–1, 181–2, 186–91, 192, 208–9
  immigrant writers 64, 65–8, 193–4
  literary theory 200, 221–4
  see also arts; books; Commonwealth Literary Fund; publishers
Little Black Princess, The 47, 51
Lindsay, Norman 186
Lippmann Committee 97
Locke-Elliott, Sumner 111
London 74, 94, 188
Longley, Kateryna 64–5
Lovell, Avon 187
Lowenthal, David 181
Lyons, Enid 128
Lyons, Joseph 82, 128

Mabo Ruling 9, 10, 38
Mad Max see Gibson, Mel; Kennedy Miller
McAllister, Ian 78
McAuley, James 193, 202
McCallum, Douglas 94
McConnan, Leslie 166
McCrann, Terry 204–5
MacCullum, Mungo 216, 217
McGowan, Lord 167
McGregor, Craig 158
McGuinness, P.P. 209, 210
McHugh, Jeanette 137
MacKay, Hugh 155, 184
McKie, Ronald 54
McLean, Marie 225
McMahon, William 129, 170
McNeill, B. 37–8
McPhee Gribble 190–1
McQueen, Humphrey 7, 42, 219
McQuilton, F.J. 8
Mahabharata 68–9
Malaysia 69, 70, 79, 202
Malouf, David 1, 14, 37, 191, 193
Mandl, Fritz 194
Mann, Chris 209
Marshall, A.J. 154
Marshall, T.H. 94–5, 102, 107
marxism 66, 87, 141, 146, 211, 218, 219, 220, 222, 224, 227
'Master of the Ghost Dreaming' 11
mateship 43, 59, 60, 63, 69, 75–6, 143
Mathews, Iola 130
Mayer, Henry 146, 154, 156, 193
media 85, 91, 110

Index

see also Australian Broadcasting Commission; *names of newspapers*; Special Broadcasting Service
Melbourne   16, 17, 80, 183, 200, 219
'Men who made Australia, The'   43
Menzies, R.G.   20, 66–7, 151, 156, 157, 163, 165, 168, 169, 176, 187
Merry-go-round in the Sea, The   17–18
Métin, Albert   142, 143, 144
Michaels, Eric   51, 201
Milner, Andrew   106, 186
Mishra, Vijay   45, 48, 60–1
Mitchell, Susan   184
Moffatt, Tracy   9
Molnar, Georg   195
monarchy   77–8, 88
Moore, Clover   113
Moran, Cardinal   82
Morgan, Sally   49, 63
Morris, Meaghan   221, 222, 226, 227
Mouffe, C.   101
Ms magazine   129, 137
Mudrooroo   11, 52, 62, 64
Mukherjee, Meenakshi   70
Muller, Laurie   189
multiculturalism   15, 64, 67, 81, 82, 103, 151, 228, 229–30
  attitudes to   81, 103–4
  opposition to   64–5, 81, 84–6, 87
  as policy   79–81, 84–5, 86–7, 100, 101, 113
  see also conservatives; immigration
Mulvaney, D.J.   28, 37–8
Murray Islands   38
Murray, Les   12–13, 61, 107
Mussen, Gerald   166
My Place   49, 63

Nadel, George   185
Narogin, Mudrooroo *see* Mudrooroo
nation   6, 87, 101, 126, 139, 162, 184, 187, 213, 216, 222, 223
nation building   41, 44, 48, 94, 97
National Institute of Dramatic Art   183
National Times   19, 129
nationalism   12, 21, 36–7, 41, 43, 44, 74, 77, 82, 87, 162, 163, 200, 203, 208, 216, 217, 222
  conservative   78, 82–3, 85, 90, 97–8, 218
  and ethnicity   60
  feminist critiques   60
  and mythology   89, 141

and national type   42, 43–4, 54, 59, 162, 203
radical nationalists   45, 74–5, 85, 218, 219, 222, 223
and war   14, 58–9
New Diversity   182
New Hebrides   3–4
New South Wales   34, 144, 149, 152, 155
New South Wales Bookstall Co.   189, 190
New Theatre   183
New York Times   129, 209
New Zealand   4, 25–6, 69, 144, 202
Newbolt, Henry   216
Newcastle   80, 182
Nile, Fred   115, 121
Nolan, Sidney   14, 192
Noonuccal, Oodgeroo   63

O'Farrell, Patrick   14
Oldfield, Audrey   126
One Day of the Year, The   21, 59, 183, 187
O'Neil, Lloyd   190
Opera in the Park   183
Optus   152
Orie, Muta   69
Oxford University Press   190
Ozolins, Uldiz   217

Palmer, Nettie   44–5
Palmer, Vance   44, 45, 183, 190, 191–2
Pa On   69
Paterson, (Banjo) A.B.   42
Penguin Books   191
Pergamon Press   194
Perth   17–18, 49, 66, 70, 78
Phillip, Arthur   25, 94
Phillips, A.A.   42, 60, 185, 191, 199, 202
Phillips-Fox, E.   199
political culture   146, 169, 170, 175
  Australian   143–4, 149, 153, 158, 159
  definition   141–2
  and homosexuality   110, 121
political institutions   141, 144, 145, 146, 168
politicians   75, 137, 144, 154
politics   24, 38, 75, 76, 80, 85, 91, 101, 104, 107, 128, 129, 141, 142, 143, 144–8, 155–8, 166, 168, 170, 173, 174, 176, 177, 185, 215, 219, 222, 225, 226, 230

Index

see also political culture; political institutions; politicians
Pollock, Jackson   187
post-colonialism   223–4
post-modernism   228, 230, 231
post-structuralism   224, 225, 227, 228, 229, 230
Pram Factory (Melbourne)   183
Prichard, Katharine Susannah   190
Pringle, J.D.   4
Pringle, Rosemary   227, 228
publishers, publishing   188–91, 194, 209, 213
Pusey, Michael   153
Pybus, Cassandra   55

Queensland   34, 38, 149
Queensland University Press   190
Quiros, Pedro de   3–4

race relations   18, 26, 90, 99, 107
  see also Aborigines, immigration, multiculturalism
racism   42, 44, 47–9, 75, 76, 77, 82, 83, 86, 193
Reagan, Ronald   153
Reid, Elizabeth   125
Reid, George   144
Reid, Ian   221
religion   21, 28, 53, 75, 76, 77, 80, 81, 83, 85, 143, 158, 199, 206, 231
Remembering Babylon   14
republicanism   20, 75, 82, 88, 93, 151
Returned Services' League   76
Reynolds, Henry   48
Roberts, David   220
Robinson, W.S.   166
Romeril, John   59, 183
Rose, Lionel   9
Ross, Lloyd   165, 166
Roughsey, Dick   32, 52
Rowse, Tim   141–2, 166, 167
Rubinstein, Bill   184
Rudd, Steele   190
Rundell, John   220
Rusden, George   25
Ryan, Mary   165
Ryan, Susan   131, 132, 133, 137
Ryle, Gilbert   205

Sahlins, Marshall   28
Salzman, Paul   182
Samuel, Peter   20
Santamaria, B.A.   122
Savage, James   10

Schaffer, Kay   212
Scheinberg, Gisella   194
science   26, 30–1, 41, 54, 181, 182, 206, 210, 231
Scripsi   221
Serious, Yahoo   4
Serle, Geoffrey   211
Seymour, Alan   21, 59, 183, 187
Sex Discrimination Act (1984)   134
Sharifar, Omah   69
Sheridan, Greg   210
Shoemaker, Adam   61
Siegfried, André   142, 144
Sinclair, Keith   26
Singapore   14, 69, 74, 79, 204
Singh, Kerpal   70
Smith, Terry   184
society   76, 94, 105, 167, 194, 206, 220
  Aboriginal   25, 28–30, 32
  composition of   78, 80, 83–7
  and culture   221, 230–1
  democratic/egalitarian   55, 76, 94
  nature of   55, 60, 105, 180, 211
  nineteenth-century   34, 50, 52, 63, 216
  participation in   101–5, 136
  and political culture   141
  and political leaders   153–4
  study of   185, 221
  women's role   128, 136
  see also citizenship; class; multiculturalism; rights
Solomos, John   99
South Africa   74, 75
Southern Review   221
Special Broadcasting Service   110
Spence, Bruce   183
Spender, Dale   224
Stanner, W.E.H.   26–7, 53–4
Stead, Christina   186, 204
Steinem, Gloria   129
Stirling, James   35
Stolen Continents   7
Stow, Randolph   17–18, 67
Stretton, Hugh   205
Striking Chords   64–5
structuralism   224
Summer of the Seventeenth Doll   183
Summers, Anne   137–8
Sun-Herald (Sydney)   129
Sunday Telegraph   129
Sweet, Georgina   165
Swift, Jonathan   3, 4
Sydney   17, 25, 27, 33, 37, 79, 80, 84, 183, 189, 194

INDEX

tall poppy sydrome   155, 184
Tangney, Dorothy   128
Tasmania   34, 55
Tatz, Colin   9, 10
technology   8, 16, 195
television   38, 59, 64, 91, 157, 158, 182, 183
Thatcher, Margaret   159, 204
theatre   194, 200
Thompson, E.P.   219
Thonemann, H.E.   45–6
Tibor, Paul   195
Tinter, Georg   195
Tocqueville, Alexis de   142–3, 144, 145, 148, 153
trade unions   75, 77, 82, 99, 146, 150
   see also women
Tranquerah   70
Tsaloumas, Dimitris   193
Turnbull, Robert   129
Turner, Graeme   218
Turner, Ian   219

unemployment *see* employment
United Australia Party   165, 168
   see also Liberal Party; Menzies, R.G.
United Kingdom   74, 144, 147, 187, 188
United Nations   15, 126, 136, 148
United States of America   86, 142, 143, 153, 183, 212
universities   27, 59, 65, 126, 135, 164, 182, 185, 186, 195, 211, 217, 218, 225
   Australian National   25
   Birmingham   218
   Curtin   221
   La Trobe   229
   London   181
   Macquarie   219
   Melbourne   165, 185, 194, 217, 221
   Murdoch   221
   Oxford   156, 190
   Queensland   190, 218
   Sydney   45, 83, 157, 192, 195, 216, 217
   Technology, Sydney   225
   Western Australia   65

Vanishing Kingdoms   14
Victoria   99, 152, 209
Viennese Theatre   194
Vietnam War   219
visual arts *see* arts, artists
Voss   11, 12

Walford, Frank   186
Walker, David   186
Wallace Line   18
Ward, Russel   24, 33, 41, 191
We of the Never-Never   47, 48
Webb, Beatrice   142
Webb, Sydney   142
Wedgewood, Ralph   167
Weiniger, Peter   200
West, John   25
Western Australia   9–10, 32, 35, 67
White Australia Policy   78–9, 84
   see also immigration
White, Patrick   4, 11, 12, 77, 118
White, Richard   42
Whiteley, Brett   192
Whitlam, E.G.   84, 113, 130, 176
   government   76, 125, 150, 170–1, 187
   personality   19–20, 156, 157, 158
   and social reform   97, 113, 125, 130
Wilding, Michael   219
Williams, Raymond   106, 215, 219, 220, 232
Williamson, David   183
Windows on to Worlds   217
Wolfsohn, Hugo   186, 192, 193
women   36, 59, 90, 125–39, 212
   Affirmative Action Act (1986)   134–5
   equality   69, 76, 89, 90, 98, 121–2, 125, 131, 134, 135, 136, 139, 148, 165
   National Agenda for   136
   United Council for Women's Suffrage   127
   Women's Electoral Lobby   104, 125, 128–30, 131, 136, 137, 138
   and work   1–3, 79, 91, 125, 126, 128, 134–5, 184
   see also Aborigines; employment
Wood, Thomas   182
Worker, The   156
Workers' Educational Association   165
Working Papers   221
Wotherspoon, Garry   111–12
Wran, Neville   84, 115
Wright, Judith   11, 55, 212
Wright, Ronald   7

Yugoslavia   75, 80